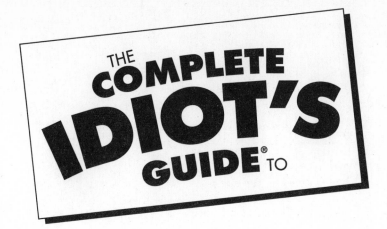

THE
COMPLETE
IDIOT'S
GUIDE® TO

Copywriter's
Words and Phrases

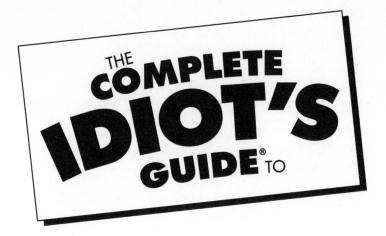

THE
COMPLETE
IDIOT'S
GUIDE® TO

Copywriter's
Words and Phrases

by Kathy Kleidermacher

ALPHA

A member of Penguin Group (USA) Inc.

ALPHA BOOKS

Published by the Penguin Group

Penguin Group (USA) Inc., 375 Hudson Street, New York, New York 10014, U.S.A.

Penguin Group (Canada), 10 Alcorn Avenue, Toronto, Ontario, Canada M4V 3B2 (a division of Pearson Penguin Canada Inc.)

Penguin Books Ltd, 80 Strand, London WC2R 0RL, England

Penguin Ireland, 25 St Stephen's Green, Dublin 2, Ireland (a division of Penguin Books Ltd)

Penguin Group (Australia), 250 Camberwell Road, Camberwell, Victoria 3124, Australia (a division of Pearson Australia Group Pty Ltd)

Penguin Books India Pvt Ltd, 11 Community Centre, Panchsheel Park, New Delhi—110 017, India

Penguin Group (NZ), cnr Airborne and Rosedale Roads, Albany, Auckland 1310, New Zealand (a division of Pearson New Zealand Ltd)

Penguin Books (South Africa) (Pty) Ltd, 24 Sturdee Avenue, Rosebank, Johannesburg 2196, South Africa

Penguin Books Ltd, Registered Offices: 80 Strand, London WC2R 0RL, England

Copyright © 2005 by Kathy Kleidermacher

International Standard Book Number: 1-59257-425-4
Library of Congress Catalog Card Number: 2005929451

07 06 05   8 7 6 5 4 3 2 1

Interpretation of the printing code: The rightmost number of the first series of numbers is the year of the book's printing; the rightmost number of the second series of numbers is the number of the book's printing. For example, a printing code of 05-1 shows that the first printing occurred in 2005.

Printed in the United States of America

Publisher: *Marie Butler-Knight*
Editorial Director: *Mike Sanders*
Senior Managing Editor: *Jennifer Bowles*
Senior Acquisitions Editor: *Renee Wilmeth*
Development Editor: *Christy Wagner*
Senior Production Editor: *Billy Fields*

Copy Editor: *Nancy Wagner*
Cartoonist: *Shannon Wheeler*
Cover/Book Designer: *Trina Wurst*
Indexer: *Aamir Burki*
Layout: *Becky Harmon*
Proofreading: *Donna Martin*

Contents

Keywords

3 Promotional Power   **171**

Foreword

Write on!

A pun and a call to action.

Plus an accurate description of what any of us will be able to achieve after a quick read-through of this invaluable, no-nonsense guide.

Open it once, and you'll use it often, because Kathy Kleidermacher covers all the bases in an easy style that not only provides the essential guidelines to writing solid, selling copy, but equally important, makes those guidelines simple to follow—and fun.

Writing effective copy is a craft. That doesn't mean it should be a daunting proposition. It does require a little thought before you start: first—how to grab your readers' attention (no small feat in today's world of hypercommunication); second—how to keep and increase your readers' interest; and finally—how to convert that interest into action.

Achieving these three goals in one piece of copy can be elusive, frustrating, and above all, time-consuming. That's why this book is destined to become a dear and reliable friend.

From the tried-and-trusted to the fresh and original, Ms. Kleidermacher's personal insights and her collective wisdom enable you to speed up the copywriting process as well as your productivity. But what I believe her readers will find indispensable are her ingenious reference sections that comprise Part 1 of this book. Handily cataloged into "Dead-On Descriptions," "Buzzwords by Business," and "Promotional Power," these sections will quickly become vital tools of the trade for any writer. Here you'll discover the key words and phrases you've been searching for—the ones you need to kick-start your copy or to polish it to perfection.

Let me give readers one little warning: this book does contain a grammar section. But Ms Kleidermacher has succeeded, by demonstrating in one succinct section, how being mindful of the basics of grammar can empower your writing instead of frustrating it. She shows you how to avoid the most common and most egregious grammatical errors and also explains why, as a copywriter, you can bypass many of grammar's restrictions. So do yourself a service—even if you think you're great at grammar—and check out the grammar chapter.

The Complete Idiot's Guide to Copywriter's Words and Phrases is perfect for fledgling writers and pros alike. It's packed with practical tips and jammed with gems you either forgot or never thought of. It makes you stop, it makes you think, and it helps you write the best-selling copy you've ever written.

John Fallon

John Fallon is associate creative director at Corbett-Accel Healthcare Group in New York. He began as a copywriter in his native Dublin, Ireland, and has won many national and international awards for his TV, radio, and print advertising. His most recent novel, *A Relative Matter*, is currently in print.

Introduction

When I was little, I used to prop up the cereal box in front of me while I ate my breakfast and devour the words on the box. Little did I know then that what I was reading was "copy." Copy really just means "words."

The term *copy* is used in certain professional settings, primarily in newspapers, magazines, and advertising, to distinguish it from the other part of the package—art. So a newspaper editor might say, "We need more copy on this page, because we didn't get the photo in time for the deadline." Or an ad executive might tell his staff, "I think we should go for lots of graphics in this ad and not too much copy." This book deals specifically with the latter type of copy—copy that's meant to sell products and services or to persuade people—to support a cause, for example, or to make a donation.

In advertising and marketing, copy can appear in a print ad, on a TV commercial, in a catalog, on a poster, in a letter to customers, in a brochure, on the product's actual package—and lots of other odd places. And someone has to write it all. You guessed it—that's where the copywriter comes in.

I have no idea why we use the term *copy* instead of *words*, but I do know a lot about how to write marketing copy because I've been doing it professionally for 16 years, learning all the while. And in this book, I tell you what I've learned, as well as offer you a lot of useful words and phrases to make your job easier. It can help you write effective copy if you're …

- A copywriter—full-time, freelance, or aspiring.

- A small-business owner doing your own marketing.

- Someone who needs to write marketing and selling copy as a part of his or her job.

- An eBay entrepreneur, a fund-raiser, or anyone who wants to sell more successfully.

If you've already written some marketing copy (or written just about anything, for that matter), you've probably experienced The Dreaded Blanks:

"I need a word like this, but not exactly this."

"I need another way to say it."

"It's right on the tip of my tongue …"

This book will help you out of all these situations and guide you to just the right words to fit your copy.

How This Book Is Set Up

The heart of this book, **Part 1, "From Action-Packed to Zingy,"** is a one-of-a-kind resource that can help you conquer The Dreaded Blanks. I include more than 200 primary entries, or keywords—words and terms that we tend to use frequently in copy.

The keywords are divided into three chapters, each organized alphabetically. Chapter 1 contains adjectives to describe your product or service (or the results of using it): big, beautiful, happy, durable, shiny, affordable, clean, up-to-date, unusual, and many more. Chapter 2 is industry-specific—you'll find lists of useful words for cosmetics, cars, food, weddings, and other fields. Chapter 3 includes terms common to many businesses: *best, child-friendly, free*, etc. Also included are words for *sale*, for common sales events tied to seasons and holidays, and for promotional concepts like *bonus*. You might find helpful ideas in each of these subsections, depending on your assigned task.

Under the keywords, you will find words and terms falling under the following sub-headings:

◆ **Synonyms.** Just like a thesaurus, this book gives you words that are the same, or very similar, in meaning to a specific word. Unlike a thesaurus, though, this book gives you some very extensive selections—for example, you'll find 50 words that mean "big." So if you need to avoid being repetitive, you have lots of options—*abundant, ample, jumbo, monster*, and more. You'll also find a range of connotations—subtle shades of meaning—for those times when you need the word for *big* that strikes exactly the right tone for your particular product or audience.

◆ **Related Words, Phrases, and Expressions.** These lists expand on the synonym lists, offering a more wide-ranging selection of terms that can help you give shape to your message and create an ad or piece of copy that's lively and unusual. The related words and phrases aren't substitute words for the main entry. Rather, they take off from the main entry to help you fly creatively. It's a common copywriter's technique to play off of familiar quotations and expressions, so many of these are included here as well. You can use them just to pick up a few useful phrases for your copy, but you can also use them to help you come up with headlines, slogans, and larger creative concepts. So under "big," you'll find, for example, *big cheese, big Kahuna, too big for his britches*, and *larger than life*, as well as *speak softly and carry a big stick*.

◆ **Symbols.** If you're a small business owner, you might be putting together an ad on your own—including both copy and art. If you're doing a corporate job, you may or may not communicate closely with an art department. If you work at an agency, you might be teamed with an art director, working side by side from square one to develop a concept. But even if you're not involved in the artistic side of things—or if your ad won't include any illustration whatsoever—these lists of symbols can serve as a creative spark. These are visual or cultural images of the main entry, things that are closely associated with its meaning—the "big" list includes *800-pound gorilla*, *Texas*, and *Empire State Building*.

Accept No Imitations!

An important cautionary note: some public figures, fictional characters, partial song lyrics, and other entries on these lists should not be represented as themselves in any advertising. I have marked these with an asterisk (*) to represent a cautionary note: *do not use or portray these in your work without researching the legality first and obtaining any necessary legal agreements with the proper parties (which may be prohibitive for those with a small marketing budget).* These are included here for creative purposes only—to help you come up with more complex concepts when you are working on an ad. Though some may be acceptable for use in some forms and under some circumstances, you need to be sure to avoid legal problems. Exercise good judgment, and do research. Using an elephant in your ad to suggest "big" is cool, but using the Incredible Hulk, the trademarked character from Marvel Comics, is not. Still, meditating on the Incredible Hulk just might give you a great idea for a character of your own, and that's why he's included here.

◆ **Antonyms.** If you're writing an ad for a restaurant and want to emphasize how big the portions are, you might want to contrast them with the *paltry* or *chintzy* portions that have disappointed your readers at other restaurants in the past. Antonym lists in Chapter 1 offer words with the opposite meaning of the main entry—usually (though not always) with negative connotations, because they'll be used to describe the problems that your product or service will solve, or to point out why your product or service is better than the competition's. So under "big," you'll find negative-sounding words meaning "small." But under "small," you'll find negative-sounding words meaning "big." Depending on what you're advertising, sometimes bigger is better (hotel rooms)—and sometimes it's not (cell phones).

Most of the keywords in this book include lists for all four categories, with some variations depending on the word. To get even more out of the book, familiarize yourself with all the primary entries, and do some browsing from time to time. On the simplest level, this book can provide you with a substitute word, but it can also get you into full brainstorming mode. You'll likely find yourself making connections and expanding on what's already on the lists, leading to bright ideas that otherwise would have been out of reach. And in most cases, more than one main entry will be useful to you on any particular job.

Of course, some keywords don't lend themselves to antonyms (what's the opposite of purple?), but they are included on all entries for which they're appropriate.

And to help you navigate your way around the book, I've set some of the words in bold type for cross-referencing purposes. When you see a word in a listing set in **bold,** that's your signal that there's another keyword you might find useful within the book. For example, under "Computers," you'll see **Fast** set in bold, indicating that "Fast" is also a keyword, and there are lots more words and phrases for it under "Fast."

In **Part 2, "A Quick Course in Copywriting,"** you'll find advice on the basics and subtleties of copywriting. Chapter 4 lists these qualities and specific ways to develop each. Chapter 5 helps you identify your goals and find more effective ways to achieve them. Then Chapter 6 teaches you techniques frequently used by professional copy-writers to grab and keep readers' attention. Chapter 7 gives you grammar essentials to remember and common mistakes to avoid. Finally, Chapter 8 offers important advice for anyone seeking to pursue copywriting as a career.

As a bonus, the back of the book offers you some additional information—lists of resources, both in print and online, for further reference and reading, and resources for job-seekers. Some valuable tools are here—both creative and practical—for any-one who writes marketing copy. Plus, you'll find a step-by-step analysis of this book's cover copy explaining just why we chose the words we did to try to sell you this book!

Also, you'll find sidebars throughout the book that expand on the content. Look for these for extra info:

Why Pay More?
Here you find time- and money-saving hints.

Accept No Imitations!
These warnings keep you on the right track, in your copy and in your copywriting career.

The Experts Agree
This box contains quotes and tips from professional copywrit-ers, marketing executives, and other assorted sages.

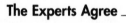

Free Sample!
Look here for examples of out-standing real-life copy—with short explanations of what makes them work so well.

Acknowledgments

I've had lots of help putting this book together from some real pros at Alpha Books: acquisitions editor Renee Wilmeth, development editor Christy Wagner, senior production editor Billy Fields, and copy editor Nancy Wagner. Creating a reference book with so much information in it takes a lot of organizational skill, and it's lucky for me (and you the reader) that they have so much of it. Their clear thinking and sharp edits really helped make this a smoother read and a better resource.

Trademarks

All terms mentioned in this book that are known to be or are suspected of being trademarks or service marks have been appropriately capitalized. Alpha Books and Penguin Group (USA) Inc. cannot attest to the accuracy of this information. Use of a term in this book should not be regarded as affecting the validity of any trademark or service mark.

Part 1

From Action-Packed to Zingy

Dive into Part 1 and discover thousands of words and phrases that can help you punch up your copy, find the term that says exactly what you want to say, and brainstorm new ideas and new twists on old favorites. Chapter 1 contains keyword adjectives frequently used in sales and marketing. Then, Chapter 2 offers industry-specific keywords, so if you're working on a clothing catalog, you'll find lists tailored especially for the job. Finally, Chapter 3 features words and terms employed by marketers and business people to communicate effectively about special sales, deals, services, and more.

I have arranged each chapter in alphabetical order for quick reference, but you may also find that browsing is a valuable technique for those times when you need to get started on a job or when you're stuck for a new angle. Try choosing an entry at random, and see where it takes you creatively!

Chapter 1

Dead-On Descriptions

Affordable	Excellent	Long-Lasting	Scary
Assorted	Exciting	Luxurious	Scented
Attractive	Famous	Multipurpose	Sexy
Authentic	Fancy	Natural	Shiny
Beautiful	Fast	New	Slim
Big	Fun	Old-Fashioned	Small
Black	Funny	Orange	Smart
Blue	Gentle	Perfect	Soft
Brown	Global	Pink	Spacious
Caring	Gold	Popular	Special
Clean	Gray	Powerful	Strong
Cold	Green	Practical	Stylish
Colorful	Happy	Prestigious	Trendy
Comfortable	Healthful	Profitable	Unique
Complete	Healthy	Proven	Unusual
Convenient	Helpful	Purple	Up-to-Date
Cool	High-Tech	Red	Useful
Custom-Made	Hot	Refreshing	Valuable
Daring	Important	Relaxing	Warm
Delicious	Informative	Reliable	White
Different	Inspiring	Rich	Yellow
Durable	Interesting	Romantic	Young
Easy	Lightweight	Safe	
Educational	Local	Satisfying	

Affordable

Synonyms

Bargain	Discount/discounted	Priced-to-move
Bargain-basement	Economical	Priced-to-sell
Bargain-priced	Half-price	Reasonable
Budget	Inexpensive	Reasonably priced
Cheap	Low-cost	Reduced
Competitively priced	Low-priced	Rock-bottom
Cost-efficient	Marked-down	Sale-priced
Cut-rate	Near-wholesale	Specially priced
Dirt-cheap	No-frills	

Related Words, Phrases, and Expressions

A deal	Easy on your wallet	On the cheap
A penny saved is a penny earned	Frugal	Pocket the difference
	Great buy	Purse strings
A steal	Haste makes waste	Small change
Cheapskate	If you have to ask, you can't afford it	Smart shopper
Clearance		Stretch your dollar
Closeout	More for your money	Value
Compare	Next to nothing	Waste not, want not
Cut corners	Nickels and dimes	Within your means
Don't get taken for a ride	On a shoestring	You get what you pay for

Symbols and Metaphors

$	Scissors
Piggy bank	

Antonyms

Budget-busting	Jacked-up	Rip-off
Dear	Overpriced	Wasteful
Expensive	Premium	
Inflated	Retail	

Assorted

Synonyms

Different

Miscellaneous

Mixed

Varying

Related Words, Phrases, and Expressions

A little of this, a little of that

Assorted colors

Assorted flavors

Choice

Colorful

Different strokes for different folks

Every color of the rainbow

For every taste

Grab bag

Many

Mixed bag

Multiple choice

Potpourri

Range

Selection

Something for everyone

Spectrum

Take your pick

The luxury of choice

Variety

Variety is the spice of life

Wide-ranging

Symbols and Metaphors

Box of chocolates

Box of donuts

Fruit basket

Patchwork quilt

Antonyms

Uniform

One-note

*What do the **bold** terms mean? These are other keywords in the book that might help with what you're looking for. See the Introduction for more information.*

Attractive

Synonyms

Appealing	Exotic	Pleasing
Artful	Finely crafted	Polished
Artistic	Flattering	Pretty
Attention-getting	Glowing	Put-together
Beautiful	Good-looking	Riveting
Charismatic	Gorgeous	Seductive
Charming	Graceful	**Sexy**
Compelling	Great-looking	Stimulating
Coordinated	Handsome	Striking
Cute	Inviting	**Stylish**
Darling	Lovely	Vivid
Delightful	Magnetic	Well-designed
Dreamy	Manicured	Well-groomed
Elegant	Neat	

Related Words, Phrases, and Expressions

A thing of beauty is a joy forever (John Keats)	Design	Presence
Aesthetic	Desire	Senses
Appeal	Image	Shape
Appearance	Like a moth to a flame	Visual
Can't take your eyes off of it	Lines	Want
Color	Look	You attract more flies with honey than with vinegar
Composition	Opposites attract	
	Picture	

Symbols and Metaphors

Bee and flower	Magnet

Antonyms

Boring	Messy	Unappealing
Clashing	Ordinary	Unattractive
Dreary	Repellent	Uncoordinated
Dull	Ugly	Unflattering
Forgettable	Unaesthetic	

Authentic

Synonyms

Authenticated	Genuine	Original
Bona fide	Homegrown	Real
Certified	Homemade	Sincere
Classic	Honest	Traditional
Down-home	Legitimate	True
First	Official	Valid

Related Words, Phrases, and Expressions

Keep it real	The real deal	True blue
Not an imitation	The real McCoy	

Symbols and Metaphors

100 percent	Official seal
Certificate of authenticity	

Antonyms

Affected	Ersatz	Phony
Artificial	Fake	Pseudo
Bogus	Faux	Replica
Contrived	Imitation	Sham
Copy	Inauthentic	Simulated
Counterfeit	Invented	Synthetic

Beautiful

Synonyms

Alluring	Fine	Pretty
Appealing	Foxy	Pulchritudinous
Attractive	Glowing	Radiant
Beauteous	Good-looking	Ravishing
Bonny	Gorgeous	Ravishing
Comely	Handsome	Striking
Cute	**Hot**	Stunning
Enchanting	Lovely	

Related Words, Phrases, and Expressions

A sight for sore eyes

A thing of beauty is a joy forever (John Keats)

American beauty

Babe

Beauty and the beast

Beauty is in the eye of the beholder

Beauty is only skin deep

Beauty pageant

Beauty salon/beauty parlor

Beauty spot/beauty mark

Black Beauty

Doll

Easy on the eyes

Eye candy

Face that launched a thousand ships

Fox

Knockout

Looker

Mirror, mirror on the wall, who's the fairest one of all?

Natural beauty

Pretty as a picture

Pretty is as pretty does

Pretty sight

She walks in beauty, like the night (Lord Byron)

Sight for sore eyes

Sleeping Beauty

The beauty part

Truth and beauty

"Truth is beauty and beauty truth"—that is all ye know on earth, and all ye need to know (John Keats)

'Twas beauty killed the beast

Visual

You must have been a beautiful baby, 'cause baby, look at you now*

Symbols and Metaphors

Mirror   Helen of Troy

Antonyms

Hideous	Ugly	Unappealing
Plain	Unaesthetic	Unattractive

What's the asterisk (*) for? See the sidebar in the Introduction for more information.

Big

Synonyms

Abundant
Ample
Bountiful
Broad
Brobdingnagian
Bulky
Colossal
Comprehensive
Considerable
Countless
Economy-size
Enormous
Extra
Extravagant
Gargantuan
Generous
Giant

Gigantic
Great
Healthy
Hefty
Huge
Immense
Jumbo
Large
Lavish
Macro
Magnum
Majestic
Major
Mammoth
Massive
Maximum
Mega

Mighty
Monster
Monumental
Myriad
Oversized
Plus
Significant
Sizable
Spacious
Substantial
Super
Tall
Towering
Tremendous
Vast
XL/XXL

Related Words, Phrases, and Expressions

Big break
Big cheese
Big city
Big day
Big deal
Big dreams
Big game
Big heart
Big Kahuna
Big league
Big news
Big picture
Big shot
Big sky

Big story
Big time
Big top
Big wheel
Bigger than life/larger than life
Bigwig
Bring out the big guns
Crowds
Hordes
Large and in charge
Living large
Make it big/making it big

Speak softly and carry a big stick (Theodore Roosevelt)
The big 4-0
The Big Apple
The Big Easy
The bigger the better
The bigger they are, the harder they fall
Think big
Too big for his britches
Top banana
Top dog
When you dream, dream big

continues

Big   *(continued)*

Symbols and Metaphors

800-pound gorilla	Empire State Building*	Paul Bunyan
All the tea in China	Goliath	Queen bee
California	Incredible Hulk*	Texas
Cornucopia	King Kong*	Whale
Elephant	Moby Dick	

Antonyms

Chintzy	Minor	Skimpy
Insubstantial	Minuscule	Stingy
Insufficient	Minute	Tiny
Miniature	Paltry	Undersized
Minimal	Shrimpy	

Black

Synonyms

Ebony	Onyx	Sable
Jet	Raven	

Related Words, Phrases, and Expressions

Black and white	Black market	Black-eyed Susan
Black as night	Black pearl	Blackjack
Black belt	Black pepper	Blackout
Black cat	Black sheep	Coal black
Black cloud	Black stallion	In the black
Black coffee	Black tie	Little black book
Black gold	Black velvet	Little black dress
Black humor	Blackbird	Pitch black
Black light	Blackboard	The Man in Black
Black magic	Black-eyed peas	The new black

Symbols and Metaphors

Clubs and Spades	Raven
Johnny Cash	

Blue

Synonyms

Aqua	Cyan	Royal
Aquamarine	Ice	Sapphire
Azure	Indigo	Sky
Cerulean	Midnight	Teal
Cobalt	Navy	Turquoise
Cornflower	Robin's-egg	Ultramarine

Related Words, Phrases, and Expressions

A bolt from the blue	Blue spruce	Little boy blue, come blow your horn
Baby blues	Blue suede shoes	Once in a blue moon
Between the devil and the deep blue sea	Blue velvet	Out of the blue/out of the clear blue sky
Blue cheese	Blue whale	Red, white, and blue
Blue chip	Bluebells	"Rhapsody in Blue"
Blue collar	Blueberry	Rhythm and blues
Blue jay	Bluebird	Something old, something new, something borrowed, something blue
Blue jeans	Blueblood	Talk a blue streak
Blue law	Bluegrass	The blues
Blue movie	Bluenose	True blue
Blue pencil	Blueprint	Turning blue
Blue period	Bluestocking	
Blue ribbon	In fourteen hundred ninety-two, Columbus sailed the ocean blue	

Symbols and Metaphors

Sea

Sky

Brown

Synonyms

Beige

Bronze

Chocolate

Copper

Earth

Sienna

Tan

Related Words, Phrases, and Expressions

Autumnal

Bronze age

Brown nose

Brownie points

Brownstone

Copper penny

Copperhead

Down to earth

Earth tones

Earthy

Golden brown

Hash browns

Muddy

Wood

Symbols and Metaphors

Autumn leaf

Dirt

Caring

Synonyms

Attentive

Committed

Concerned

Considerate

Generous

Gentle

Good-hearted

Kind

Nice

Philanthropic

Selfless

Sensitive

Soft-hearted

Supportive

Sweet

Thoughtful

Unselfish

Warm-hearted

Related Words, Phrases, and Expressions

A friend in need is a friend indeed

Caregiver

Caretaker

Charity begins at home

Friend

Give something back

Handle with care

Heart of gold

Hero

Home care

Hospice care

If you want to lift yourself up, lift up someone else (Booker T. Washington)

It's better to give than to receive

Lend a hand

Make a difference

Needy

No act of kindness, no matter how small, is ever wasted (Aesop)

Open your heart

Others

Pay it forward

Share the wealth

Share/sharing

Take care

The less fortunate

There when you're needed

Time of need

Times of trouble

Symbols and Metaphors

Chicken soup

Good Samaritan

Hug

Volunteer

Antonyms

Cold-hearted

Indifferent

Insensitive

Scroogelike

Self-centered

Selfish

Uncaring

Clean

Synonyms

Antiseptic
Clear
Dirt-free
Dust-free
Fresh
Gleaming
Grease-free

Hygienic
Immaculate
Laundered
Neat
Oil-free
Organized
Polished

Pristine
Sanitary
Scoured
Scrubbed
Shining
Sparkling
Spotless

Tidy
Uncluttered
Uncontaminated
Unpolluted
Unsullied
Washed

Related Words, Phrases, and Expressions

A place for everything and everything in its place
Bathe
Batting cleanup
Clean air
Clean as a whistle
Clean break
Clean getaway

Clean house
Clean language
Clean sweep
Clean up
Clean up your act
Clean water
Clean your plate
Clean-cut

Cleanliness is next to godliness
Cleanse
Clear the air
Come clean
Disinfect
Good, clean fun
In a lather

Keep it clean
Neatness counts
Scour
Soap and water
Soapbox
Spring cleaning
Squeaky-clean
Take a bath

Symbols and Metaphors

Bubbles

White glove

Antonyms

Cluttered
Dingy
Dirty
Disorganized
Dull/dulled
Dusty
Filthy

Gray
Greasy
Grimy
Gritty
Grubby
Grungy
Messy

Muddy
Oily
Sloppy
Sooty
Stale
Tarnished
Unfresh

Unhygienic
Unkempt
Unwashed
Yellowed

Cold

Synonyms

Arctic	Frigid	**Refreshing**
Chilly/chilled	Frosty	Shivery
Cool	Frozen	Siberian
Crisp	Icy	Wintry
Freezing	Polar	

Related Words, Phrases, and Expressions

Below freezing	Cold shoulder	Freeze frame
Chill	Cold snap	Ice-cold
Chill pill	Cold sober	Low temperature
Chilled to the bone	Cold spell	Makes your blood run cold
Cold as ice	Cold storage	Out cold
Cold call	Cold war	Stone-cold
Cold case	Cold-hearted	Teeth-chattering
Cold cash	Come in from the cold	Wind chill factor
Cold cream	Common cold	**Winter**
Cold feet	Deep freeze	Zero degrees
Cold front	Down cold	

Symbols and Metaphors

Ice cream	Igloo	Siberia
Ice cube	North Pole	Snowflake
Icicle	Refrigerator	Snowman

Antonyms

Hot	Overheated	Sweaty
Lukewarm	Stifling	**Warm**
Oppressive	Stuffy	

Colorful

Synonyms

Bright	**Rich**	Vivid
Lively	Vibrant	

Related Words, Phrases, and Expressions

Color guard	Earth tones	Pastels
Color my world*	Every color of the rainbow	Primary colors
Color scheme	Full color	Shades
Color TV	Hues	Spectrum
Coloring book	Jewel tones	Tints
Colors	Multicolored	Tones

Symbols and Metaphors

Artist's palette	Jellybeans
Garden/bouquet	Rainbow

Antonyms

Black and white	Faded	Sepia
Colorless	Muddy	
Dull	Muted	

Comfortable

Synonyms

Casual	Laid-back	Roomy	Unburdened
Comfy	Loose	Slow-paced	Unhurried
Cozy	Low-stress	Snug	**Warm**
Cushy	**Luxurious**	**Soft**	Welcoming
Easy	Padded	Soothing	
Gentle	Painless	**Spacious**	
Informal	Relaxed	Stress-free	

Related Words, Phrases, and Expressions

Ahhhh	Comfort level	Easy life/easy living	Snug as a bug in a rug
At ease	Comfortable fit	Embrace	Stretch
Breathe easy	Comfortable pace	In comfort	Take comfort
Breeze	Comforter	Kick back	Unwind
Chill out	Curl up	Kick off your shoes	Wrap
Cold comfort	Ease	Loose as a goose	
Comfort food	Easy chair	Put up your feet	

Symbols and Metaphors

Bubble bath	Fireplace	Recliner
Coffee/tea/hot cocoa	Hammock	Slippers
Couch	Lounge chair	Teddy bear
Easy chair	Milk and cookies	Winter scarf/ mittens
	Quilt	

Antonyms

Awkward	Fast-paced	Sore	Tense
Buttoned-up	Formal	Stiff	Tight
Chilly	Hard	Strained	Uncomfortable
Competitive	Intense	Straitlaced	Uptight
Cramped	Overloaded	Stressful/stressed	
Drafty	Pressured	Stuffy	

Complete

Synonyms

All-encompassing

All-inclusive

Comprehensive

Exhaustive

Finished

Full

Thorough

Total

Related Words, Phrases, and Expressions

100 percent

All in one

All you need

A-to-Z

Complete set

Everything but the kitchen sink

From soup to nuts

Whole kit and caboodle

Whole nine yards

You complete me

Symbols and Metaphors

Circle

Finish line

Antonyms

Incomplete

Half-baked

Lacking

Short

Shy

Undone

Unfinished

Convenient

Synonyms

Accessible	Handy	Opportune
Easy	Hassle-free	Quick
Efficient	Low-stress	Simple
Fast	Nearby	

Related Words, Phrases, and Expressions

A breeze	**Convenient location**	On your own schedule
A convenient excuse	Easy to find	Push-button
A snap	Easy to store	Store out of sight
At your convenience	Easy to use	There when you need it
At your fingertips	Marriage of convenience	Waiting for you
Close at hand	No fuss, no muss	Within your reach
Convenience store	On the spot	

Symbols and Metaphors

24-hour store	Microwave
ATM	Private driveway

Antonyms

Awkward	Hard-to-find	Remote
Complicated	Inconvenient	Tedious
Demanding		

Cool

Synonyms

Autumnal	Brisk	Chilly
Bracing	Calm	Nippy

Related Words, Phrases, and Expressions

Cool and collected	Cool it	Cool-headed
Cool breeze	Cool million	It's cool
Cool cat	Cool off	Keep cool
Cool customer	Cool your heels	Play it cool

Symbols and Metaphors

Beach umbrella	Jazz musician	Sunglasses
Fan	Lemonade	The Fonz
Ice cube	Mint	

Antonyms

Overheated	**Warm**
Stuffy	

Custom-Made

Synonyms

Bespoke	Customized	Personalized
Custom-built	Individualized	Tailored
Custom-designed	Made-to-order	

Related Words, Phrases, and Expressions

As you like it	Expressly for you	To your liking
Designed with you in mind	Made to fit	To your specifications
Engraved	To each his own	To your taste

Symbols and Metaphors

Measuring tape	Monogram
Mixed tape	

Antonyms

Common	Mass-produced	Ordinary
Cookie-cutter	Off-the-rack	Run-of-the-mill
Machine-made	One-size-fits-all	

Daring

Synonyms

Adventurous

Audacious

Bold

Brave

Courageous

Edgy

Fearless

Gutsy

Intrepid

Nervy

Plucky

Risky/risk-taking

Risqué

Related Words, Phrases, and Expressions

All in

Chutzpah

Color outside the lines

Dare to dream

Daredevil

Dive in

Do you dare?

Double dare

Double or nothing

Explore

Fortune sides with him
  who dares

Frontier

Gambler

High stakes

"I dare you"

Innovator

Make a statement

On a dare

Push the envelope

Put it on the line

Risk-taker

Roll the dice

Rules are made to be broken

Take a chance

Take the lead

Test the limits

Truth or dare

Up for anything

You only live once

You've got some nerve

Symbols and Metaphors

Astronaut

Bungee jumper

Explorer

Lion tamer

Stuntman

Wright brothers

Antonyms

Careful

Cautious

Inhibited

Meek

Mousy

Shy

Timid

Delicious

Synonyms

Appetizing	Luscious	Succulent
Delectable	Mouthwatering	Tasty
Flavorful	Savory	Yummy
Lip-smacking	Scrumptious	

Related Words, Phrases, and Expressions

A matter of taste	Gimme some sugar	Sweet life
A taste of honey	Good taste never goes out	Sweet mystery of life
Aftertaste	of style	Sweet spot
Ambrosia	Gourmet/gourmand	Sweet tooth
Bite	Hint	Take a bite out of life
Bitter	In good taste	Tangy
Bittersweet	Leaves a bad taste	Taste
Bold	Medley	Taste buds
Connoisseur	Nibble	Taste of heaven
Craving	Nosh	Tasteful
Creamy	Palate	Texture
Crispy	Salty	Tongue
Crunchy	Sour	Variety is the spice of life
Eat, drink, and be merry	Spicy	Wholesome
Fresh	Subtle	Yum
Fruity	Sweet	Zingy

Symbols and Metaphors

Chocolate-covered strawberry	Spice rack
Salt and pepper	Sugar cube

Antonyms

Bland	Tasteless
Flavorless	

Different

Synonyms

Alternate/alternative

Contrasting

Creative

Distinct

Exotic

Foreign

Innovative

New

Original

Special

Uncommon

Unique

Unusual

Related Words, Phrases, and Expressions

Apples and oranges

Dare to be different

Different strokes for
different folks

Individual

March to the beat of a
different drum

Night and day

Off the beaten path

On the fringe

Out of the ordinary

Same thing, different day

Something different

Standout

Which one of these is not
like the other?

Why is this night different
from all other nights?

Symbols and Metaphors

Foreigner

Vacation

Antonyms

Alike

Boilerplate

Cookie-cutter

Everyday

Mundane

Ordinary

Repetitive

Routine

Run-of-the-mill

Same

Same-old

Similar

Standard

Template

Usual

Durable

Synonyms

Enduring	Professional grade	Tough
Hard	Shatterproof	Unbreakable
Indestructible	Solid	Well-built
Lasting	**Strong**	Well-made
Long-lasting	Sturdy	

Related Words, Phrases, and Expressions

Built to last	Generation after generation	Rock-solid
Fifteen rounds		Stands up to wear and tear
For the duration	Goes all the way	Strong as an ox
For the long term	Heirloom quality	

Symbols and Metaphors

Diamond	Oak tree	Steel
Fruitcake	Rock	Turtle

Antonyms

Cheap	Flimsy	Poorly made
Disposable	Fragile	Short-lived

Easy

Synonyms

Effortless

Painless

Simple

Smooth

Straightforward

Stress-free

Uncomplicated

Related Words, Phrases, and Expressions

A breeze

A cakewalk

A cinch

A snap

Anyone can do it

As easy as 1-2-3

Easy as pie

Easy chair

Easy money

Easy street

Easygoing

Go easy

Lobbing softballs

Piece of cake

Take it easy

The easy life

Symbols and Metaphors

E-Z

2+2

Antonyms

Challenging

Complex

Complicated

Confusing

Difficult

Hard

Tough

Educational

Synonyms

Brain-building
Broadening
Enlightening

Informative
Instructive

Knowledge-
enhancing
Skill-building

Skill-enhancing
Skill-sharpening

Related Words, Phrases, and Expressions

Assignment
Book-learning
Brains
Brainy
Bright
Campus
Class
College
Course
Course of action
Cram
Dean's list
Develop
Distance learning
Do your homework
Give a man a fish and you feed him for a day; teach a man to fish and you feed him for a lifetime

Grow
Hands-on learning
Homework
Honor roll
Idea
If you think educa-tion is expensive, try ignorance
Know-it-all
Knowledge
Learn
Learn from your mistakes
Learn the hard way
Lecture
Lesson
Lesson plan
Library
Library card
Mentor

Online course
Only the educated are free
Pop quiz
Potential
Prep school
Preparatory
Private school
Public school
Pulling an all-nighter
Pupil
Quiz
Quiz show
School
School of hard knocks
School's out
Sharp as a tack
Smart
Smarts

Student
Studious
Study
Study hall
Summa cum laude
Take notes
Teach
Teach your children well*
Test
Textbook
This is not a test
Tutor
Valedictorian
Wisdom
You can't teach an old dog new tricks
You learn something new every day

Symbols and Metaphors

Backpack
Blackboard

Books
Lightbulb

Mortarboard
Owl

Report card

Antonyms

Mind-numbing
Pointless

Time-wasting
Useless

Worthless

Excellent

Synonyms

Amazing
Astonishing
Awesome
Awe-inspiring
Brilliant
Dope
Dynamite
Extraordinary
Fabulous
Fantastic
First-class
First-rate
Glorious

Great
High-end
High-quality
Impressive
Incredible
Magnificent
Marvelous
Outstanding
Phat
Primo
Radical/rad
Sensational
Sublime

Super
Superb
Superior
Supreme
Terrific
Top-drawer
Top-notch
Top-of-the-line
Top-performing
Top-quality
Top-shelf
Wonderful

Related Words, Phrases, and Expressions

Excellence and moderation
Genius
Merit
Out of this world
Performance

Quality
Some are born great; some
    achieve greatness, and
    some have greatness
    thrust upon them
    (William Shakespeare)

The bomb
The joint
Tops

Symbols and Metaphors

A+
Blue ribbon

Trophy
Gold medal

Gold star

Antonyms

Average
Cheap
Flimsy
Inferior

Junky
Lame
Low-quality
Mediocre

Poor
Poor-quality

Exciting

Synonyms

A thrill a minute	Exhilarating	Sensational
Action-packed	Mind-blowing	Spine-tingling
Arousing	Provocative	Stimulating
Compelling	Pulse-pounding	Stirring
Electric	Riveting	Thrilling
Electrifying	Rousing	Titillating

Related Words, Phrases, and Expressions

A tingle in the air	Pumped	Thrill
Buzz	Rush	Tingle
Edge-of-your-seat	Sets your heart aflutter	What's all the excitement about?
Excite your senses	Shock	
Jazzed	The shock of the new	

Symbols and Metaphors

Roller coaster

Antonyms

Blah	Humdrum	Slow
Boring	Lame	Tedious
Dreary	Mind-numbing	Unstimulating
Dull	Routine	Yawn-inducing
Everyday	Run-of-the-mill	
Ho-hum	Sleep-inducing	

Famous

Synonyms

Celebrated	Known	Renowned
Eminent	Legendary	Well-known
Famed	Notable	Widely known
High-profile	Noted	World-famous
Illustrious	Prominent	World-renowned

Related Words, Phrases, and Expressions

Boldface name	Household name	Of the moment
Celebrity	In front of the camera	Paparazzi
Fame and fortune	In the future everyone will be famous for 15 minutes	Star
Familiar face		Star quality
Famous face	"It" girl	Superstar
Glitterati	Name brand	
Hollywood	Notorious	

Symbols and Metaphors

Marquee	Star on dressing-room door
Spotlight	

Antonyms

Anonymous	Unknown
No-name	

Fancy

Synonyms

Elaborate

Embellished

Decked-out

Dressed-up

Frilly

Gussied-up

Intricate

Ornamented

Ornate

Ostentatious

Posh

Showy

Snazzy

Swanky

Tricked-out

Related Words, Phrases, and Expressions

Bells and whistles

Dressed to the nines

Fancy dress

Fancy footwork

Fancy pants

Fancy that

Footloose and fancy free

In the spring a young man's fancy lightly turns to thoughts of love (Alfred, Lord Tennyson)

Nothing fancy

Razzle-dazzle

Whatever strikes your fancy

Whatever tickles your fancy

Symbols and Metaphors

Chandelier

Ribbons and bows

Top hat

Tuxedo

Antonyms

Austere

Bare

Casual

Dressed-down

Everyday

Plain

Spare

Spartan

Unadorned

Fast

Synonyms

Accelerated	High-velocity	Racing	Swift
Brisk	Hurried	Rapid	Whirlwind
Express	Immediate	Rocketing	Zippy
Fast-paced	Instantaneous	Rushing/rushed	
Hasty	Lightning-paced	Speedy/speeding	
High-speed	Quick	Supersonic	

Related Words, Phrases, and Expressions

100-yard dash	Fast lane	Left in the dust	Speed of sound
Blur	Fast talker	Lickety-split	Split second
BPS (bits per second)	Fast track	Like the wind	Turbo
Burning rubber	Fasten your seatbelt	MPH	Velocity
Colorfast	Feast and fast	On your mark, get set, go	Vroom
Dart	Flash	Playing fast and loose	Warp speed
Dash	Fly	Rapid-fire	Whitewater
Fast and furious	Gathering speed	RPM	Whizzing by
Fast asleep	Haste makes waste	Rush hour	Whoosh
Fast buck	Hold fast	Speed of light	Zero-to-sixty
Fast forward	Hurry up and wait		Zip
Fast friends	Hyperspeed		Zoom

Symbols and Metaphors

Cheetah	Jet	Race car	The Flash*
Gazelle	Lightning	Rocket	Torpedo
Hummingbird	Rabbit	Speedy Gonzales*	

Antonyms

Draggy/dragging	Lumbering	Snail-like	Time-wasting
Drawn-out	Slow	Stagnant	
Glacial	Sluggish	Time-consuming	

Fun

Synonyms

Adventurous

Diverting

Enjoyable

Entertaining

Festive

High-spirited

Jocular

Lively

Merry

Recreational

Related Words, Phrases, and Expressions

Frolic

Fun and games

Fun for the whole family

Fun in the sun

Fun-filled

Get in on the fun

Good, clean fun

Joie de vivre

Just for fun

Let the good times roll

Making fun

Making merry

Symbols and Metaphors

Amusement park

Beach ball

Playground

Antonyms

Boring

Demanding

Draining

Dull

Mundane

Routine

Serious

Funny

Synonyms

Amusing

Comical

Farcical

Giggle-inducing

Goofy

Hilarious

Humorous

Hysterical

Ironic

Laugh-a-minute

Laugh-out-loud

Light

Rib-tickling

Riotous

Satiric

Sharp-witted

Side-splitting

Uproarious

Witty

Related Words, Phrases, and Expressions

Absurd

Banter

Belly laugh

Burst out laughing

Can't keep a
    straight face

Chuckle

Comedy = tragedy
    + time

Comic relief

Crack up

Dry wit

Funny bone

Funny face

Funny pages

Gas

Giggle

Glee

Grin

Guffaw

Ha ha

He who laughs,
    lasts

He who laughs last
    laughs best

Hoot

Howl

In on the joke

In stitches

Inside joke

Jest

Joke

Knee-slapper

Last laugh

Laugh

Laugh until you cry

Laughter is the
    best medicine*

LOL

Many a truth is said
    in jest

One-liner

Pun

Punch line

Repartee

Riot

Roaring

Rolling in the aisles

Scatological

See you in the
    funny papers

Sense of humor

Slapstick

Smile

Snicker

Snort

The joke's on me

Wit and wisdom

Symbols and Metaphors

Clown

Comedy mask

Court jester

Hyena

Sitcom

Standup comic

Antonyms

Boring

Dull

Flat

Humorless

Lame

Unfunny

Witless

Gentle

Synonyms

Careful	Light	**Soft**
Delicate	Low-impact	Tender
Easy	Nonirritating	
Kind	Sensitive	

Related Words, Phrases, and Expressions

A gentleman never kisses and tells	Gentle giant	Tread lightly
An officer and a gentleman	Gentle reader	Walk on eggshells
Do not go gentle into that good night (Dylan Thomas)	Gentleman	
	Handle with kid gloves	
	Light touch	

Symbols and Metaphors

Breeze	Rose petal
Feather	

Antonyms

Abrasive	Insensitive	Rough
Grating	Irritating	Rude
Harsh	Pushy	Tactless

Global

Synonyms

International   Worldwide
Universal

Related Words, Phrases, and Expressions

Across the globe   Everywhere   Planet
All over the map   Global epidemic   Think globally, act locally
Around the globe   Global warming   Universal language
Around the world   Here, there, and every- World
Earth   where

Symbols and Metaphors

Globe

Antonyms

Limited   National
Local   Provincial

Gold

Synonyms

Champagne   Topaz

Honey

Related Words, Phrases, and Expressions

14k

All that glitters is not gold

Bling

Fool's gold

Gold digger

Gold lamé

Gold medal

Gold mine

Gold record

Gold rush

Gold standard

Gold star

Gold tooth

Golden girl/boy

Golden Rule

Golden years

Good as gold

Goose that laid the golden egg

He who has the gold makes the rules

Make new friends and keep the old, one is silver and the other gold

Shimmering

Sparkling

Strike gold

White gold

Yellow gold

Symbols and Metaphors

Gold bar   Wedding ring

Treasure chest

Gray

Synonyms

Ash

Charcoal

Gunmetal

Silver

Smoke

Titanium

Related Words, Phrases, and Expressions

Cloudy

Going gray

Gray area

Gray day

Gray flannel suit

Gray hair

Gray matter

Overcast

Shades of gray

Symbols and Metaphors

Elephant

Storm cloud

Green

Synonyms

Chartreuse

Emerald

Hunter

Jade

Kelly

Kiwi

Lime

Loden

Mint

Moss

Olive

Seafoam

Teal

Related Words, Phrases, and Expressions

Cross on the green, not in between

Environmental

Go

Green around the gills

Green beans

Green grass

Green light

Green thumb

Green vegetables

Green with envy

Greenbacks

It's not easy being green

Little green men

On the green

Salad greens

The grass is always greener on the other side of the fence

The wearin' of the green

Symbols and Metaphors

Dollar bill

Frog

Lawn

Plants/trees

Shamrock

Vegetables

Happy

Synonyms

Blissful/blissed-out
Celebrating/celebratory
Cheerful/cheery
Content/contented
Delighted
Giddy

Gleeful
Joyful
Joyous
Light-hearted
Merry
Overjoyed

Pleased
Rejoicing
Satisfied
Smiling
Thrilled

Related Words, Phrases, and Expressions

Come on, get happy
Don't worry, be happy
Follow your bliss
Grinning from ear to ear
Happiness is a warm
  puppy*
Happy as a clam
Happy birthday
Happy camper
Happy days

Happy feet
Happy occasion
Happy talk
Happy to help
Heaven
If you're happy and you
  know it, clap your hands*
Ignorance is bliss
In heaven
Let a smile be your
  umbrella

Life, liberty, and the pur-
  suit of happiness
Nirvana
On cloud nine
Paradise
Purring
Seventh heaven
Walking on air
Warm your heart
"You made my day!"

Symbols and Metaphors

☺
Bluebird

Smile
Sun

Antonyms

Blue
Bummed/bummed-out
Depressed
Disappointed
Discontented
Displeased

Dissatisfied/unsatisfied
Distressed
Down
Frustrated
Gloomy
Glum

Miserable
Sad
Sorrowful
Unhappy
Woeful
Yearning

Healthful

Synonyms

Additive-free
Balanced
Beneficial
Caffeine-free
Enriched
Fortified

Healing
Health-promoting
Invigorating
Nourishing
Nutrient-packed
Nutritious

Sensible
Strengthening
Vitamin-packed
Wholesome

Related Words, Phrases, and Expressions

An apple a day keeps the
    doctor away
Enjoy it in good health
Good for you
Health and fitness
Health and happiness
Health care
Health club

Health food
Health insurance
Health nut
Health plan
Heart-healthy
I've still got my health
In sickness and in health
Mental health

Minerals
Nutrients
Nutritional value
To your health
Vitamins
Wear it in good health
Well-being
Wellness

Symbols and Metaphors

Apple
Stethoscope

Antonyms

High-fat
High-salt
Junky

Processed
Sedentary
Sugary

Unbalanced
Unhealthy/unhealthful

Healthy

Synonyms

Balanced

Energetic

Flexible

Flourishing

Robust

Strong

Supple

Thriving

Well

Related Words, Phrases, and Expressions

Clean bill of health

Early to bed and early to rise makes a man healthy, wealthy, and wise

Fit as a fiddle

Glowing with health

Health and fitness

Health care

Health club

Health food

Health **insurance**

Health nut

Health plan

Healthy and happy

Healthy appetite

Healthy attitude

Healthy curiosity

Healthy glow

In the pink

Vital/vitality

Well-being

Wellness

You're the picture of health

Symbols and Metaphors

Scale

Weights

Yoga pose

Antonyms

Achy

Ailing

Fatigued

Ill

Run-down

Sedentary

Sick

Sluggish

Suffering

Unbalanced

Unhealthy

Helpful

Synonyms

Attentive

Encouraging

Responsive

Supportive

Useful

Related Words, Phrases, and Expressions

Aid

Assist

Enable

Every little bit helps

Get help

Guidance

Happy to help

Help and hope

Help me, Rhonda*

Help out

Helping hand

Helping professions

Helpless

Helpmate

Here to help

Hired help

Mother's little helper*

Relief

Serve

Succor

There for you

With a little help from my
friends*

You can't get good help
these days

Symbols and Metaphors

Barn raising

Bucket brigade

Crutch

Eyeglasses

Flare

Nurse

PDA

SOS

Stepladder

Antonyms

Discouraging

Hurtful

Inattentive

Indifferent

Uncaring

Unhelpful

Unresponsive

Unsupportive

Useless

High-Tech

Synonyms

Advanced	Futuristic	State-of-the-art
Cutting-edge	Next-generation	

Related Words, Phrases, and Expressions

Advancements	Fine-tuned	Push-button
Ahead-of-the-curve	High-speed	Quantum leap
Change	**Information** age	Robotic
Computerized	Intelligent	Scientific
Developments	Latest research	Space-age
Digital	Leading	Technology
Efficient	**New**	Tomorrow
Electronic	Next	Up-to-the-minute
Engineered	On the cutting edge	Wireless

Symbols and Metaphors

e	Plug
Mouse	

Antonyms

Analog	Cut-and-paste	Obsolete
Bricks-and-mortar	Low-tech	**Old-fashioned**

Hot

Synonyms

Blazing

Equatorial

Caribbean

Heated

High-temperature

Radioactive

Searing

Sizzling

Spicy

Steaming/steamy

Sultry

Summery

Sweltering

Torrid

Related Words, Phrases, and Expressions

Beat the heat

Giving off heat

Heat and eat

Heat and serve

Heat of the
moment

Heat wave

Hot air

Hot and spicy

Hot cocoa

Hot cross buns

Hot dog

Hot flash

Hot legs

Hot lights

Hot mama

Hot off the presses

Hot on his heels

Hot on the trail

Hot pants

Hot pepper

Hot plate

Hot pot

Hot potato

Hot property

Hot pursuit

Hot rod

Hot sauce

Hot spot

Hot story

Hot stuff

Hot toddy

Hot under the collar

Hot wax

Hot-blooded

Hotfooting it

Hothead

Hothouse

Hotline

Hotshot

If you can't take the
heat, get out of
the kitchen

In hot water

In the hot seat

Out of the frying
pan, into the fire

Piping hot

Radiating heat

Running hot and
cold

Selling like hot-
cakes

Steam heat

The heat is on

Too hot to handle

You can fry an egg
on it

Symbols and Metaphors

Beach

Desert

Fire

Fireplace

Jalapeño pepper

Radiator

Space heater

Steam

Stove/oven

Sun

Antonyms

Cold

Chilly

Frigid

Icy

Lukewarm

Room-temperature

Important

Synonyms

Basic

Consequential

Critical

Crucial

Essential

Fundamental

Indispensable

Key

Life-changing

Momentous

Necessary

Pivotal

Serious

Significant

Urgent

Related Words, Phrases, and Expressions

A must

An important distinction

ASAP

Big deal

Don't sweat the small stuff

Emergency

If it's important, it'll come
  back to you

In order of importance

Must-have

Priority

Required

Top of the pile

VIP

You've got your health, and
  that's the most important
  thing

Symbols and Metaphors

!

*

Yellow highlighter

Antonyms

Frivolous

Inconsequential

Insignificant

Unimportant

Informative

Synonyms

Educational	Fact-filled	Instructive
Enlightening	Illuminating	Revealing

Related Words, Phrases, and Expressions

411	In the know	Reference
Breaking news	Imparting **information**	Research
Bulletin	Information age	Shedding light
Classified information	Information, please	**Smart**
Data	Information superhighway	Source
Dirt	Informed opinion	Special report
Dish	Just the facts, ma'am	The lowdown
Fact-finding mission	Keep me informed	The scoop
Fact-finding tour	Knowledge	The word
Film at 11	Memo	Updates
Fully informed	Need-to-know basis	Wise
FYI	On top of the story	

Symbols and Metaphors

Computer/hard drive/database	Encyclopedia	Newspaper
Dictionary	Information desk	**Phone**
	Library	Search engine

Antonyms

Biased	Secretive	Uninformative
Confusing	Slanted	Withholding
Misleading	Unenlightening	

Inspiring

Synonyms

Cheering
Encouraging
Energizing
Galvanizing

Heartening
Heartwarming
Inspirational
Motivating

Moving
Rousing
Soul-stirring
Stimulating

Related Words, Phrases, and Expressions

Believe in miracles
Creative inspiration
Determination
Dose of inspiration
Fire the imagination
Hero
Inspired idea

Inspired to act
Inspiring example
Inspiring figure
Make miracles
Never, never, never, never give up
Overcoming the obstacles

Persistence
Spirit
Spurred on
Success is 1 percent inspiration and 99 percent perspiration

Symbols and Metaphors

Butterfly
Knute Rockne*
Pep rally

Preacher
Sunrise

Antonyms

Cynical
Defeating
Demotivating

Depressing
Discouraging
Downbeat

Fatalist
Pessimistic
Uninspiring

Interesting

Synonyms

Absorbing	**Exciting**	Riveting
Attention-getting	Fascinating	Spellbinding
Compelling	Gripping	Thought-provoking
Engrossing	Intriguing	

Related Words, Phrases, and Expressions

An interesting turn of events	High interest	People are buzzing
Attract a crowd	Interest rates	Person of interest
Capture your interest	Interest-free	Pique your interest
Earning interest	Low interest	Point of interest
Focus of attention	May we interest you in _____?	Spark interest
Get their attention	Much-discussed	Verrry interesting

Symbols and Metaphors

Crowd	Museum display
Front page of newspaper	Spotlight

Antonyms

Boring	Mind-numbing	Tedious
Dull	Slow-moving	Uninteresting
Ho-hum		

Lightweight

Synonyms

Airy	Featherweight	Space-saving
Comfortable	Portable	

Related Words, Phrases, and Expressions

Carry-on	Grab it and go	Take it anywhere
Easy to carry	Lay down your burdens	Unencumbered
Easy to move	Light as a feather	Won't weigh you down
Emotional baggage	Light as air	You can't take it with you
Float	Lighten your load	
Freedom of movement	Ounces	

Symbols and Metaphors

Backpack	Helium balloon
Feather	

Antonyms

Awkward	Burdensome	Oppressive
Big	Clunky	Oversized
Bulky	Heavy	Uncomfortable

Local

Synonyms

Close	Familiar
Convenient	Nearby

Related Words, Phrases, and Expressions

From the people you know and trust	Just around the corner	Shop locally
In the vicinity	Locally grown	Think globally, act locally
In your community	Neighborly	We know where you live
Just a short trip away	Quick trip	Within walking distance

Symbols and Metaphors

Bike	Walking shoes
Main Street	

Antonyms

Distant	**Global**	Out-of-the-way
Faraway	Inconvenient	Strange
Foreign	National	Unfamiliar

Long-Lasting

Synonyms

Durable

Continuing

Enduring

Extended-use

Extended-wear

Lasting

Long-wearing

Permanent

Related Words, Phrases, and Expressions

All day long/all night long

Around the clock

For the duration

For the long haul

Keeps working

Lasting effects

Lasting relationship

Never say die

To the finish line

Waterproof

Won't fade away

Won't let you down

Won't peter out

Won't quit

Symbols and Metaphors

Calendar

Clock

Marathon runner

Antonyms

Disappearing

Flash-in-the-pan

Passing

Quick-fading

Temporary

Luxurious

Synonyms

Comfortable	Lavish	**Soft**
Deluxe	Opulent	Splendid
Grand	Padded	Sumptuous
High-quality	Plush	
Indulgent	Ritzy	

Related Words, Phrases, and Expressions

Advantage	Little luxuries	Luxury and necessity
Amenities	Living in luxury	Luxury item
At your service	Luxuriate	Luxury tax
Extras	Luxuriously appointed	The luxury of choice
Lap of luxury	Luxuriously furnished	The luxury of time

Symbols and Metaphors

Bubble bath	**Jewelry**	Sofa
Caviar	King-size bed	Yacht
Champagne	Limousine	
Cruise ship	Silk	

Antonyms

Austere	Minimal	Spartan
Bare-bones	Necessary	Uncomfortable
Basic	No-frills	
Economical	Spare	

Multipurpose

Synonyms

Adaptable

All-purpose

Multi-use

Versatile

Related Words, Phrases, and Expressions

A multitude of uses

All-in-one

Does it all

Double duty

Efficient

Jack of all trades

Multiple attachments

Multiple settings

Multi-talented

Renaissance man

Triple threat

Symbols and Metaphors

Baking soda

Gal Friday

Junk drawer

Swiss Army knife*

Utility infielder

Natural

Synonyms

Additive-free	Raw	Untainted
Genuine	Unadulterated	Whole
Organic	Unprocessed	Wholesome
Pure	Unrefined	

Related Words, Phrases, and Expressions

A natural	Mother Nature	Natural selection
All you gotta do is act naturally*	Natural beauty	Natural state
	Natural childbirth	Nature of the beast
All-natural	Natural fiber	Nature trail
Back to the earth	Natural history	Nature vs. nurture
Communing with nature	Natural look	Nature walk
From the earth	Natural number	No artificial ingredients
Good-natured	Natural order	Occurring in nature
Human nature	Natural progression	You make me feel like a natural woman*
It's only natural	Natural resource	
Laws of nature	Natural science	

Symbols and Metaphors

Family farm	Vegetable garden
Garden of Eden	

Antonyms

Altered	Machine-made	Phony
Artificial	Made-up	Processed
Contrived	Manipulated	Synthetic
Laboratory-made	Manmade	Unnatural

New

Synonyms

All-new	Late-model	Re-engineered
Brand-new	Latest	Refreshed/refreshing
Contemporary	Mint	Rejuvenated
Creative	Modern	Renewed
Cutting-edge	Original	Unprecedented
Fresh	Recent	Updated
Innovative	Redesigned	Up-to-date

Related Words, Phrases, and Expressions

Debut	New era	New Year's Day
For the first time	New idea	New Year's resolution
Introducing	New Jersey	New York
Like new	New lease on life	Newbie
Make new friends and keep the old, one is silver and the other gold	New Mexico	Newcomer
	New millennium	News
Never before	New moon	Now available
New Age	New opportunity	Premiere
New and **improved**	New twist	The shock of the new
New day	New Wave	There's nothing new under the sun
New England	New World	Try something new

Symbols and Metaphors

Baby	Chick	**Spring**
Bow	January 1	Tags
Bud	Shrink-wrap	

Antonyms

Ancient	Old-hat	Stale
Antique	Outdated	Tired
Dated	Over	Used
Obsolete	Raggedy	Vintage
Old	Rickety	Worn-out
Old-fashioned		

Old-Fashioned

Synonyms

Antique	Old-style	Time-honored
Folksy	Old-time	Traditional
Home-style	Retro	Vintage
Nostalgic	Simple	
Old-school	Small-town	

Related Words, Phrases, and Expressions

Another time	Good old days	Time-tested
Back in the day	Good, old-fashioned	Tradition
Back to basics	Original recipe	Tried-and-true
Built to last	Passed down through gen-	Wisdom
Bygone days	erations	Yesteryear
Common sense	Through the years	

Symbols and Metaphors

General store	Rotary phone	Tire swing
Grandma	Soda jerk	White picket fence
Norman Rockwell*	Tail fins	

Antonyms

Factory-made	Newfangled	Shoddy
Faddish	Plastic	Synthetic
Mass-produced		

Orange

Synonyms

Cantaloupe

Melon

Peach

Pumpkin

Rust

Saffron

Tangerine

Related Words, Phrases, and Expressions

Eat a peach

Orange blossom

Orange juice

Orange you glad I didn't
    say banana again?

Peachy

Peachy-keen

Pumpkin pie

Symbols and Metaphors

Florida

Hunting vest

Traffic cone

Perfect

Synonyms

Consummate	Ideal	Ultimate
Faultless	Mint	Unblemished
Flawless	Model	Unspoiled

Related Words, Phrases, and Expressions

4.0	Just right	Perfect score
100 percent	Nobody's perfect	Perfect stranger
A+	Perfect 10	Perfect tense
I never said I was perfect	Perfect circle	Perfect timing
I'm not perfect, but I'm all I've got	Perfect fit	Perfection
	Perfect game	Perfectionist
In a perfect world	Perfect match	Striving for perfection
It ain't perfect, but it'll do	Perfect pitch	

Symbols and Metaphors

Bull's-eye
Nadia Comeneci*

Antonyms

Faulty	Imperfect
Flawed	Second-rate

Pink

Synonyms

Blush

Coral

Fuchsia

Rose

Seashell

Related Words, Phrases, and Expressions

Hot pink

In the pink

Pink and blue

Pink elephant

Pink eye

Pink lemonade

Shocking pink

Tickled pink

Symbols and Metaphors

Baby girl

Cotton candy

Pig

Popular

Synonyms

Beloved	**Hot**	**Trendy**
Best-selling	Much-loved	Well-liked
Chart-topping	Preferred	
Favored	Sought-after	

Related Words, Phrases, and Expressions

#1	In demand	The people have spoken
All the rage	Phenomenon	The people's choice
By popular demand/back by popular demand	Pop	The popular crowd
	Popular culture	Universally embraced
Craze	Popular misconception	Voted most popular
Everybody's doing it	Popular opinion	Vox populi
Everyone's talking about it	Popular parlance	Widely loved
Golden girl/golden boy	Popularity	
Hit		

Symbols and Metaphors

Cheering crowd	Star athlete
Cheerleader	

Antonyms

Also-ran	Rejected
Disliked	Unpopular
Outcast	

Powerful

Synonyms

Alpha

Authoritative

Commanding

Compelling

Dominant

Effective

Forceful

Fully charged

High-impact

High-powered

Influential

Mighty

Potent

Power-packed

Strong

Related Words, Phrases, and Expressions

Absolute power corrupts absolutely

Balance of power

Battery power

Corridors of power

Electric power

Executive powers

Fight the power*

Flower power

Fuel

Full power

Horsepower

Impact

In charge

Knowledge is power

Leader of the pack

Power breakfast

Power failure

Power is the ultimate aphrodisiac

Power lifter

Power lunch

Power mower

Power of attorney

Power of movement

Power of positive thinking

Power of speech

Power plant

Power struggle

Power suit

Power surge

Power to the people

Power tools

Power trio

Powerhouse

Powers that be

Purchasing power

Seat of power

Sisterhood is powerful

Solar power

Superpowers

Top dog

Water power

Willpower

Symbols and Metaphors

Battery

Lightbulb

Plug

Weightlifter

White House

Windmill

Antonyms

Disenfranchised

Feeble

Ineffectual

Lame-duck

Powerless

Weak

Practical

Synonyms

Applied

Bottom-line

Down-to-earth

Economical

Effective

Efficient

Functional

Goal-oriented

Hands-on

Handy

Helpful

Level-headed

Logical

Multipurpose

Purposeful

Realistic

Real-life

Real-world

Results-oriented

Sensible

Smart

Solid

Useful

Related Words, Phrases, and Expressions

Bottom line

Gets the job done

How do I get to Carnegie Hall? Practice

Immediate results

In theory and in practice

Makes sense

Measurable

Practical effect

Practical use

Practice makes perfect

Results

Use it or lose it

Visible difference

Visible results

Symbols and Metaphors

Eyeglasses on chain

Paper clip

Patched jeans

Sensible shoes

Store coupons

Swiss Army knife*

Tape measure

Toolkit

Umbrella

Antonyms

Academic

Decorative

Impractical

Theoretical

Unrealistic

Useless

Prestigious

Synonyms

Exclusive
High-profile
High-status
Impressive

Recognized
Renowned
Respected
Selective

Status-enhancing
Top-drawer
Top-shelf

Related Words, Phrases, and Expressions

Community leader
Credentials
Dressed to impress
High standards

Make an impression
Name
Only the best
Prestige

Prestigious address
Social standing
Status
Status symbol

Symbols and Metaphors

Corner office
First-class cabin
Four-star general
Ivy League

Lectern
Limousine
Park Avenue
Penthouse

Presidential suite
Reserved parking space
Reserved restaurant table

Antonyms

Average
Common

Low-profile
Low-status

Second-class
Unrecognized

Profitable

Synonyms

Enriching	High-yield	Productive
Gainful	Income-generating	Rewarding
High-dividend	Lucrative	Wealth-producing
High-paying	Moneymaking	

Related Words, Phrases, and Expressions

A handsome profit	Not for profit	Profitable investment
Bottom line	Payoff	Profitable venture
Buy low, sell high	Percent	Returns
Earn	Profit and loss	Revenues
Growth	Profit margin	What does it profit a man to gain the world and lose his soul?
In the black	Profit sharing	
Increase	Profit-driven	Windfall profits
Make your money grow	Profitable endeavor	Worthwhile investment

Symbols and Metaphors

+	Seeds
$	

Antonyms

Losing	Unrewarding
Unprofitable	

Proven

Synonyms

Authenticated

Certified

Clinically proven

Confirmed

Established

Laboratory-tested

Substantiated

Tested

Time-tested

Validated

Verified

Related Words, Phrases, and Expressions

Burden of proof

Evidence

Exhibit A

Foolproof

Mathematical proof

Passed the test

Photographic proofs

Proof

Proof of age

Proof of identity

Proof of ownership

Proofreader

Prove it

Proven results

Proving grounds

Test drive

Theory

Time-tested

Trust, but verify

Symbols and Metaphors

Coat check ticket

Driver's license

Receipt

Scale

Seal of approval

Sealed evidence bag

Antonyms

Experimental

Hypothetical

Unproven

Untested

Purple

Synonyms

Amethyst	Eggplant	Lilac
Aubergine	Grape	Plum
Burgundy	Hyacinth	Puce
Carmine	Lavender	Violet

Related Words, Phrases, and Expressions

I've never seen a purple cow	Purple prose	Turn purple
Purple mountains' majesty	Shrinking violet	When I am old, I shall wear purple*

Symbols and Metaphors

Grapes

Mauve

Red

Synonyms

Burgundy	Garnet	Vermilion
Carmine	Puce	Wine
Cinnamon	Ruby	
Crimson	Scarlet	

Related Words, Phrases, and Expressions

Beet-red	Red pepper	Red-faced
Blood-red	Red ribbon	Redhead
Caught red-handed	Red robin	Red-hot
In the red	Red Sea	Red-letter day
Red carpet/red-carpet treatment	Red tape	Rockets' red glare
Red eye	Red wine	Roll out the red carpet
Red flag	Red, white, and blue	Seeing red
Red fox	Red-blooded	What's black and white and red all over? A newspaper
Red light	Redcoats	

Symbols and Metaphors

Red apple	Ruby slippers

Refreshing

Synonyms

Battery-charging
Bracing
Brightening
Brisk
Chilled
Cool/cooling

Delightful
Energizing
Iced
Invigorating/reinvigorating
Rejuvenating
Renewing

Restorative
Reviving
Soothing
Thirst-quenching

Related Words, Phrases, and Expressions

A refreshing breeze
A refreshing change
A refreshing difference
Feel like a new man/woman
Fresh
Fresh as a daisy

Fresh talk
Good as new
New coat of paint
Out of the ordinary
Perked up
Recharged

Refresh my memory
Refresh your drink
Refresh your makeup
Refreshing scent
Refreshments will be
  served

Symbols and Metaphors

Coffee break
Ice cream
Lemonade

Lipstick
Mint
Swimming pool

Water fountain/water
  cooler
Wet Paint sign

Relaxing

Synonyms

Calming

Casual

Comfortable

De-stressing

Easy

Freeing

Free-flowing

Informal

Lazy

Low-pressure

Peaceful

Placid

Serene

Slow-paced

Soothing

Spontaneous

Tranquil

Unrestrictive

Worry-free

Related Words, Phrases, and Expressions

Come as you are

Ease the tension

Hair relaxer

Impromptu gathering

Let go

Let it all hang out

Let your hair down

Lower your blood pressure

Put your feet up

Recuperate

Relax, this won't hurt a bit

Relax and enjoy

Relax and unwind

Relaxed atmosphere

Relaxed standards

Relaxing the rules

Rest

Sit back and relax

Slack off

Snooze

Stretch

Take your time

Unclench

Symbols and Metaphors

Bare feet

Bubble bath

Casual Friday

Chamomile tea

Hammock

Lavender

Massage

Nap

Recliner

Sleep mask

Slippers

Sofa

Spa

Weekend

Whirlpool

Antonyms

Fist-clenching

Formal

Headache-inducing

High-pressure

Oppressive

Restrictive

Stressful/stress-inducing

Uncomfortable

Uptight

White-knuckle

Reliable

Synonyms

Accurate

Committed

Dependable

Devoted

Faithful

Loyal

Predictable

Prompt

Punctual

Responsible

Solid

Steadfast

Steady

Trustworthy

Unfailing

Unwavering

Related Words, Phrases, and Expressions

As sure as the sun rises in
  the east

At your beck and call

Count on it

Faithful servant

Keeping promises

Lean on me*

Like clockwork

Meeting obligations

On-time performance

There when you need us

Symbols and Metaphors

Big Ben*

Mountain

Old Faithful*

St. Bernard

Sunrise

Swiss watch

Antonyms

Flighty

Inaccurate

Undependable

Unpredictable

Unreliable

Untrustworthy

Rich

Synonyms

Affluent

Flush

Fortunate

Loaded

Prosperous

Wealthy

Well-heeled

Well-off

Well-to-do

Related Words, Phrases, and Expressions

A good name is better than riches

An embarrassment of riches

Billionaire

Cushion

Elite

Fat cat

For richer or poorer

From rags to riches

Get rich quick

I've been poor and I've been rich—rich is better

If I were a rich man*

Inheritance

It's easier for a camel to pass through the eye of a needle than for a rich man to enter the kingdom of heaven

Millionaire

Money

Paid in full

Rich and creamy

Rich and famous

Rich man's table

That man is the richest whose pleasures are the cheapest (Henry David Thoreau)

The rich are different from you and me

The rich get richer, the poor get poorer

Symbols and Metaphors

$

Bulging wallet

Caviar

Champagne

Croesus

Diamonds

First-class cabin

Gold

Limousine

Mansion

Mr. and Mrs. Howell/the millionaire and his wife*

Mr. Burns*

Roll of bills

Swimming pool

Tennis court

Top hat

Yacht

Antonyms

Broke

Deprived

Destitute

Dirt-poor

Down-at-the-heels

Flat-broke

Hard-up

Insolvent

Needy

Penniless

Poor

Struggling

Unfortunate

Romantic

Synonyms

Amorous
Flowery
Heartfelt

Heartwarming
Ideal
Mushy

Passionate
Sentimental
Sexy

Related Words, Phrases, and Expressions

4-eva
A match made in heaven
Across a crowded room*
Affection
All the world loves a lover
All you need is love*
All's fair in love and war
Apple of my eye
Attachment
Ballad
Beloved
Cherished
Courtship
Crazy for you
Crush

Fairy tale
Falling for you
First love
Happily ever after
Head over heels
Heartbeat
Hearts and flowers
Honeymoon
Hugs and kisses
I only have eyes for you*
In the mood
It's better to have loved and lost than never to have loved at all
Knight in shining armor
Love at first sight

Love conquers all
Love is blind
Love makes the world go round
Love song
Love story
Love thy neighbor as thyself
Love your enemies
Love-forty
Lovebirds
Lovesick
Lovey-dovey
Made for each other
Make love, not war
Man/woman of your dreams
One true love

Pet names
Puppy love
Romance novel
Romantic comedy
Romantic getaway
Romantic ideal
Romantic interest
Romantic love
S.W.A.K.
Sonnet
Starry-eyed
The course of true love never did run smooth
Whirlwind romance

Symbols and Metaphors

Candlelit dinner
Cupid
Gondola

Heart
Ice-cream soda with two straws

Initials carved in tree
Locket

Porch swing
Red rose
XOXO

Antonyms

Businesslike
Calculated

Formal
Impersonal

Practical
Sensible

Unromantic

Safe

Synonyms

Childproof
Dependable
Encrypted
Fully insured
Harmless

Locked-up
Low-risk
Nonviolent
Password-protected
Peaceful

Protective/
  protected
Prudent
Reliable
Risk-free

Secure
Sheltered
Tamper-proof
Well-guarded
Worry-free

Related Words, Phrases, and Expressions

24-hour surveillance
All clear
Backup
Breathe easy
Caution
Guard
Health and safety
Making the world
  safe for democ-
  racy
No worries
On guard

Out of harm's way
Peace of mind
Play it safe
Precautions
Rest assured
Safe and sound
Safe at home
Safe bet
Safe-deposit box
Safe house
Safe investment
Safe place

Safe zone
Safecracker
Safeguard
Safekeeping
Safety belt
Safety first
Safety goggles
Safety in numbers
Safety latch
Safety patrol
Safety pin
Safety razor

Secure the perim-
  eter
Security
Security guard
Serenity
Someone to watch
  over me*
Under lock and key
We've got you cov-
  ered
We've got your
  back

Symbols and Metaphors

Backup disk
Crossing guard
Flashlight
Gated community

Helmet
Lock
Oven mitts
Police

Seatbelt
Tank
Thimble

Umbrella
Vault

Antonyms

Chancy
Dangerous
Exposed

Fly-by-night
High-risk

Risky
Vulnerable

Satisfying

Synonyms

Complete	Gratifying	Satisfactory
Filling	Pleasing	
Fulfilling	Satiating	

Related Words, Phrases, and Expressions

At peace	Get what you want	Satisfy your appetite
Climax	**Happy**	Satisfy your craving
Coming full circle	I can't get no satisfaction*	Satisfy your curiosity
Content/contented	Sated	Satisfy your hunger
Don't be satisfied by anything less	Satisfaction guaranteed	Satisfy your needs
Don't settle for second best	Satisfied	Satisfy your thirst
Get what you need	Satisfied customer	Satisfying ending
	Satisfy the requirements	Satisfying meal

Symbols and Metaphors

Clean plate	Completed puzzle
Completed checklist	Punch line

Antonyms

Frustrating	Unacceptable
Incomplete	Unsatisfying

Scary

Synonyms

Anxiety-inducing	Eerie	Haunting	Nerve-racking
Blood-chilling	Fearsome	Heart-stopping	Petrifying
Bloodcurdling	Frightening	Horrific	Spooky
Chilling	Frightful	Horrifying	Terrifying
Disturbing	Hair-raising	Intimidating	Unsettling

Related Words, Phrases, and Expressions

Afraid	Haunted house	Run screaming	The only thing we have to fear is fear itself
Afraid of his own shadow	Hide	Scare tactics	
Anxiety	Horror movie	Scared out of your wits	Things that go bump in the night
Boo	Jittery	Scared senseless	Tremble with fear
Don't be afraid of the dark	Jumpy	Scared silly	Warning
Fear	Nervous	Scared straight	Weak in the knees
Fear and loathing	Nightmare	Scared to death	You don't scare me
Fear and trembling	Panic	Scary movie	You gave me a scare
Fearless	Panic attack	Scream	
Freedom from fear	Phobic/phobia	Shiver	
	Reign of terror	Terror	

Symbols and Metaphors

Black cat	Grizzly bear	Snake	Witch
Cemetery	Jack-o'-lantern	Vampire	Wolves
Ghost	Monster	White knuckles	
Grim Reaper	Shark		

Antonyms

Harmless	Unintimidating
Innocuous	

Scented

Synonyms (Good-Smelling)

Aromatic	Fruity	Spicy
Flowery	Musky	Sweet-smelling
Fragrant	Perfumed	
Fresh	Redolent	

Related Words, Phrases, and Expressions

Aroma	On the breeze	Something smells fishy
Bouquet	On the scent	Stop and smell the roses*
Breath/breathe	Potpourri	The sweet smell of success
Come out smelling like a rose	Powder	Waft
	Refreshing	Wake up and smell the coffee
Fragrance	Sachet	
Hint	Scratch and sniff	Whiff
I love the smell of napalm in the morning*	Sniff	Whisper

Symbols and Metaphors

Bloodhound	**Flowers**	Rose
Cinnamon bun	Perfume bottle	Skunk
Nose		

Antonyms (No Smell or Bad Smell)

Fetid	Pungent	Smelly
Foul	Putrid	Sour
Fragrance-free	Rank	Sterile
Malodorous	Reeking	Stinky
Odorless	Rotten	Unscented

Sexy

Synonyms

Alluring
Appealing
Arousing
Attractive
Desirable
Erotic
Exciting
Flirtatious
Frisky
Hot
Hunky

Magnetic
Manly/womanly
Masculine/feminine
Passionate
Playful
R-rated
Racy
Red-hot
Revealing
Risqué
Seductive

Sensual
Spicy
Steamy
Stimulating
Tantalizing
Uncensored
Uninhibited
Virile
Wild
X-rated

Related Words, Phrases, and Expressions

Aphrodisiac
Babe
Bare
Chemistry
Come-hither look
Desire
Dirty dancing*
Get a room
Hot and bothered

Hot and heavy
Hot stuff
Hottie
Hunk
Kiss
Melt
Passion
Sex appeal
Sex scene

Sex sells
Sex symbol
Sex, lies, and videotape*
Sexpot
Sexual politics
Siren
Strip poker
Striptease
You sexy thing*

Symbols and Metaphors

Aphrodite
Belly dancer
Candlelight
Do Not Disturb sign

Fireman
High heels
Librarian taking off glasses
Lingerie

Rumpled sheets
X

Antonyms

Bland
Censored
G-rated

Inhibited
Platonic
Prudish

Sexless
Squeaky-clean
Unappealing

Shiny

Synonyms

Bright
Brilliant
Burnished
Dazzling
Gleaming
Glimmering
Glittery/glittering

Glossy
Glowing
Light-reflecting
Lustrous
Polished
Radiant
Reflective

Sequined
Shimmering
Slick
Sparkling
Sunny
Twinkling

Related Words, Phrases, and Expressions

A polished performance
A shining performance
Broad stripes and bright stars
Chrome
Don't hide your light under a bushel
Evening star
Falling star
From sea to shining sea*
Gloss over the problem
Gold
Light

Moonshine
Oil
Patina
Rise and shine
Sheen
Shine on, you crazy diamond*
Shining jewel
Shining star
Shiny and new
Shiny happy people*
Shoeshine/shoe polish

Shooting star
Silver
Stardust
Starfish
Starlight
Starry night
Sunshine
Sunshine of your love*
Twinkle, twinkle, little star
Wax
You are the sunshine of my life*

Symbols and Metaphors

Firefly
Mirror

Satin
Sequins

Star
Sun

Antonyms

Cloudy
Dim
Drab
Dreary

Dull
Dusty
Faded

Lackluster
Matte
Powdery

Slim

Synonyms

Delicate
Fit
Lanky
Lean
Lithe
Narrow

Petite
Skinny
Sleek
Slender
Slinky

Svelte
Thin
Trim
Willowy
Wiry

Related Words, Phrases, and Expressions

Fit as a fiddle
Narrow victory
Out of thin air

Rail-thin
Slim chance
Slim pickin's

Stick-thin
Walking a thin line

Symbols and Metaphors

Pipe cleaner
The Thin Man*

Twiggy*

Antonyms

Beefy
Bulky
Chubby
Chunky
Fat

Heavy
Hefty
Large
Overweight

Rotund
Sturdy
Thick
Wide

Small

Synonyms

Bite-size

Dainty

Handheld

Lilliputian

Little

Miniature/mini

Petite

Pocket-size

Subtle

Tiny

Travel-size

Wee

Related Words, Phrases, and Expressions

A little of this, a little of that

A small favor

All creatures great and small

Convenient

Don't sweat the small stuff

Easy to store

Fits in the palm of your hand

Gem

Good things come in small packages

How many angels can dance on the head of a pin?

Lightweight

Little Boy Blue

Nearly invisible

Portable

Small business

Small change

Small comfort

Small fry

Small is beautiful

Small parts

Small pieces

Small potatoes

Small scale

Small talk

Small time

Small town

Small wonder

Take two, they're small

The small hours

Tiny Tim*

Symbols and Metaphors

Ant

Atom

Baby

Chihuahua

Gymnast

Hummingbird

Jockey

Liechtenstein

Mouse

Pea

Rhode Island

Studio apartment

Tom Thumb

Antonyms

Awkward

Big

Bulky

Clunky

Huge

Large

Lumbering

Ostentatious

Oversized

Swollen

Smart

Synonyms

Astute	Gifted	Learned	Swift
Brainy	High-IQ	Perceptive	Well-informed
Bright	Informed	Quick-thinking	Well-read
Brilliant	Ingenious	Quick-witted	Wise
Clever	Intellectual	Scholarly	
Educated	Intelligent	Sharp	
Erudite	Knowledgeable	Shrewd	

Related Words, Phrases, and Expressions

A word to the wise	Human intelligence	Penny wise, pound foolish	Think again
Artificial intelligence	Idea	Quick on the uptake	Think fast
Book-smart	In the know	Sharp as a tack	Three wise men
Brain food	Intelligence gathering	Smart aleck	Two heads are better than one
Bright idea	Intelligentsia	Smart mouth	Wisdom tooth
Dean's List	IQ	Smarty-pants	Wise guy
Early to bed and early to rise makes a man healthy, wealthy, and wise	It is not wisdom to be only wise	Straight-A	Wisecrack
Genius	Know thyself	Street-smart	Wit and wisdom
Get smart	Knowledge is power	Summa cum laude	
Honor roll	None the wiser	The fear of the Lord is the beginning of wisdom	
	Old enough to know better	The smart money	

Symbols and Metaphors

Albert Einstein*	Encyclopedia	Lightbulb	Wise man on top of mountain
Books	Glasses	Ph.D.	

Antonyms

Brainless	Dull-witted	Misinformed	Uninformed
Clueless	Dumb	Slow-witted	Unintelligent
Dim-witted	Foolish	Stupid	
Dopey	Ignorant	Uneducated	

Soft

Synonyms

Cushy

Delicate

Feathery

Flexible

Flowing

Gentle

Lush

Luxurious

Padded

Plush

Satiny

Silky

Snuggly

Supple

Tender

Velvety

Whisper-soft

Yielding

Related Words, Phrases, and Expressions

A soft answer turneth away
  wrath

Fabric softener

Killing me softly with his
  song*

Soft breeze

Soft drink

Soft focus

Soft in the head

Soft landing

Soft lights

Soft money

Soft **music**

Soft pedal

Soft rock

Soft sell

Soft shell

Soft **shoe**

Soft shoulder

Soft spot

Soft to the touch

Soft touch

Softball

Soft-boiled

Soft-hearted

Soft-spoken

Software

Speak softly and carry a big
  stick (Theodore
  Roosevelt)

Tread softly

Symbols and Metaphors

Candlelight

Cloud

Comforter

Cotton ball

Feather

Kitten

Moonlight

Pillow

Rabbit

Rose petal

Snow

Whisper

Winter scarf

Antonyms

Coarse

Glaring

Hard

Harsh

Rough

Sharp

Stiff

Unyielding

Wooden

Spacious

Synonyms

Airy

Big

Accommodating

Capacious

Cavernous

Comfortable

Expansive

Generous

Grand

Large

Large-capacity

Roomy

Vast

Related Words, Phrases, and Expressions

A room with a view

Breathing room

Buffer zone

Comfort zone

Cubic feet/yards

Dining room

Environment

High ceilings

Horizon

King size

Leg room

Living room

Oh beautiful for spacious
  skies*

Outer space

Parking space

Passing lane

Personal space

Room for one more

Room to move

Space and time

Space flight

Space program

Space ship

Space station

Space travel

Spacecraft

Spacesuit

Spread

Square footage

Storage room

Stretch your legs

Visual-spatial ability

Walk-in

Wide berth

Wide-open spaces

Symbols and Metaphors

Big sky

Corner office

Desert

Grand Canyon

Hotel suite

Ottoman

Oversized **clothing**

Palace

Stretch limo

Two-**car** garage

Walk-in closet

Antonyms

Claustrophobic

Close

Close-fitting

Closet-sized

Cramped

Crowded

Hole-in-the-wall

Overstuffed

Snug

Tight

Special

Synonyms

Beloved	Exceptional	Significant
Cherished	Meaningful	**Unusual**
Dear	Remarkable	

Related Words, Phrases, and Expressions

Blue-plate special	Something special	Special price
Breakfast special	Special case	Special purchase
Especially	Special day	Special treat
Extra-special	Special delivery	Special treatment
Hold dear	Special effects	Standout
Nothing special	Special occasion	
Someone special	Special order	

Symbols and Metaphors

*	Bow
Award	Frame

Antonyms

Average	Regular	Standard
Insignificant	Routine	Usual
Ordinary		

Strong

Synonyms

Brawny
Buff
Built
Durable
Forceful
Formidable

Hard-shelled
Heavy-duty
Mighty
Muscular
Potent
Powerful

Reinforced
Rock-solid
Sound
Steady
Steely
Strapping

Sturdy
Tough
Unbreakable
Vigorous
Well-built
Well-muscled

Related Words, Phrases, and Expressions

800-pound gorilla
An iron fist in a
    velvet glove
Barbell
Bench press
Brains and brawn
Bring it on
Built to last
Bulging biceps
Carries a heavy
    load
Feats of strength
Free weights
Full force

God give me
    strength
Holds up under
    pressure
In unity there is
    strength
Muscle in
Nothing is stronger
    than habit
Only the strong
    survive
Pile it on
Position of
    strength
Professional grade
Resistance

Rules with an iron
    fist
Six-pack
Stand strong
Stands up
Steel-toe
Stiff drink
Strength
Strength in num-
    bers
Strength of your
    convictions
Strengths and
    weaknesses
Strong and steady
    win the race

Strong feeling
Strong language
Strong medicine
Strong possibility
Strong-arm
Stronghold
Strongman
Superhuman
    strength
Tough as nails
Tough talk
Tower of strength
Weightlifting/
    weight training

Symbols and Metaphors

Ant
Atlas
Backpacker
Brick

Chin-up bar
Elephant
Hammer
Heavyweight boxer

Lion
Oak
Ox
Paul Bunyan

Spider web
Tank
Weightlifter

Antonyms

Flabby
Flimsy
Frail

Puny
Shoddy
Skinny

Spineless
Unsound
Weak

Wispy

Stylish

Synonyms

Best-dressed	Flattering	Pulled-together	Suave
Chic	Glamorous	Refined	Tailored
Coordinated	Haute-couture	Sleek	Tasteful
Designer	High-fashion	**Smart**	Understated
Distinctive	High-style	Sophisticated	Urbane
Elegant	Polished	Striking	Well-dressed

Related Words, Phrases, and Expressions

Accent	Dressed to kill	Individual style	Out of style
Accessorize/ **accessories**	Dressed to the nines	Inimitable style	Panache
Appearances can be deceiving	*Élan*	It suits you	Pizzazz
By design	Every girl's crazy 'bout a sharp-dressed man*	Keeping up appearances	Runway
Classic style	Flair	Look	Sense of style
Don't judge a book by its cover	Freestyle	Look like a million bucks	Style and substance
Dressed for success	Hairstyle	Looking good	The elements of style
	In style	Not my style	Vision
			You look marvelous!

Symbols and Metaphors

Convertible	Hat	Little black dress	Paris
Full-length mirror	High heels	Mannequin	Sunglasses
Handbag	Lipstick	Milan	Supermodel

Antonyms

Frumpy	Ill-fitting	Scruffy	Uncoordinated
Gaudy	Poorly dressed	Sloppy	Unflattering
Haphazard	Schlubby	Tacky	

Trendy

Synonyms

Current	Hip	Modish	Red-hot
Faddish	**Hot**	Must-have	**Stylish**
Fashionable	In	Of-the-moment	**Up-to-date**
Fresh	In-demand	Omnipresent	Up-to-the-minute
Happening	Latest	**Popular**	White-hot

Related Words, Phrases, and Expressions

À la mode	Flying off the shelves	On fire	Status symbol
Ahead of the curve	Hard to find	Object of desire	Sweeping the nation
All the rage	Hard to get	Overnight sensation	The tipping point
Au courant	Hit	Passing fad	This season
Buzz	Hot off the runway	Phenomenon	Those in the know
Can't keep them in stock	Hot property	Riding the current	Trendsetter
Craze	In favor	Right now	Trend-spotting
Cutting edge	In vogue	Scene	Update your look
Downward trend	**New** sensation	Selling like hot-cakes	Upward trend
Everyone's doing it	Newest	Sensation	Wave
Exploding	Next	Sold out	What they're wearing
Fashion forward	Now	Spreading like wildfire	

Symbols and Metaphors

Boutique	Mood ring	Teenagers
Hula hoop	Runway model	

Antonyms

Out	Out-of-favor	Stale
Outdated	So-5-minutes-ago	Unfashionable
Out-of-date	So-last-year	Unhip

Unique

Synonyms

Incomparable

Individual

Inimitable

Once-in-a-lifetime

One-and-only

One-of-a-kind

Only

Peerless

Singular

Unequaled

Unmatched

Unparalleled

Related Words, Phrases, and Expressions

A breed apart

Beyond compare

Custom-made

Handcrafted

Handmade

Imprint

Like no other

Nothing compares

Nothing else like it

One-in-a-million

Only you

Rare

Signature

Standout

Stands apart

Sui generis

There's no comparison

Trademark

Unique opportunity

Uniquely qualified

Unusual

Work of art

Symbols and Metaphors

DNA

Fingerprint

Signature

Snowflake

Antonyms

Boilerplate

Common

Dime-a-dozen

Everyday

Mass-produced

Standard

Unusual

Synonyms

Different
Exceptional
Exotic
Extraordinary
Fascinating
Hard-to-find

Nonconformist
Out-of-the-ordinary
Quirky
Rare
Remarkable
Seldom-seen

Special
Surprising
Uncommon
Unconventional
Unexpected
Unorthodox

Related Words, Phrases, and Expressions

A find
Against all odds
Dare to be different
Different take
Element of surprise
Escape the everyday
Expect the unexpected
Limited edition
Not your everyday
Off the beaten path

On the edge
On the fringe
One-in-a-million
Rare bird
Rare example
Rare find
Rare sighting
Rare specimen
Special case
Stands out in the crowd

Subculture
The exception to the rule
There's something you
 don't see every day
Treasure
Valuable
With a difference
With a twist

Symbols and Metaphors

Fancy hat
Manx cat

Orchid
Pearl in oyster

Antonyms

Boring
Common
Everyday
Expected
Habitual
Ho-hum

Ordinary
Predictable
Regular
Routine
Run-of-the-mill
Same-old

Unexceptional
Unsurprising
Unremarkable
Usual

Up-to-Date

Synonyms

Advanced

Current

Cutting-edge

Fashionable

Latest

Modern

Recently-updated

State-of-the-art

Timely

Trendy

Updated

Up-to-the-minute

Up-to-the-moment

Related Words, Phrases, and Expressions

As it happens/as it's hap-
  pening

As the story unfolds

Au courant

Breaking news

Current events

Fully automated

Fully informed

Fully updated

Immediate

In the loop

Keep pace

Keep up

Keeping up

Latest and greatest

Latest developments

Latest fashion

Latest **information**

Latest news

Latest research

Latest technology

Latest word

Live

On top of

Plugged in

Stay tuned

This just in

This year's model

Today's

Tune in

Symbols and Metaphors

News bulletin

Software upgrade

Antonyms

Dated

Discontinued

Irrelevant

Obsolete

Old

Outdated

Out-of-date

Out-of-step

Stale

Useful

Synonyms

Effective

Functional

Handy

Helpful

Indispensable

Practical

Usable

Utilitarian

Valuable

Related Words, Phrases, and Expressions

Appliance

Asset

Assists

Does the work for you

Easy to use

Enables

Function

Form follows function

Grammar and usage

Helpful hint

Helps

I could use the money

I could use some help

I feel used

Job

News you can use

Proper use

Put to good use

Put to immediate use

Resources

Serves its purpose

Slightly used

Task

That's using your noodle

Tool

Use a coaster

Use everything at your disposal

Use it; don't abuse it

Use it or lose it

Use it up, wear it out, make it do, or do without

Use what you've got

Used car

Used or new

Used up

Useful advice

Useful information

Utility/**utilities**

Utility belt

What's the use

You could use

Symbols and Metaphors

Corkscrew

Dumbwaiter

First-aid kit

Key ring

Paper clip

Pocket

Toolkit

Antonyms

Decorative

Extraneous

Impractical

Pointless

Trivial

Useless

Worthless

Valuable

Synonyms

Costly

Expensive

High-priced

High-value

Indispensable

Invaluable

Irreplaceable

Precious

Priceless

Profitable

Rare

Related Words, Phrases, and Expressions

A bargain at any price

A good reputation is more
   valuable than money

Appraised

Assessed

Asset

Cherished

Collector's item

Cultural values

Family values

Fortune

Hoard

Increases in value

King's ransom

Market value

Mathematical value

Monetary value

Moral values

More valuable than **gold**

MVP

My most valuable possession

Precious gem

Precious metals

Prized

Production values

Property values

Relative value

Retail value

Sentimental value

Societal values

The value of X

The value of your time

Time is the most valuable
   thing a man can spend

Treasure

Valuable lesson

Valuable prizes

Valuables

Value judgment

Valued

Vault

What is a cynic? A man
   who knows the price of
   everything and the value
   of nothing

Worth

Worth every penny

Worth its weight in gold

Symbols and Metaphors

Diamonds

Gold

Museum display case

Oil well

Price tag

Safe

Stock ticker

Antonyms

Cheap

Disposable

Flimsy

Junky

Valueless

Worthless

Warm

Synonyms

Balmy

Cozy

Fresh-baked

Heated

Insulated

Lined

Springlike

Sunny

Related Words, Phrases, and Expressions

Death warmed over

Fresh from the oven

Happiness is a warm
  puppy*

Heartwarming

Keep warm

Still warm

Warm and dry

Warm bath

Warm breeze

Warm embrace

Warm feelings

Warm greetings

Warm milk

Warm reception

Warm up dinner

Warm up exercises

Warm up to

Warm water

Warm welcome

Warm wishes

Warm your hands

Warm-blooded

Warm-hearted

Warm-up band

Warm-up suit

You're getting warmer

Symbols and Metaphors

Fireplace

Mittens

Palm tree

Quilt

Antonyms

Bitter

Bone-chilling

Chilly

Cold

Cool

Freezing

Unheated

White

Synonyms

Blank	Ivory	Pearl	Titanium
Colorless	Pale	Pure	

Related Words, Phrases, and Expressions

Black and white

Clean slate

Don't shoot until you see the whites of their eyes

Egg whites

Great white shark

Here comes the bride, all dressed in white

I'm dreaming of a white **Christmas***

Lily white

Never wear white shoes after Labor Day

Pearly whites

Red, white, and blue

Snow White

Tennis whites

The Great White Way

Tighty-whities

White as a ghost

White as a sheet

White as snow

White Christmas

White cliffs of Dover

White collar

White elephant

White flag

White flour

White gold

White hair

White horse

White hot

White House

White knight

White knuckles

White lace

White lie

White noise

White paper

White picket fence

White rabbit

White rice

White space

White tie

White tiger

White **wedding**

White whale

White wine

Whitecaps

Whiteout

Whitewash

Whitewater

Symbols and Metaphors

Bleach	Egg	Salt	Sugar
Bridal gown	Ghost	Sand	Sunlight
Chalk	Pearl	Snow	
Cloud	Polar bear		

Yellow

Synonyms

Dandelion	Lemon
Golden	

Related Words, Phrases, and Expressions

What are you, yellow?	Yellow journalism	Yellow peppers
Yellow fever	Yellow light	Yellow with age
Yellow **gold**	Yellow Pages*	Yellow-bellied
Yellow jacket		

Symbols and Metaphors

Banana	Lemon
Corn	Sunshine

Young

Synonyms

Childlike

Dewy

Energetic

Fresh

Innocent

New

Ripe

Supple

Teenage

Unlined

Youthful

Related Words, Phrases, and Expressions

And the children shall lead them

Baby

Bloom of youth

Boy

Early

Flush with youth

From the mouths of babes

Girl

How old would you be if you didn't know how old you were?

Infant/infancy

Junior

Kid

Kid stuff

Kitten

Live fast, die young, and leave a good-looking corpse

Never trust anyone over 30

Newborn

Old enough to know better

Puppy

Puppy love

Put away childish things

Salad days

Spring

You don't look a day over 25

You're only as old as you feel

You're only young once

Young at heart

Young guns

Youth is wasted on the young

Youthful rebellion

Symbols and Metaphors

Baby

Gymnast

Rosebud

School

Antonyms

Aged/aging

Ancient

Beaten-down

Desiccated

Dried-out

Drooping/droopy

Elderly

Haggard

Lined

Middle-aged

Old

Sagging/saggy

Senior

Slow

Stiff

Stooped

Worn-out

Wrinkled

Buzzwords by Business

Accessories
Art
Athletic Equipment
Baby Supplies
Books
Business Supplies/Services
Careers
Cars
Catering/Parties
Charity
Clothing
Computers
Cosmetics
Crafts
Dental Care
Drink
Education
Exercise/Fitness

Flowers
Food
Furniture
Gardening
Hair Care
Hardware
Hotel
Housewares
Information
Insurance
Jewelry
Law
Medical/Pharmaceutical
Money/Financial Services
Movies
Music
Personal Grooming
Pet Care

Phone/Phone Service
Photography
Real Estate
Restaurants
Shoes
Skin Care
Spiritual/New Age
Sports Events
Taxes
Television
Theater
Toys/Games
Transportation
Travel
Utilities
Vision Care
Weddings

Accessories

Synonyms

Accents

Accoutrements

Extras

Finishing touches

Related Words, Phrases, and Expressions

A touch of _____

Accessorize

Accessory to the crime

Bag of tricks

Brighten

Carry it off

Distinctive

Eye-catching

Funky

Garnish

Highlight

Icing on the cake

Individual

It's in the bag

Jaunty

Jazz up

Keep it under your hat

Let the cat out of the bag

Liven

Make it your own

Not my bag

Ornament

Personalize

Pièce de résistance

Pull it all together

Set off

Splash of **color**

Stylish

Tighten your belt

Top it off

Touch

Trimmings

Vary

Symbols and Metaphors

Bow on package

Cherry on sundae

Handbag

Jewelry

Scarf

Sunglasses

Art

Synonyms

Objets d'art

Related Words, Phrases, and Expressions

Abstract

Artistic license

Arts and crafts

Avant-garde

Beautiful

Beauty is in the eye of the beholder

Bold

Collage

Color

Color scheme

Composition

Con artist

Display

Exhibit

Expression

Folk art

Found art

Frame

Gallery

I don't know much about art, but I know what I like

Image

Imagination

Is it art?

Landscape

Line

Masterpiece

Meditation

Mixed-media

Multimedia

Museum

Original

Palette

Picture

Picture **perfect**

Piece

Pretty as a picture

Portrait

Print

Provocative

Representational

Sculpture

Shape

Show

Starving artist

Statement

Striking

Suitable for framing

Talent

Texture

The art of _____

Three-dimensional

Transgressive

Unique

Vision

Work of art

Symbols and Metaphors

Ballet shoes

Beret

Brush

Child's drawing on refrigerator

Drop cloth

Easel

Frame

Palette

Pedestal

Velvet rope

Wine and cheese

Athletic Equipment

Synonyms

Sporting goods   Sports equipment

Related Words, Phrases, and Expressions

Ace
Achieve
Advantage
Aerodynamic
Aggressive
Batter up
Batting cleanup
Breathable
Buzzer
Catch a break
Champ
Competition
Diamond
Double play
Edge
Equipment manager
Excel
Field goal
Finish line
First string
Free throw
Free weights
Game

Game on
Gear
Gear up
Get in gear
Get in the game
Goal
Good sport
Grand slam
Hat trick
He's got game
Have a ball
Hole in one
In a league of your own
In your corner
It's not whether you win or lose, it's how you play the game
Jock
Knockout
Marathon
Movable
Nice guys finish last

Nice save
On the ball
Out of bounds
Out of the park
Overtime
Pennant
Pep talk
Perfect game
Play
Play ball
Points
Position
Powerful
Pro
Record-breaker
Rush
Save
Sales pitch
Score
Shutout
Slam dunk
Star
Starting lineup
Suit up

Team spirit
Teamwork
The ball's in your court
There's no *I* in *team*
Tiebreaker
Touch base
Touchdown
Training
Triple Play
Triumph
Trophy
Trophy case
Trophy wife
Trounce
Uniform quality
Victory
Well-equipped
We're here to serve you
Win
Winning isn't everything; it's the only thing

Symbols and Metaphors

Gym bag
Jousting armor

Locker
Medal

Pennant
Trophy

Baby Supplies

Synonyms

Baby care

Baby needs

Baby products

Infant supplies

Newborn supplies

Related Words, Phrases, and Expressions

Babe in the woods

Baby blanket

Baby bonnet

Baby doll

Baby face

Baby **food**

Baby New Year

Baby on board*

Baby pictures

Baby steps

Baby talk

Baby's first _____

Babying

Baby-sitter

Bib

Booties

Born free

Born to run*

Bouncing baby boy

Change is good

Cooing

Crawling

Diaper change

Diaper service

Diapers

Goo goo ga ga

Gurgle

High chair

It's a boy

It's a girl

Little ones

Lullaby

Maternity leave

New addition

New arrival

New member of the family

New parents

Nursery

Nursing

Oh, baby

Out of the mouths of babes

Paternity leave

Peek-a-boo

Pink and blue

Rock a bye baby

Rubber baby buggy
  bumpers

Sleep deprivation

Small

Teething

Tiny

Wee

You and me and baby
  makes three

Symbols and Metaphors

Baby birds in nest

Booties

Bronzed baby shoes

Carriage

Car seat

Cigar

Cradle

Ducklings following mother

Mobile

Newly hatched chick

Pacifier

Rattle

Rocking chair

Stork

Stroller

Books

Synonyms

Reading materials	Tomes
Texts	Volumes

Related Words, Phrases, and Expressions

Acclaimed	Cover to cover	Novel	Rulebook
Address book	Cover-up	On the same page	Saga
Airplane reading	Dog-eared	One for the books	Shelf
Appointment book	Engrossing	Open book	So many books, so little time
Author	Epic	Pages	
Award-winning	Extra, extra, read all about it	Paperback	Softcover
Banned book		Phone book	Story
Beach read	Finally in paperback	Print	Story time
Bedtime story	**Funny** pages	Read and write	Tale
Best-seller	Guidebook	Read him his rights	The full story
Bibliophile	Handbook	Read him like a book	The last word
Book a room	Hard copy		The word is out
Book a table	Hardcover	Read him the riot act	The word on the street
Book learning	Illustrated		
Book bag	In black and white	Read in bed	Turn the page
Book 'em, Danno	**Interesting**	Read it and weep	Undercover
Bookmark	Library	Read me a story	We've got it covered
Bookworm	Literary	Read the fine print	
Can't put it down	Literature	Read the writing on the wall	Who wrote the book of love?*
Chapter	Lost in a good book		
Comic book	Lyrical	Reading glasses	Word
Compelling	No more pencils, no more books, no more teachers' dirty looks	Reading in bed	You can look it up
Cook the books		Reading lamp	You can't judge a book by its cover
Cookbook		Record book	
Cover		Reference	You have our word

Symbols and Metaphors

Beach chair	Bookworm	Hammock	Reading lamp
Bookmark	Fountain pen	Reading glasses	Recliner

Business Supplies/Services

Synonyms

Business needs

Office supplies

Related Words, Phrases, and Expressions

A **clean** desk is a sign of a sick mind

Agenda

Another day at the office

ASAP

Assistant

Bad business

Bean counter

Because I'm the boss, that's why

Board

Boardroom

Boss

Business cards

Business equipment

Business plan

Business school

Business sense

Business suit

Business tools

Busywork

Calculate

Calendar

Casual Friday

CC

CEO

Circular file

Clear your desk

Clerical

Client

Clutter

Coffee break

Committee

Computers

Conference room

Copy

Corner office

Corridors

Desk

Desk drawer

Desktop

Details

Dirty business

Documents

Drowning in paperwork

Efficient

Executive

Executive dining room

Executive powers

Executive privilege

Executive washroom

Fax

File

File under _____

Folder

Fringe benefits

FYI

Get down to business

Give him the business

Goals

Good business

Grunt work

Half staff

Hardware and software

Helpful

High-tech

Hole puncher

Home office

Homework

Human resources

I already gave at the office

I must have missed the memo

I'm taking my business elsewhere

In working order

Inbox

Industrial-strength

It's nothing personal, it's just business

Lead

Legwork

Mailroom

Make it work

Manage

Meeting

Memo

Motivate

MYOB/Mind your own business

New incentive plan: work or get fired

Nine to five

No one ever says on their deathbed, "I wish I'd spent more time at the office"

None of your business

Notes

Number crunching

Office complex

Office **furniture**

Office gossip

Office hours

Office park

Office party

Operations

Organize

continues

Business Supplies/Services *(continued)*

Related Words, Phrases, and Expressions

Outbox
Paper
Paper clip chain
Paper clips
Paper pusher
Paper trail
Paper trained
Paperweight
Paperwork
Perks
Photocopy
Productive
Professional-quality
Profitable
Project
Promotion

Punching the clock
Raise
Reception
Rubber band
Rubber-band ball
Rush hour
Secretarial
Skyscraper
Staff
Stapler
Stationery
Staying late at the office
Storage
Supply and demand
Supply chain

Supply closet
Supply room
Systems
Team
Telecommute
Temporary help
The business of America is business
Three-martini lunch
To err is human; to really foul things up requires a computer
To-do list
Watching the clock

Water cooler
Window office
Work at home
Work it
Work it out
Work the room
Workflow
Working overtime
Working through lunch
Workload
Workout
Workup
You can't get good help these days
You're not the boss of me

Symbols and Metaphors

Briefcase
Cubicle
Desk calendar

Elevator
File cabinet
Laptop case

Nameplate
Office building
Overflowing waste-basket

Paper clip
Pen and pencil holder
Tabbed file folders

Careers

Synonyms

Career counseling   Career services   Employment services   Job training

Related Words, Phrases, and Expressions

Ability
Advance
Any job worth doing is worth doing well
Application
Apply yourself
Assistance
Career change
Career satisfaction
Chosen field
Classified
Classified information
Climb the ladder
Coach
Connections
Cover letter
Dead-end job
Develop
Do more
Do what you love
Entry level
Expand your horizons
Expand your opportunities

Find
Find your place
Fit
Follow up
Fulfillment
Full-time
Get a foot in the door
Get a job
Get paid
Gig
Grow
Guidance
Help
Help wanted
Human resources
In-demand
Initiative
Interview
It's not what you know, it's who you know
Job fair
Job market
Join the team
Leads

Learn
Life's work
Make a difference
Make more **money**
Make your move
Match
Moving on up
New start
No experience necessary
On the job
On-the-job training
Opening
Opportunity
Opportunity doesn't knock twice
Part-time
Path
Personnel
Placement
Position
Potential
Pounding the pavement
Purpose

References
Resumé
Search
Skills
Snow job
Start fresh
Start over
Strengths
Suit
Talent
Talent search
That's not my job
The right person for the job
Title
Will work for food
Work at home
Work it
Work it out
Work the room
Working overtime
Workout
Workup
You're hired

Symbols and Metaphors

Briefcase
Classified ad

Help Wanted sign
Ladder

Resumé
Work Area sign

Cars

Synonyms

Autos

Automobiles

Rides

Vehicles

Wheels

Related Words, Phrases, and Expressions

Accelerate

Along for the ride

Asphalt

Automatic

Baby, you can drive my car*

Backseat

Backseat driver

Blacktop

Body

Brake

Bucket seats

Buggy

Bumper

Bumper sticker

Bumper-to-bumper

Car **service**

Car stereo

Carfare

Carpool

Carport

Carsick

Change lanes

Climate control

Clutch

Cruise

Cruise control

Designed

Destination

Detour

Drive time

Drive you crazy

Drive you wild

Drive-in

Driven

Driver

Driveway

Drive-thru

Easy Street

Engine

Engineered

Exit

Fast lane

Fasten your seat-belt

Free ride

Fuel-efficient

Fuel-injection

Garage

Gas up

Glove compartment

Highway

Horsepower

Hybrid

Ignition/ignite

In the driver's seat

Iron horse

Jalopy

Journey

King of the road*

Late-model

Legroom

Lemon

Lift

Limo

Loaded

Machine

Mechanic

MPG (miles per gallon)

MPH (miles per hour)

Muscle car

My way or the highway

No pressure

Off-road

On a roll

On the road

One way

Open road

Options

Own the road

Park yourself

Passenger

Powerful

Pump

Quiet

Race car

Rent a car

Road test

Road trip

Roll

Roll out

Seat belt

Shift

Showroom

Smooth ride

Speed limit

Steering committee

Stick

Sticker shock

Street

Street smart

Stop

Test drive

Ticket to ride

Tire

Traffic

Traffic jam

Transport

Trip

Trolley car

Trunk

Turn

Turn on a dime

Under the hood

Warranty protected

Yield

Your turn

Zero to sixty

Symbols and Metaphors

Driving gloves

Green light

Highway divider line

Keys

Route 66 sign

Steering wheel

Tire

Valet parking

Catering/Parties

Synonyms

Entertaining

Event planning

Party planning

Related Words, Phrases, and Expressions

An evening to remember

All you have to do is show up

Ambience

Appetizers

Atmosphere

Bash

Birthday party

Blast

Blowout

Buffet

Cater to your needs

Catered affair

Catering hall

Celebration

Coordinate

Dance the night away

Details

Dinner party

Eat, **drink**, and be merry

Elegant

Enjoy your own party

Extravaganza

Feast

Festive

Festivities

For all occasions

Formal

Full service

Fun

Gathering

Get down

Get the party started

Get-together

Guest list

Guest of honor

Guests

Hors d'oeuvres

Host

Hostess with the mostest

House party

Informal

Invite/invitation

It's my party, and I'll cry if I want to*

Leave the work to us

Let us entertain you

Let's party

Live it up

Make your guests feel welcome

Mingle

No need to **clean** up afterward

No need to slave in a **hot** kitchen

Office party

On-premises

Open bar

Party

Party animal

Party favors

Party hearty

Party time

Preparation

Presentation

Rehearsal dinner

Serve/**service**

Shindig

Sit-down dinner

Special event

Special occasions

Special touch

Tent

Thank you for a wonderful evening

Throw a party

Valet parking

View

Wedding party

Symbols and Metaphors

Balloons

Bed piled with coats

Buffet table

Centerpiece

Champagne glasses

Dancing couple

Disco ball

Engraved invitations

Outdoor lights

Place cards

Punch bowl

Streamers

Tent

Tray

Charity

Synonyms

Fund-raising

Philanthropy

Related Words, Phrases, and Expressions

A **better** tomorrow

A better world

Aid

Appeal

Appreciation

Assist

Benefactor

Bequest

Bestow

Build

Charitable

Charity begins at home

Community

Contribute

Do well by doing good

Do-gooder

Donate/donation

Donate online

Drive

Established

Every little bit helps

Every penny counts

Extend a hand

Faith, hope, and charity

For a good cause

Fund

Generous

Gift in honor of

Gift in memory of

Give/giving

Give something back

Grateful

Help

Helping hand

In a position to help

Invest in their future

Lend a hand

Love thy neighbor

Make a difference

Make the time

Matching gift

Needy

Pass it on

Pay it forward

Pitch in

Raise

Reach out

Recognized

Relief

Reputable

Share the wealth

Stop the suffering

Support

Tax-deductible

Thank you

Thanks to you

The less fortunate

Those in need

Tithe

Trust

Volunteer

We can't do it without you

We depend on you

Whatever you do to the least of my brothers, that you do unto me

With your help

With your support

Worthy cause

Write a check

Your help is needed

Symbols and Metaphors

Breadline

Cup

Checkbook

Soup kitchen

Clothing

Synonyms

Apparel | Attire | Clothes

Related Words, Phrases, and Expressions

A stitch in time
saves nine

Ace up your sleeve

Appearance

Beautiful

Best-dressed

Blue collar

Boxers or briefs

Bra burners

Button up

Buttons and bows

Casual

Casual Friday

Classic

Cling

Close-knit

Clothes closet

Clothes make
the man

Clotheshorse

Clothesline

Clothing drive

Coat of paint

Color

Comfortable

Coordinated

Costume

Cotton to

Custom-made

Cut

Debonair

Designer

Devil with a blue
dress on*

Dog collar

Don't get fleeced

Dress code

Dress down

Dress for success

Dress **shoes**

Dress up

Dressed to impress

Dressed to kill

Dresser

Dressing on the
side

Duds

Durable

Eight ball in the
corner pocket

Every girl's crazy
'bout a sharp-
dressed man*

Fabric

Family ties

Fancy

Fancy pants

Fashion plate

Fashion victim

Fashion-forward

Feminine

Fit

Flattering

Flow

Formal dress

Form-fitting

Getup

He puts his pants
on one leg at a
time like anyone
else

Hemmed in

Hot button

In cuffs

In the stretch

It suits you

It's a stretch

It's a tie

Lawsuit

Lipstick on his
collar

Look

Lost his shirt

Masculine

Material

Mini golf

Model

Name brand

Natural fiber

Nights in **white**
satin*

No shirt, no shoes,
no service

Off the cuff

Off the rack

Out of the closet

Outfit

Play it close to the
vest

Pocket change

Pocket the differ-
ence

Pull the wool over
their eyes

Push button

Roll up your
sleeves

School ties

Shape

Shiny

Skirt the question

Smarty pants

Snappy

Snazzy

Sock it to me

Sock puppet
Soft
Stocking cap
Stocking feet
Stretch the truth
Stretch your legs
Stretchy
Stuffed shirt
Stylish
Suit your taste
Suits
Synthetic
Tailored

Tie clip
Tie one on
Tie tack
Uniform
Up his sleeve
Use it up, wear it out, make it do, or do without
Vested
Vintage
Wardrobe
Warm
Wash and wear
Wear it in good health

Wear out
Wear your heart on your sleeve
Well-cut
Well-suited
White collar
Who are you wearing?
Wild and woolly
Wind sock
Wolf in sheep's clothing
Yellow jacket
Zip your lip

Symbols and Metaphors

Closet
Fig leaf
Garment bag
Hanger

Iron
Mannequin
Paper doll
Sewing machine

Suit of armor
Washing machine

Computers

Synonyms

Computer accessories

Hardware

ISP (Internet service providers)

Personal computing

Search engines

Software

Websites

Related Words, Phrases, and Expressions

A quick read

A real find

All access

Beat the system

Bit

Blog

Boot up

Byte

Call off the search

Calling for backup

Cat and mouse

Click

Code

Code blue

Code red

Command and control

Connect the dots

Connections

Crack the code

Crash and burn

Crash at your place

Crash course

Crash test dummy

Crash the party

Crashing bore

Cyberspace

Data

Database

Desktop

Digital

Do not enter

Does not compute

Driver's seat

Driver's side

E

Electronic

Enter if you dare

Enter the dragon*

En-terrrr!*

Explicit content

Fast

Fine print

Fingerprint

Get the message

Get with the program

Gig

Guest speaker

Hall monitor

Hard sell

Heavy load

Hidden message

High-tech

High-wire act

Icon

In the system

Information

Job search

Key

Laptop

Lightweight

Link in the chain

Link sausage

Log in

Make your connection

Message in a bottle

Missing link

Monitor your progress

Mouse hole

Mousetrap

Navigate

Network news

Nice save

No strings attached

Offline

Online

On-site

PDA

Plug

Powerful

Process

Programmed for _____

Programmed to _____

Pull the plug

Quiet as a mouse

Reliable

Safety monitor

Save money

Save my seat

Save the whales

Saved by the bell

Screen time

Screen your calls

Search and rescue

Search for buried treasure

Search near and far

Search party

Search the premises

Secret code

Secret message

Secure

Senior moment
Small print
Soft sell
Speak now
Speak up
Speaking in code
Storage facility
Storage room
Subliminal message
Subtext

Support
System failure
Talent search
Textbook
Thanks for the memories*
The check is in the mail
To err is human, to really mess things up requires a computer

TV program
'Twas the night before Christmas and all through the house, not a creature was stirring, not even a mouse
Under my command
Up-to-date
Virtual

Visit
Weakest link
Wide load
Wire fraud
Wire money
Wired up

Symbols and Metaphors

Attic
Binary code

Brain
HAL*

Mouse
Plug

Cosmetics

Synonyms

Beauty aids   Beauty products   Makeup

Related Words, Phrases, and Expressions

Accent

Application

Art/artist

Base

Beautiful

Beautify

Beauty

Blush

Blushing bride

Body makeup

Bone structure

Bright/brighten

Bring out

Clarifying

Clear

Color

Conceal

Concealer

Contour

Cool

Cosmetic purposes

Cosmetic surgery

Dark/darken

Daytime/nighttime

Demure

Don't give me
any lip

Dramatic

Earthy

Effect

Eye color

Eye shadow

Eyeliner

Face

Face that launched
a thousand ships

Facelift

Features

Formula

Foundation

Gel

Gentle

Glimmer

Glisten

Glitter

Gloss

Glow

Hide

Highlight

Hydrating

Kiss and make up

Kiss and tell

Kissable

Lengthen

Light/lighten

Line

Lip color

Lip gloss

Lip liner

Lipstick

Liquid

Long-lasting

Long-wearing

Makeover

Makeup exam

Mascara

Matte

Moisture/
moisturizing

Nail color

Nail polish

New coat of paint

Natural

Noncomedogenic

Oil-free

Paint

Paint the town **red**

Palette

Play up/play down

Potion

Powder

Powder puff

Pretty

Pucker up

Put on a **happy** face

Put your **best** face
forward

Putting on my face

Radiant

Repair

Replenishing

Shade

Shadow

Shape

Shimmer

Shiny

Smooth

Smudge-proof

The eyes are the
windows of the
soul

There is no cos-
metic for beauty
like happiness

Thicken

Tone

Touch

Touchable

Transform

Translucent

War paint

Warm

Waterproof

Symbols and Metaphors

Applicator brushes   Compact   Lighted makeup   Lipstick print
                                               mirror

Crafts

Synonyms

Arts and crafts   Craft supplies   Hobbies

Related Words, Phrases, and Expressions

A compelling yarn

A cut above

A noticeable pattern

A stitch in time saves nine

A stitch in your side

Album

All the trimmings

Art

Beads

Beady eyes

Birthday candles

Build

Burn the candle at both ends

Can't hold a candle to it

Candlelight dinner

Candlestick

Card party

Card table

Close-knit

Craftwork

Create

Crimp

Crochet

Crystal ball

Cut and dried

Cut and paste

Cut it out

Director's cut

Draw a breath

Draw a card

Draw your own conclusions

Fabric

Feet of clay

Finishing touch

Gift

Great on paper

Handiwork

Handmade

Hanukkah candles

High wire act

Hobby horse

In stitches

In the cards

It's a draw

It's better to light a candle than to curse the darkness

Keepsake

Knit 1, purl 2

Layout

Make the cut

Memory book

Needlework

Needling the competition

Newspaper

On the wire

Out of your gourd

Page me

Page through

Paint the town **red**

Paperwork

Prime cut

Project

Put your stamp on it

Quick draw

Quilting bee

Scrapbook

Soap dish

Soap opera

Soapbox

Spycraft

Stagecraft

Stamp out

Statecraft

Stencil

Stick to him like glue

Textured

Tools

Trimming the tree

Unique

When they made you, they broke the mold

Wreath

You need a hobby

You're such a card

Symbols and Metaphors

Ball of yarn

Beads

Jewelry box

Scarf

Scissors

Dental Care

Synonyms

Dental hygiene

Dentistry

Mouth care

Oral hygiene

Orthodonture

Related Words, Phrases, and Expressions

A brush with _____

A smile that lights up a
  room

Bite the bullet

Bonding

Brace yourself

Breathe **easy**

Bridge

Brightening

Brush

Brush up

Cavity search

Chattering teeth

Checkup

Chew the fat

Chew up the scenery

Clean/cleaning

Cosmetic

Crown

Dentist's-office music

Filling

Floss

Gentle

Grinning from ear to ear

Grit your teeth

Gums

Healthy

Incisor

Let a smile be your
  umbrella*

Long in the tooth

Molar

Mouth off

Open wide

Painless

Pearly whites

Polishing

Refreshing

Relax

Rinse

Say cheese

Sink your teeth into _____

Smart mouth

Smile for the camera

Soothing

Spit

Straightening

Strong

Sweet tooth

Take a bite out of life

Tooth fairy

Toothsome

Toothy

White/whitening

Winning smile

Wisdom teeth

Symbols and Metaphors

Cheshire cat

Dentist's chair

Saber-tooth tiger

Shark

Tooth fairy

Toothbrush

Vampire

Drink

Synonyms

Alcoholic beverages	**Hot** drinks	Soft drinks
Beverages	Juices	

Related Words, Phrases, and Expressions

A **cold** one	Eat, drink, and be merry	It's raining, it's pouring	Rehydrate
Aromatic	Essential	Java	Rich
Bar	Fine	Joe	Saloon
Bartender	Fizz	Jug	Salud
Bold	Flavorful	Keg	Savor
Bottle	Fortified	Kick	Sip
Brew	Fountain of youth	Last call	Sippy cup
Cheers	Fresh	Light	Smooth
Chill	Fresh-brewed	Liquid	Soak
Chug	Fresh-ground	Mix	Sommelier
Clear improvement	Fresh-squeezed	Mix and match	Sparkling
Cocktail dress	Fruity	Mix it up	Spill the beans
Cocktail hour	Get up and go	Not my cup of tea	Splash
Cocktail party	Golden	Nutritious	Subtle
Coffee klatsch	Good morning	On tap	Swallow
Coffee shop	Gulp	Parched	Sweet
Coffee, tea, or me*	H_2O	Pour	Tall drink of water
Cream and sugar	**Happy** hour	Proof	Tap
Creamy	Herbal	Prosit	Tap dance
Daily grind	Hint	Pulp	Tea for two
Draft	Hurricane	Pure	Tempest in a teacup
Drench	Hydrate	Quench	The difference is clear
Drink and dial	Ice cold	Rain	The proof of the pudding is in the eating
Drink in	Imported	Reading tea leaves	
Drink to _____	*In vino veritas*	**Refreshing**	
Drink up			

continues

Drink *(continued)*

Related Words, Phrases, and Expressions

Thirst

Toast

Top shelf

Water, water every-
where and not a
drop to drink

Wet

Wet your whistle

Wine cellar

Wine list

Symbols and Metaphors

Corkscrew

Fountain

Glass

Mini-umbrella

Mug

Oasis

Olive

Pitcher

Spring

Straw

Swizzle stick

Waterfall

Education

Synonyms

Classes

Courses

Learning

Lessons

Schools

Universities

Related Words, Phrases, and Expressions

Assignment

Book learning

Brain-building

Broadening

Campus

Class

Course

Course of action

Cram

Develop

Distance learning

Do your homework

Educational

Enlightening

Get the facts

Give a man a fish and you feed him for a day; teach a man to fish and you feed him for a lifetime

Grade

Grow

Hands-on learning

Homework

Honor roll

Idea

If you think education is expensive, try ignorance

Illuminating

In the know

Informative

Informed opinion

Instructive

Know-it-all

Knowledge

Knowledge-enhancing

Learn

Learn from your mistakes

Learn the hard way

Lecture

Lesson

Mentor

Online course

Only the educated are free

Potential

Prep school

Preparatory

Private school

Public school

Pulling an all-nighter

Pupil

Reference

Research

School of hard knocks

School's out

Shedding light

Skill-building

Skill-enhancing

Skill-sharpening

Skills

Smart

Smarts

Student

Studious

Study

Study hall

Summa cum laude

Take notes

Teach

Teach your children well*

Test

Test yourself

Textbook

Tutor

Valedictorian

Wisdom

Wise

You can't teach an old dog new tricks

You learn something **new** every day

Symbols and Metaphors

Apple

Backpack

Blackboard

Book

Library

Lightbulb

Mortarboard

Owl

Report card

Search engine

Exercise/Fitness

Synonyms

Exercise equipment	Exercise videos	Fitness products	Health clubs
Exercise machines	Fitness plans	Gyms	

Related Words, Phrases, and Expressions

_____ minutes a day

A measurable difference

Achieve

Adrenaline

At your convenience

Beginners welcome

Body and mind

Body and soul

Body and spirit

Body **beautiful**

Body building

Body language

Bodywork

Built

Burn

Cardio

Classes **available**

Climb aboard

Coach

Easy

Encouragement

Endorphins

Endurance

Fat-burning

Fat-blasting

Feel the burn

Feel the difference

Firm

Fit for _____

Flat

Flexible

For all ages, shapes, and sizes

Free classes available

Friendly atmosphere

Fun

Get going

Get high naturally

Get in shape

Get moving

Get off the treadmill

Get rid of aches and pains

Goal

Guidance

Heart-**healthy**

In the comfort of your own home

In unity there is strength

Individualized fitness plan

Invest

Invigorating

Lift

Look years younger

Make it a priority

Measure your progress

Melt

Metabolism

Nature's antidepressant

New you

Nonintimidating atmosphere

Personal trainer

Plan

Program

Pull your own weight

Pumped up

Push

Put some muscle into it

Reps

Resolution

Rock hard

Rock solid

Run for your life

Runner's high

Safety-tested

Scale

Sculpt

See a difference

Sets

Shape up

Six-pack

Slim down

Smash your stress

Spacious

Start slow—just start

Stick with it

Stretch

Strong

Strongly encouraged

Strongly recommended

Support

Sweat

Take a walk

Take the first step

Tone

Trainer

Training

Trim the fat

Tune-up

Walk it off

Washboard abs

We can work it out

Weighty issue

Wide range of
  equipment

Workout

You'll feel better

Young

Youthful

Symbols and Metaphors

Barbell/dumbbell

Finish line

Lotus pose

Mat

Scale

Tape measure

Flowers

Synonyms

Arrangements   Blooms   Blossoms   Bouquets

Related Words, Phrases, and Expressions

A rose by any other name would smell as sweet (William Shakespeare)

A rose is a rose is a rose ...* (Gertrude Stein)

Anemone

Annuals

Aster

Azalea

Baby's-breath

Blooming

Boutonniere

Buds

Camellia

Candy and flowers

Carnation

Centerpiece

Chrysanthemum

Come out smelling like a rose

Corsage

Crocus

Daffodil

Dahlia

Daisy

Daisy, Daisy, give me your answer, do

Delphinium

Design

Every rose has its thorns

Floral

Flower bed

Flower pot

Flower power

Fresh as a daisy

Fresh-cut

Funeral wreath

Garden

Garden of Eden

Hearts and flowers

Hothouse flower

In full bloom

Iris

Lilac

Lily

Lily pad

Lily pond

Lily **white**

Long-stemmed

Magnolia

My luve's like a red, red rose that's newly sprung in June (Robert Burns)

Orchid

Pansy

Peony

Perennials

Petals

Petunia

Plant

Poinsettia

Poppy

Primrose

Prom

Rose

Send

Snapdragon

Spray

Sprig

Springtime

Stems

Stop and smell the flowers

Sunflower

Surprise

Sweetpea

Throwing/catching the bouquet

Tulip

Vase

Wallflower

Weddings

Where have all the flowers gone?* (Pete Seeger)

Wreath

Yellow rose of Texas

Zinnia

Symbols and Metaphors

Bumblebee   Georgia O'Keeffe   **Spring**   Vase

Food

Synonyms

Groceries

Provisions

Related Words, Phrases, and Expressions

Aisles

Ambrosia

Apple of my eye

Baby food

Bad apple

Bag it

Baker's dozen

Bearing fruit

Brain food

Brand

Bread and water

Bread box

Cakewalk

Canned

Cat food

Catering

Choice

Coffee, tea, or me*

Craving

Daily bread

Deli/delicatessen

Delicious

Dog food

Double coupons

Easter eggs

Economy size

Egg him on

Egg on his face

Ethnic food

Express lane

Family size

Feed the hungry

Feed the world

Feed your head

Fish food

Flavors

Food and **drink**

Food fight

Food for thought

Food taster

Foodie

Fresh

From soup to nuts

Frozen

Fruitful

Go bananas

Go nuts

Good egg

Gourmet/ gourmand

Grocery coupon

Grocery list

Halal

Health food

Healthful

Home **delivery**

If music be the food of love, play on (William Shakespeare)

In a jam

In a pickle

Kosher

Lactose-free

Like peas in a pod

Locally grown

Macrobiotic

Market value

Meat market

Meatless

MRE (meal ready to eat)

Nectar

Nutritious

Open market

Open-air market

Organic

Paper or plastic?

Peachy keen

Peanut butter and jelly

Peter Piper picked a peck of pickled peppers

Rations

Raw

Refreshments

Rolling in the aisles

Salt of the earth

Sandwich board

Soul food

Spice things up

Stock up

Strap on the feed-bag

Supermarket

Sweeeeet!

Sweet deal

Sweet talk

Take a bite out of life

TV dinner

Variety

Variety is the spice of life

Vegan

Vegetarian

Walking on eggshells

We accept competitors' coupons

Whole

Your grocer's freezer

continues

Food   *(continued)*

Symbols and Metaphors

Buffet table	Farmer's market	Plate	Shopping list
Cornucopia	Grocery cart	Produce bins	Tray
Cutlery	Pantry	Refrigerator	

Furniture

Synonyms

Furnishings

Home furnishings

Related Words, Phrases, and Expressions

A house is not a
 home

Accent

Adjustable

Antique

Arrangement

Bedtime

Breathing room

Brighten

Bring to the table

Casting couch

Centerpiece

Chairperson

Come home to

――――

Comfortable

Comfy

Conversation piece

Coordinated

Couch potato

Cozy

Crib

Décor

Decorator

Digs

Domain

Domestic

Easy assembly

Easy chair

Easy to **clean**

Efficient

Elbow room

Environment

Everything but the
 kitchen sink

Expandable

Feather your nest

Fixtures

Floor-to-ceiling

Focal point

Formal

Freshen

Furnished room

Gather around

Guest room

Have a seat

Head of the table

Heirloom-quality

Home base

Home is where the
 heart is

House party

In a good light

Indoor/outdoor

Interior

Interior designer

Keep your feet off
 the furniture

Layout

Lifestyle

Lighting

Living space

Luxurious

Make room for

――――

Matching

Mix and match

Modern

Nest

Nook

Offer on the table

Office furniture

On the house

On the table/off
 the table

Pad

Palace

Patio furniture

Piece

Pillow talk

Practical

Put your feet up

Rearrange

Redecorate

Refuge

Refurbish

Renovation

Rest easy

Rocking chair

Room for improve-
 ment

Room **service**

Room with a view

Roundtable discus-
 sion

Sack out

Sanctuary

Seat

Set

Set the table

Showplace

Simplify

Sit

Sitting pretty

Sleep on it

Slipcover

Snug as a bug in
 a rug

Space

Space-saving

Storage space

Sturdy

continues

Furniture *(continued)*

Related Words, Phrases, and Expressions

Suite

Surroundings

Surround yourself with _____

Table for two

The writing is on the wall

Traditional

Unclutter

Up against the wall

Update

Upholstered

Veneer

Versatile

Wall-to-wall

Well-built

Your home is your castle

Symbols and Metaphors

Carpenter

Chair

Dollhouse

Swatches

Table

Tape measure

Gardening

Synonyms

Garden supplies   Landscaping   Nurseries

Related Words, Phrases, and Expressions

A man for all seasons

*A Tree Grows in Brooklyn**

Ace of spades

All grown up

Annual event

Arbor Day

Arboretum

At first bloom

Bank branch

Bed

Bed of roses

Bed rest

Bedbug

Bedroom

Bedtime

Bloom

Blooming

Blossom

Blossoming

Bluegrass

Border

Branch out

Bring us a shrubbery*

Call a spade a spade

Clay court

Climate control

Climb a tree

Coffee grounds

Container

Crabgrass

Cultivate

Cultivate a following

Design

Dim bulb

Dirt cheap

Dirt poor

Dirty deal

Dishing dirt

Don't sit under the apple tree with anyone else but me*

Down and dirty

Down to Earth

Dying on the vine

Earth-friendly

Eat your vegetables

Evergreen

Falling leaves

Family tree

Feet of clay

Fertile

Fit and trim

Flourishing

Flowers

Foliage

Fresh air

Fresh ground

From the ground up

Gaining ground

Garden club

Garden gate

Garden of Eden

Garden party

Get your hands dirty

Going out on a limb

Grass stains

Green

Green thumb

Greenhouse

Ground

Ground cover

Ground down

Ground up

Grounds for dismissal

Grounds for divorce

Grow into

Grow up

Growing attraction

Growing fear

Growing sales

Growing tired

Growing wealth

Grows on you

Growth

Hardy

Harvest

Harvest moon

Heaven and Earth

Heaven on Earth

Hedge maze

Hedge sculpture

Hedge your bets

Higher ground

Hollywood and Vine

Hothouse flower

Hybrid

I think that I shall never see a poem lovely as a tree* (Joyce Kilmer)

In season

In the ground

Into each life a little rain must fall

Ivy League

Just a trim

Keep your feet on the ground

Landscape

Lawn party

Lawn tennis

Leaf blower

continues

Gardening *(continued)*

Related Words, Phrases, and Expressions

Leaf through
Led down the garden path
Legal grounds
Life on Earth
Lightbulb
London Underground
Loose-leaf
Lush
Manicured
Mary Mary quite contrary, how does your garden grow?
Moist
Move heaven and Earth
Mow
Mow the lawn
Mowed down
Neutral ground
Nourish
Nuclear plant
Nursery
Nursery rhyme
Nutrients

Organic
Outgrow
Perennial favorite
Perennial question
Pistil
Plant an idea
Plant yourself
Planting a seed
Potted plant
Power plant
Prune
Put down roots
Rain date
Rain or shine
Raining cats and dogs
Rock garden
Roof garden
Root around
Root cause
Root for
Root of the conflict
Root of the problem
Root out
Root, root, root for the home team*

Same time next year
Save it for a rainy day
Season
Season's greetings
Seedlings
Seeds of an idea
Seeds of love
Set down roots
Shade tree
Shady
Shovel it in
Sod
Soil
Soiled reputation
Solid ground
Someone else's turf
Sowing your wild oats
Stamen
Stem the tide
Stemming from
Sunny
Tend your own garden
The bloom of youth

The dirt on _____
The green, green grass of home*
Thriving
Thriving business
Topsoil
Tree house
Tree line
Treetops
Trim
Trim the fat
Trunk space
Turf battle
Turf war
Underground movement
Vegetable garden
Victory garden
Water/watering
Welcoming climate
Wild
Window garden
Woke up on the wrong side of the bed
You reap what you sow

Symbols and Metaphors

Flower
Flowerpot
Garden gloves
Greenhouse

Hat
Hedge maze
Leaf
Seeds

Shovel
Spade
Tree

Watering can
Window box

Hair Care

Synonyms

Hair products

Haircutting/
    hairstyling

Styling products

Related Words, Phrases, and Expressions

Auburn

Bad hair day

Bangs

Barrette

Beautiful

Black

Blond

Blow dryers

Body

Body wave

Bouffant

Bouncy

Braid

Brunette

Brush

Bun

Buzz cut

Clip joint

Color

Comb

Conditioner

Cornrows

Créme rinse

Crowning glory

Curl up

Curly

Cut and run

Dye

Enough to curl
    your hair

Extensions

Flame-haired

Frizz

Frost

Gel

Glossy

Hair

Hair accessories

Hair band

Hair color

Hair of the dog

Hairpiece

Hairspray

Hair-raising

Head

Highlights

Layers

Locks

Longhair

Mousse

Part

Permanent

Pigtails

Platinum

Ponytail

Redhead

Ribbons and bows

Salon

Sculpt

Shampoo

Shape

Sheen

Shimmering

Shiny/shine

Shock waves

Silky

Silver

Smooth

Snip

Split ends

Straight

Straight talk

Streak

Style

Styling tools

Stylish

Tangle-free

Tidal wave

Tint

Tips

Touch up

Touchable

Tresses

Trim

Updo

Wave

Wave good-bye

Wavy

Wax

Wig

Symbols and Metaphors

Barber pole

Blow dryer

Helmet dryer with
    chair

Hippies

Rapunzel

Hardware

Synonyms

Building materials

Contracting supplies

Home improvement

Tools

Related Words, Phrases, and Expressions

Adjustable

Anything worth doing is worth doing well

Bolt

Brush with greatness

Brush-off

Bucket seats

Build

Buildup

Cement the deal

Corporate ladder

Corporate tool

Counterpoint

Cut a deal

DIY (do-it-yourself)

Drill for oil

Drill sergeant

Durable

Fair and square

Finger paint

Finish the job

Finish what you started

Fire drill

Fix

Fixer-upper

Floor to ceiling

Floored

Gadgets

Grip

Hammer the point home

Hammer time*

Hammered

Hammerhead shark

Handyman

Handyman special

Hang up

Hard as nails

Hit the nail on the head

If these walls could talk

In a fix

Industrial

Install

It's a fix

Level best

Level the playing field

Lightweight

Like putty in your hands

Lumbering around

Measurable difference

Measurable results

Measure by measure

Measure twice, cut once

Measure your options

Mop up the floor with him

Nailed it

Need a fix

Paint by number

Paint it black*

Paint the town red

Peace pipe

Peter Piper

Piping hot

Plumbing the depths

Plunge in

Ply him with _____

Power

Price cut

Rake it in

Refinish

Renovate

Repair

Safety

Saw the light

Sawbones

Screw around

Screw loose

Screwball

Screwdriver

Seal the deal

Seesaw

Tacky

Take the plunge

The fix is in

The last nail in the coffin

The right tool for the job

Tool belt

Tool kit

Toolbox

Tooling around

Tough

Under our roof

Versatile

Wall-to-wall

Washer and dryer

Wet paint

Whitewash

Workshop

Wrenching

Symbols and Metaphors

Can of nails	Goggles	Tool bench	Toolbox
Dust mask	Ladder		

Hotel

Synonyms

Accommodations

Bed and breakfast

Guest house

Inn

Lodge

Lodging

Motel

Resort

Related Words, Phrases, and Expressions

A place to crash

Along the way

Bath

Bed

Breakfast **available**

Breakfast included

Breathing room

Centrally located

Check in/check out

Coffee **service**

Concierge service

Conference rooms/meeting rooms

Do Not Disturb sign

Elbow room

Enjoy your stay

Full service

Good night's sleep

Guest

Gym

Hospitality

Host

Innkeeper

Internet connection

King size/queen size

Last resort

Luxury/**luxurious**

Maid service

Newspaper **delivery**

No room at the inn

Oasis

On the road

Overnight guest

Overnight sensation

Overnight stay

Overnight success

Pool

Privacy

Put you up for the night

Quiet

Rest stop

Rest your weary bones

Room service

Room with a view

Second home

Services

Shelter from the storm

Sleep on it

Spacious

Stay a while

Suite

Travel light

Traveler

Turndown service

Turn in for the night

Vacancy

Wake-up call

Weekend

Welcome

Welcome mat

Welcome with open arms

Within walking distance of _____

You're welcome

Symbols and Metaphors

Bellhop

Do Not Disturb sign

Gideon Bible

Ice machine

Key

Luggage

Miniature soap

Mint on pillow

Robe

Room service cart

"Sanitized for your protection" strip

Tray outside door

Vacancy sign

Housewares

Synonyms

Household items

Related Words, Phrases, and Expressions

A bun in the oven
A cut above
A house is not a home
Accent
Another kettle of fish
Bring to the table
Cabinet meeting
Chopping block
Clean your plate
Coffee break
Cook up
Cooking with gas
Cookware
Countertop
Curio
Dish it out
Dishing
Dishwasher-safe
Fork in the road
Fork it over
Gadget
Help yourself

Home for the holidays
Home is where the heart is
Home on the range*
Home plate
Household name
I'd like to make a toast
Kettle drum
Kitchenware
Linen closet
Microwave-**safe**
Mix it up
Money-saver
My cup of tea
My cup runneth over
Now you're cooking
On a silver platter
Out of the frying pan and
  into the fire
Pass the salt
Pots and pans
Push-button
Put the kettle on

See-through
Serve up
Silver spoon
Silverware
Space-saver
Spoon fed
Stackable
Stir it up
Storage
Stovetop
Table service
Table setting
Tchochke
Tea for two
Tempest in a teacup
There's no place like home
Throw in the towel
Time-saver
Tools
Unbreakable
Wedding gift
Welcome home

Symbols and Metaphors

Apron
Blender
Bridal shower

Kitchen cabinet
Napkin ring
Oven mitt/potholder

Place setting
Toaster

Information

Synonyms

Data   Facts   Reference materials

Related Words, Phrases, and Expressions

411

A little knowledge
  is a dangerous
  thing

At your fingertips

A-to-Z

Aware

Bits

Bytes

Brief

Clued in

Clueless

Crunch the num-
  bers

Data entry

Database

Dirt

Dish

Evidence

Exclusive

Fact and fancy

Fact and myth

Fact and opinion

Fact or fiction

Fact sheet

Fact-finding
  mission

Facts of life

Get a clue

Hip

I've made up my
  mind; don't con-
  fuse me with the
  facts

Important

In on it

In the know

Info

Information age

Information desk

Information net-
  work

Information revo-
  lution

Information super-
  highway

Informative

Informed

Inside information

Inside scoop

IT (information
  technology)

Just the facts,
  ma'am

Know your limits

Know your rights

Know-it-all

Knowledge
  workers

Lowdown

Memory

Numbers

Nutrition facts

Organized

Practical

Privileged informa-
  tion

Processing

Proven

Quick-reference

Refer

Reliable

Reliable informa-
  tion

Report

Scoop

Search

Search engine

Sensory informa-
  tion

Storage

Substantiated

Top secret

True

Up-to-date

Useful

Valuable

Verified/verifiable

We regret to
  inform you

Well-informed

You could look
  it up

Symbols and Metaphors

Book

Chart

Computer

Dictionary

Encyclopedia

Footnotes

Graph

Microchip

Newspaper

Phone book

Insurance

Synonyms

Coverage

Related Words, Phrases, and Expressions

Affordable
Backup
Benefits
Breathe **easy**
Care
Choice
Claim
Co-pay
Count on us
Cover me
Cushion
Depend on us
Eligible
Emergency
Fast approval
Fast payout

Financially **healthy**
For a rainy day
For better or worse
Get through the hard times
Health
Honesty is the **best** policy
In good times and bad
In sickness and in health
Misfortune
Options
Peace of mind
Policy
Premium
Prepared
Preventive maintenance is
  less costly than repairs
Protection

Reimbursement
Reliable
Rest easy
Ride out the storm
Risk
Rough patch
Safe
Safety net
Secure their future
Security
See your own doctor
Sensible
Shelter
Think ahead
We've got you covered
We've got your back

Symbols and Metaphors

Bib
Helmet

Shield
Slipcover

Tarp

Jewelry

Synonyms

Bling

Gems

Jewels

Related Words, Phrases, and Expressions

A diamond is a
  girl's best friend*

Accessory

Ankle bracelet

Antique

Appraisal

Aquamarine

Bangle

Bejeweled

Birthstone

Body jewelry

Bracelet

Brilliant

Brooch

Carat

Catch the light

Chain

Charm

Charming

Choker

Clarity

Clasp

Class ring

Classic

Clip-on

Costume jewelry

Crystal

Crystal clear

Cubic zirconia

Cut

Design

Diamond

Diamond district

Diamond in the
  rough

Drop earrings

Elegant

Emerald

Emerald City*

Engagement ring

Facets

Faux

Flash

Flawless

Funky

Garnet

Give me a ring

Glitter

Glow

Gold

Handcrafted

Handmade

Hearts and dia-
  monds

Heirloom

Hoop earrings

Ice

Jade

Jewel tones

Jewelry box

King of diamonds

Locket

Luster

Marcasite

Mood ring

Mother-of-pearl

Necklace

Nose ring

Onyx

Opal

Pearl

Pearl beyond price

Pendant

Peridot

Pierced

Pin

Platinum

Pop the question

Precious

Precious metals

Priceless

Queen of diamonds

Reflect

Rhinestone

Ring

Rock

Ruby

Sapphire

Semi-precious

Setting

Shimmer

Shiny

Silver

Silver spoon

Sparkle

Stones

Stud earrings

Tennis bracelet

Toe ring

Topaz

Turquoise

Valuable

Watch

Wedding ring

Symbols and Metaphors

Oyster

Treasure chest

Velvet box

Zsa Zsa Gabor*

Law

Synonyms

Legal counsel

Legal representation

Legal services

Related Words, Phrases, and Expressions

Acquit

Advise

Advocate/advocacy

Agreement

Appeal

Approach the bench

Argument

Asked and answered

Attorney/attorney at law

Barrister

Basketball court

Blue laws

Breach of contract

Briefcase

Browbeating

Capital case

Character witness

Charges

Circumstantial evidence

Civil

Civil disobedience

Civil unrest

Closing arguments

Code

Common-law marriage

Contract

Court date

Court disaster

Court of public opinion

Court officer

Court stenographer

Courtside seats

Crime

Criminal

Cross-examine

Custody

Damages

Decision

Defense

De-fense! De-fense!

Don't make a federal case out of it

Don't settle for less

Emotional duress

Esquire

Fair

Firm

Firm commitment

Get what you're entitled to

Grand jury

Hanging judge

Hearing

Hearsay

Here comes the judge

Hostile witness

I fought the law, and the law won*

I rest my case

I'll see you in court

If it doesn't fit, you must acquit

Illegal

Impaired judgment

Indefensible

Indict

Injustice

In-law

Interrogation

Judge, jury, and executioner

Judge Dredd*

Judge not lest ye be judged

Judgment call

Jury

Jury duty

Jury pool

Justice

Justice is blind

Justice is served

Know your rights

Law and order

Law of averages

Law of gravity

Law of the jungle

Law of the land

Lawgiver

Lawmaker

Laws of nature

Laws of physics

Lawyer

Lay down the law

Leading the witness

Legal brief

Legal eagle

Legally binding

Legally blind

Legislation

Let the record show

Litigation

Make your case

Maneuver

Material witness

continues

Law *(continued)*

Related Words, Phrases, and Expressions

Miscarriage of justice

Misdemeanor

Mistrial

Objection

Offense

On the bench

On the books

Order in the court

Outlaw

Overruled

Oyez

Physical evidence

Plea

Presiding

Proceedings

Prosecution

Protection

Represent

Rights

Scopes monkey trial

Sentence

Settlement

Small claims

Special case

Star witness

Suit

Summation

Suspended sentence

Sustained

Tennis court

Test case

The ball's in your court

The best defense is a good offense

The truth, the whole truth, and nothing but the truth

Transcripts

Travesty of justice

Trial by jury

Trial of the century

Trials and tribulations

Trials and triumphs

Try

Uncivil

Value judgment

Verdict

Vs.

We stand up for you

Witness

Worst-case scenario

You can't judge a book by its cover

Symbols and Metaphors

Briefcase

Courthouse

Gavel

Jury box

Moses

Perry Mason*

Scales of justice

Witness stand

Medical/Pharmaceutical

Synonyms

Clinics

Doctors

Drugs

Drugstores

Hospitals

Labs

Medical care

Medical services

Medical treatment

Nursing care

Pharmacies

Physicians

Related Words, Phrases, and Expressions

A shot in the arm

Adding insult to
  injury

Admitting privileges

Advanced

Affiliated

Affordable health
  care

Alternative medicine

Annual checkup

Assessment

Attentive

Battery of tests

Bed rest

Bedside manner

Body check

Caregiver

Caring

Chart

Checking up on you

Checkup

Chill pill

Clean bill of health

Cold and flu season

Concerned

Consultation

Cure

Diagnosis

Doc

Doctor's note

Doctor's orders

Enough to make
  you sick

ER (emergency
  room)

Examination

Facility

First do no harm

Fix

Get well soon

Healing

Healing hands

Healing touch

Health care

Healthy, wealthy,
  and wise

Hippocratic oath

Hospice

Hospital food

House call

In sickness and in
  health

Inpatient

Lab on premises

M.D.

Medic

Medical emergency

Medical journal

Medical records

Medical waste

Medicine ball

Mental health

Not yourself

Nurse practitioner

Nurse you back to
  health

Nursing home

Office hours

Office visit

On call

OR (operating
  room)

Outpatient

Patient

Patient care

Payment plan

Physician, heal thy-
  self

Practitioner

Preventive

Private room

Procedure

Professional

Prognosis

Recover

Recuperate

Red-carpet treat-
  ment

Remedy

Reputable

Results

Road to recovery

Rounds

Rx

Semi-private room

Shift

Sick as a dog

Silent treatment

Special treatment

Spin doctor

Staff

Standard of care

State-of-the-art

Sterile

continues

Medical/Pharmaceutical *(continued)*

Related Words, Phrases, and Expressions

Strong medicine	Thorough	Trustworthy	We accept _____
Take care	Time heals all wounds	Urgent care	X-ray vision
Take your medicine		Vital signs	
The **best** medicine	To your health	Walk-in	

Symbols and Metaphors

Bed tray	Golf clubs	Prescription	White coat
Beeper	Hospital gown	Scrubs	X-ray
Blood pressure cuff	Lollipop	Stethoscope	
Diplomas	M.D. plates	Surgical mask	
Exam table	Paper gown	Waiting room	

Money/Financial Services

Synonyms

Account	Dimes	Moolah	Quarters
Assets	Dinero	Nest egg	Riches
Bank	Dollars	Net worth	Roll
Bankroll	Dough	Nickels	Savings
Benjamins	Euros	Nickels and dimes	Shekels
Bread	Fortune	Paycheck	Silver
Bucks	Funds	Pence	Treasure
Capital	**Gold**	Pennies	Treasure chest
Cash	**Green**	Pesos	Wealth
Cash money	Greenbacks	Pounds	Yen
Coins	Interest	Principal	
Deutschmarks	Means	Profit	

Related Words, Phrases, and Expressions

Accumulate	**Easy** money	Income	Money isn't every-thing
Affluent	Easy street	Interest	Money makes the world go 'round*
An embarrassment of riches	Finance	Invest	Money shot
Billionaire	For love or money	It takes money to make money	Moneybags
Billions	Future/futures	It's only money	Moneymaker/moneymaking
Bonds	Get paid	Jackpot	Net worth
Bonus	Good life	Liquid	Opportunity
Budget	Grand	Living large	Options
Cash flow	Grow/growth	Luxury	Pay
Cost	**Healthy**, wealthy, and wise	Means	Pay the piper
Crime doesn't pay	High end	Millionaire	Pay through the nose
Cut your losses	If I were a **rich** man	Millions	Payday
Dividends	In for a penny, in for a pound	Money, that's what I want*	Payoff
Don't spend it all in one place	In the black	Money changes everything*	Pays for itself
Don't throw good money after bad	In the money		

continues

Money/Financial Services *(continued)*

Related Words, Phrases, and Expressions

Peace of mind

Penny wise and
  pound foolish

Price

Principal

Prospects

Returns

Reward

Rich/riches

Salary

Save

Save it for a
  rainy day

Security

Socked away

Spend

Stashed away

Stocks

Surplus

Take stock

The $64,000 ques-
  tion

The love of money
  is the root of all
  evil

Time is money

Top drawer

Top of the line

Top shelf

We're in the money

Wealth

Who wants to be a
  millionaire?

Worth

You're money, baby

Your money is no
  good here

Your money or
  your life

Symbols and Metaphors

Beverly Hills

Bill Gates*

Champagne

Country club

Croesus

Diamonds/**jewelry**

Fifth Avenue

Hamptons

Las Vegas

Mansion

Money clip

Monte Carlo

Mr. and Mrs.
  Howell/the mil-
  lionaire and his
  wife*

Mr. Burns*

Park Avenue

Piggy bank

Pocketbook

Poker chips

Purse

Rockefeller*

Scrooge

Treasure chest

Vault

Wallet

Wall Street

Yacht

Movies

Synonyms

Films

Flicks

Motion pictures

Related Words, Phrases, and Expressions

Academy Award winner*

Acclaimed

All-star cast

Animated

Audience

Based on a true story

Big picture

Big screen

Big-budget

Box office

Chick flick

Cinema

Cinematic

Classic

Critic's favorite

Crowd-pleaser

Date movie

Did you miss it?

Documentary

Double feature

Dream

Ensemble cast

Epic

Escape

Exciting

Extravaganza

Family-friendly

Filmed on location

First run

From the director who brought you _____

From the studio that brought you _____

Funny

Hit

Indie

Inspired by a true story

Laugh-out-loud

Low-budget

Matinee

Magic

Movie star

Movie studio

Must-see

Now **available** on video/DVD

Now playing

Only in theaters

Onscreen

Premiere

Reel you in

Saga

Scary

See it again

See it on the big screen

See it with someone you love

Silver screen

Sleeper

Smash

Soundtrack

Starring

The movie everyone is talking about

Thrills and chills

Twists and turns

Unforgettable

Visual

Symbols and Metaphors

Drive-in

Film reel

Marquee

Popcorn

Usher

Music

Synonyms

Sounds

Tunes

Related Words, Phrases, and Expressions

A little night music

Acoustic

Airplay

Album

All that jazz

Ambient

Amped up

Amplified

Anthem

Aria

Background music

Ballad

Band

Beat

Beatbox

Belt it out

Blow

Bluegrass

Boombox

Brass

B-side

Cassette

Catchy

CD

Change your tune

Chart-topper

Choir

Choir of angels

Chorus

Classic

Classical

Collection

Composer

Concept album

Country and western

Crooner

Cut

Dance

Digital

Disco

Diva

DJ

Download

Driving

Duet

Ear candy

Easy listening

Eight-track

Electronica

Family album

Fiddling around

Folk

Free sample

Funk

Gold record

Gospel

Grammy winner*

Groove

Harmony

Haunting

Have you heard?

Heavy metal

Hip hop

Hit

Hit a high note

Hits all the right notes

Hook

Horns

Hymn

I sing the body electric

If music be the food of love, play on (William Shakespeare)

It's got a good beat and you can dance to it

Jazz

Key

Keyboard

Listen up

Live

Love song

LP

Lush

Lyrics

March

March to the beat of a different drum

Masterpiece

Melodious

Melody

Mood music

MP3

Music has charms to soothe the savage breast

Music library

Music to your ears

New Age

No strings attached

Note

Now hear this

Opera

Orchestra

Our song

Percussion

Piano bar

Platinum record

Platters

Pop
Power trio
Punk
Radio
Raised voices
Range
Rap
Reggae
Rhythm and blues/R&B
Rhythm method
Rock
Rock 'n' roll
Rock on

Rock solid
Salsa
Same old song and dance
Sample
Scale
Score
Sheet music
Show tunes
Shred
Sing it
Singing another tune
Song

Song and dance
Songbird
Sonic boom
Soul
Sound advice
Sound investment
Sound off
Soundtrack
Spare
Speakers
Spin
Strings
Supersonic
Symphony

Techno
Tickling the ivories
Top 40
Tracks
Tune in
Tune up
Verse
Vibe
Victrola*
Vocal
Wax
Wedding song
Woodwind
World music

Symbols and Metaphors

Conductor
Dancing couple
Headphones

Jukebox
Microphone
Musical note

Music stand
Pied Piper
Schroeder*

Sidewalk musician
Wandering minstrel

Personal Grooming

Synonyms

Grooming products   Health and beauty   Personal hygiene
                          aids

Related Words, Phrases, and Expressions

Annual bath

Baby shower

Bathroom break

Blowing bubbles

Bracing

Breathe **easy**

Bridal shower

Brisk

Bubble bath

Bubble gum

Car wash

Clean

Close shave

Cream and sugar

Cream puff

Creamed

Delicate

Don't burst my
  bubble

Don't get fresh

Don't sweat the
  small stuff

Dry as a bone

Dry goods

Dry run

Dry wit

Fresh

Fresh as a daisy

Fresh as the morn-
  ing dew

Fresh baked

Fresh cream

Fresh groove

Fresh squeezed

Fresh take

Fresh talk

Gentle

Groomed

Hair-free

Half bath

Hand wash

High and dry

Horses sweat; men
  perspire; women
  only glow

It's a wash

Itching to _____

Just a trim

Keep it fresh

No sweat

Not tonight, I have
  to wash my hair

Peaches and cream

Pit stop

Point shaving

Polished

Powder blue

Powder puff

Powdered sugar

Running dry

Scented

Sensitive

Shower scene

Shower with praise

Silky

Smooth

Smooth move

Smooth talk

Soak

Soothing

Success is 1 percent
  inspiration and 99
  percent perspira-
  tion

Sweat the details

Take a bath

Take a powder

The pit and the
  pendulum

The pits

Throw the baby
  out with the bath-
  water

Unscented

Wash your mouth
  out with soap

Washer and dryer

Wedding shower

Well-groomed

Whipped cream

Window washer

Without breaking a
  sweat

Symbols and Metaphors

Bathtub

Bubbles

Flowers

Loofah

Medicine cabinet

Soap dish

Steamy mirror

Towel

Well-trimmed lawn

Pet Care

Synonyms

Pet needs

Pet supplies

Veterinary care

Related Words, Phrases, and Expressions

A horse of a different color

All creatures great and **small**

Animal house

Animal instinct

Animal rights

Arf

Bark

Beast

Beg

Best friend

Birdbath

Care/**caring**

Cat's meow

Cat's pajamas

Cathouse

Companion

Cool cat

Creatures

Dog days

Dog tired

Experienced

Fat cat

Feathered friends

Fins

Fishing for compliments

Flea circus

Four-footed friends

Furry

Gentle

God's creatures

Heavy petting

Holy cow

Hot dog

Howl

I wouldn't send a dog out on a night like this

In the doghouse

Living in a fishbowl

Love

Man's **best** friend

Member of the family

Menagerie

Meow

Paws

Pet cause

Pet name

Pet peeve

Pigpen

Puppy love

Purr

Raining cats and dogs

School of fish

Something to chew on

Tails

Tail-wagger

Talk to the animals

Throw me a bone

Top dog

Toys

Treats

Whiskers

Wings

Woof

Zoo

Symbols and Metaphors

Bone

Bowl

Dr. Dolittle*

Noah's Ark

Paw prints

Phone/Phone Service

Synonyms

Telephone service

Related Words, Phrases, and Expressions

All talk, no action
Answering machine
Area code
Battery
Beep
Big talk
Busy signal
Buzz
By the minute
Call a cab
Call back
Call collect
Call forward
Call now
Call of the wild
Call waiting
Caller ID
Calling all cars
Calling area
Calling card
Calling plan
Can I call you sometime?
Car phone
Cell
Chat
Chat room
Chatterbox
Chattering class

Check in
Close call
Communication breakdown*
Connect
Cordless
Counting the minutes
Dial
Digits
Disconnect
Don't call us, we'll call you
Don't limit yourself
Every minute counts
Everyone's talking about it
Fast talk
Flip
Flip out
Flip your lid
Free speech
Get the message
Give me a call
Give me a ring
Hands-free
Hang on
Hang up
Headset

Hear ye
Hello
Hold all calls
Hold the phone
I hear you
In touch
Internet phone
Keep talking
Landline
Last call
Lifeline
Listen carefully
Listen up
Local
Long distance
Loose talk
Message
Minutes
Mobile
Nature calls
No limit
Now hear this
On hold
On the horn
Operator
Pay a call
Phone book
Phone booth
Phone home

Phone it in
Pick up
Private line
Push-button phone
Put your **money** where your mouth is
Rates
Reach
Receiver
Ring
Rotary phone
Screen your calls
Shoe phone*
Signal
Small talk
Smoke signal
Something to talk about
Speak now or forever hold your peace
Speak up
Speaker phone
Speaking of _____
Switchboard
Talk is cheap
Talk it over
Talk it up
Talk of the town

Talk the talk and
  walk the walk
Talk therapy
Talking points
Telecommunications

Telephone pole
Touch base
Video phone
Voicemail
Wait a minute

We need to talk
What we have here
  is a failure to
  communicate*
Who may I say is
  calling?

Wire
Wireless
Yammer
Yap

Symbols and Metaphors

Cord
Hollywood execu-
  tive

Phone number
  written on match-
  book

Receptionist
Switchboard
  operator

Photography

Synonyms

Cameras   Portraits   Videography

Related Words, Phrases, and Expressions

A picture is worth a thousand words
Album
Baby pictures
Black and white
Camera-ready
Camera-shy
Candid
Capture
Cherish
Class picture
Clear
Click
Color
Composition
Darkroom
Delete
Develop
Edit
Family album
Film at 11
Fix
Flash

Frame
Freeze frame
Gallery
Generations
Good shot
Head shot
High-speed
History
Image
In the picture
Lasting
Look back
Memento
Memories
Moments
Moving pictures
Occasion
Out of the picture
Paparazzi
Photographic evidence
Photojournalist
Picture **perfect**

Picture postcard
Picture show
Picture this
Posed
Precious
Preserve
Pretty as a picture
Print
Quality
Record
Remember
Remember the occasion
Remember your party
Remember your trip
Restore
Say cheese
See for yourself
Send
Share
Shoot for the stars

Shoot the moon
Shot
Shutterbug
Slide show
Smile
Snap
Souvenir
Star
Strike a pose
Take your **best** shot
The picture of _____
Through the years
Touch up
View
Vivid
Wallet size
Yearbook picture
You oughta be in pictures
Zoom

Symbols and Metaphors

Album
Backdrop screen
Filmstrip

Frame on desk or bedside
Old photo with black corner holders

Photo strip from booth
Snapshot in the corner of a mirror

Spotlight
Wallet foldout filled with photos

Real Estate

Synonyms

Buildings

Commercial properties

Homes

Houses

Land

Residential properties

Related Words, Phrases, and Expressions

A backyard for the kids

A house is not a home

A place for everything, and everything in its place

A room of one's own

Acres

Airy

Amenities

Ample parking

Architecture

Attic

Basement

Brand **new**

Bright

Built for _____

Built like a brick house

Built to _____

Busy corner

Busy street

Buy land; they're not making it anymore

CAC (central air conditioning)

Centrally located

Clean

Closet space

Come home

Comfortable

Convenient

Cook at home

Cozy

Crib

Cul de sac

Curb appeal

Deck

Decorator's dream

Doorman

Dream house

Duplex

DW (dishwasher)

Easy commute

EIK (eat-in kitchen)

Elevator

Energy-efficient

Escape the city

Established business

FDR (formal dining room)

Finished basement

Fly south for the winter

FP (fireplace)

Fresh coat of paint

Garage

Good move

Good schools

Guest bedroom

Handyman's dream

Hardwood floors

High-traffic area

Home

Home for the holidays

Home is where the heart is

Home is where you hang your hat

Home run

House hunting

House party

House rules

Investment

Land ho

Landscaped

Lifestyle

Lively

Location, location, location

Look out on _____

Lovingly maintained

Low maintenance

Luxury/**luxurious**

Make your move

Mint condition

Move up

Move-in condition

Must see

Must sell

Needs TLC

New appliances

New windows

No car needed

No more clutter

No more lugging laundry

Office space

On the house

Open house

Original detail

continues

Real Estate   *(continued)*

Related Words, Phrases, and Expressions

Outdoor space

Pad

Pay your mortgage
  with rental
  income

Pied-a-terre

Plot

Porch

Quiet

Renovated

Rent or own

Rent to own

Rental apartment

Room to entertain

Room to move

Room with a view

Space

Spacious

Square footage

Starter house

Storage

Stretch out

Summer home

Sunny

The key to _____

They don't build
  them like this
  anymore

Under my roof

Unique

Unlock

Vacation home

View

Walk to _____

Wall to wall

WD (washer and
  dryer)

Winter home

Your own parking
  space

Symbols and Metaphors

Chimney with
  smoke

Door

Keys

Mailbox

Skyline

Welcome mat

White picket fence

Restaurants

Synonyms

Diners

Dining

Eateries

Related Words, Phrases, and Expressions

A night on the town
A place to celebrate
Adventurous
Al fresco
Ambience
Atmosphere
Attentive **service**
Booster seats **available**
Breakfast
Bring to the table
Brunch
Buffet available
Cafeteria-style
Catering available
Chef
Child-friendly
Cozy
Cuisine
Dine by candlelight
Dinner
Dinner and a movie
Dinner date
Doggie bag
Don't cook tonight
Eat out
Elegant
Exotic

Experience
Exquisite
Extensive menu
Extensive wine list
Family restaurant
Family-style
Fast service
Feast
Fine dining
Fireside dining
Fully stocked bar
Gourmet
Halal
Highchairs available
Homemade desserts
Kids welcome
Kids' menu available
Kosher
Late-night dining
Live music
Lovingly prepared
Low-carb menu available
Low-fat menu available
Lunch
Macrobiotic
No reservations required
Presentation

Private booths available
Private room available
Quiet
Reservations required
Romantic
Salad bar
Senior discount available
Service
Service with a smile
Smoking section available
Sophisticated
Soup du jour
Special
Table for two
Take your time
Takeout available
Treat yourself
Try the _____
Unobtrusive service
Vegan
Vegetarian selections
View
Waited on hand and foot
We **deliver**
We use organic ingredients

Symbols and Metaphors

Checkered tablecloth
Maître d'

Menu
Place setting

Reserved sign on table
Waiter/waitress

Shoes

Synonyms

Footwear

Related Words, Phrases, and Expressions

Athletic footwear
Barefoot
Best foot forward
Boogie shoes*
Boots
Cold feet
Comfortable
Cushioned
Deck shoes
Fancy footwork
Feet first
Fit
Flat
Follow in your footsteps
Foot in the door
Foot patrol
Foot the bill
Get your feet wet
Head over heels
High heels
High-performance
Hotfoot
I could have danced all night*

Jump
Keep your feet on the ground
Kick up your heels
Knock them flat
Lace up
Land on your feet
Loafers
Long-running
No shirt, no shoes, no service
On your own two feet
One small step for man, one giant leap for mankind
Open toe
Orthopedic
Penny loafers
Pump
Put on your dancing shoes
Put one foot in front of the other
Put your feet up
Put your foot down

Put yourself in our shoes
Run
Run the show
Run wild
Saddle shoes
Sensible shoes
Shoe fetish
Shoe polish
Shoe tree
Shoehorn
Shoeshine
Skid-proof
Skip
Stay on your toes
Steel toe
Step by step
Step lively
Step off
Step on it
Step right up
Step to it
Stepping out
Strappy

Support
Take a walk
Take a walk on the wild side*
Talk the talk and walk the walk
Tennis shoes
These boots were made for walking*
Think on your feet
Toe the line
Toe-tapping
Twelve steps
Walk down the aisle
Walking on air
Walking wounded
Waterproof
Well-heeled
Wide sizes **available**
Winning pair
You can't judge someone until you've walked a mile in his shoes

Symbols and Metaphors

Bronzed baby shoes

Cinderella

Imelda Marcos*

Ruby slippers*

Skin Care

Synonyms

Body care   Complexion care

Related Words, Phrases, and Expressions

Acne treatment
Anti-aging
Astringent
Baby-**soft**
Bath/bathe
Beautiful
Beauty is skin deep
Bright
Brilliant
Butter-soft
Clarifying
Clean
Cleansing
Clear
Complexion
Cooling
Cream/creamy
Crease-proof
Deep-clean
Dermatologist
Drench
Drink
Ebony
Even
Exfoliating

Face forward
Facelift
Facial
Flawless
Formula
Fresh-faced
Gel
Gentle
Glow
Healthy
Hydrate
Hypoallergenic
I've got you under my skin
Lotion
Mask/masque
Medicating
Moisture/moisturizing
Moisturizer
Noncomedogenic
Nourishing
Oil
Oil-free
Pampered
Peaches and cream
Polished

Pore-minimizing
Quench
Relief
Scrub
Shower
Silky
Skin tone
Slough
Smooth
Soap
Soft
Soothe
Sunscreen
To the touch
Toner
Toning
Unlined
We're all alike under the skin
Wrinkle-free
You're only young once
Youth is wasted on the young
Youthful

Symbols and Metaphors

Bathtub
Loofah

Mirror
Mud mask

Spiritual/New Age

Synonyms

Alternative

Related Words, Phrases, and Expressions

Ancient	Herbal	Prayerful
Awareness	Holistic	Pure
Body and soul	Inner peace	Soothing
Body and spirit	Meditation	Soul
Communicate	Meditative	Spirit
Complementary	Mind	Timeless
Cultures	Mindful	Traditions
Discover	**Natural**	Universe
Divine	Nondenominational	Unorthodox
Eastern	Nonsectarian	Whole
Find	Open	Wisdom
Folk	Path	World
Healing	Peace	Yoga

Symbols and Metaphors

Crystals	Lotus pose
Dreamcatcher	Meditation pose

Sports Events

Synonyms

Competitions   Games

Related Words, Phrases, and Expressions

A day at the ballpark
A day at the races
Arena
Banners
Battle it out
Beer here
Behind the dugout
Bleachers
Box seats
Catch a foul ball
Championship series
Cheer
Clash of the titans
Courtside
Doubleheader
Event
Face painters
Fans

Field
Field day
Field trip
Fifty-yard line
Home and away
Home team
In town
It ain't over 'til it's over
Match up
Meet
National anthem
On the road
Opening day
Opponents
OT (overtime)
Pennant
Play ball
Playoffs

Public arena
Rematch
Ringside
Rivals/rivalry
Roar of the crowd
Root
Seventh-inning stretch
Stadium
Stands
Supporters
Tailgate
Take me out to the ball-game
Twi-night doubleheader
Visitors
Wave
Where the action is

Symbols and Metaphors

Banners
Blanket
Bleachers
Caps

Cheerleaders
Glove
Hot dogs
Mascot

Pennant
Scoreboard

Taxes

Synonyms

Tax accountant

Tax preparation

Tax **service**

Related Words, Phrases, and Expressions

1040

As **easy** as A, B, C

Avoid the red flags

Confused

CPA

Deadline pressure

Deduct our fee

Deduction

Deductive reasoning

Don't get audited

Don't give the government a penny more than you have to

Don't make a federal case out of it

Don't panic

Don't tax your brain

Don't tax your budget

Don't tax your schedule

Don't wait for the last minute

Drowning in forms

Drowning in receipts

E-file

Expenses

File for relief

File under _____

Forms

Get a bigger refund

Get a return on your investment

Get the refund you're entitled to

Get your refund faster

Itemize

Keep more **money** in your pocket

Keep more of what you earn

Legal

Many happy returns

Maximize

Minimize

Not everyone's tax return is EZ

Organized

Overtaxed

Paperwork

Professional

Refund

Save money

Save yourself a headache

Schedule an appointment

Shelter from the storm

Single file

State of anxiety

Tax cut

Tax law

Tax relief

Tax shelter

Taxation without representation

Taxing

Taxman

Taxpayer

The only sure things in life are death and taxes

Uncle Sam wants you

We find ways to save you money

We know the ins and outs

Write off

Symbols and Metaphors

Boston Tea Party

Calculator

Calendar showing April 15

Food with bite taken out

Television

Synonyms

TV   Tube   **Small** screen

Related Words, Phrases, and Expressions

Air
Airwaves
Appointment televi-
  sion
As seen on TV*
Big picture
Big screen
Boob tube
Broadcast
Cable
Cameras
Channel
Channel surf
Characters
Choice
Classic
Clear
Click
Cliffhanger
Commercials
Couch potato
Debut
Electronic baby-sitter
Emmy Award*
Episode
Event

Family hour
Film at 11
Flat screen
Freeze frame
Get the picture
Giant screen
Groove tube*
Guest appearance
Guest star
HDTV
Hiatus
Idiot box
Infomercial
Keep watch
Lineup
Live
Long-running
Made for TV
Mute
Network
On
On the air
Picture
Picture it
Picture-in-a-picture
Plasma

Premiere
Pretty as a picture
Preview
Prime time
Program
Public access
Ratings
Remote control
Remote possibilities
Rerun
Room with a view
Satellite
Schedule
Screen
Screen time
Screen your calls
Season
Season finale
Season's greetings
See for yourself
Series
Series finale
Set
Shows
Sitcom
Small screen

Soap opera
Spin-off
Station
Studio
Summer reruns
The show must
  go on
Tube top
Tune in
Tune in, turn on,
  drop out
TV dinner
TV **movie**
TV news
TV room
Vast wasteland
Video
View
Watch
Watch and wait
Watch it
Watch out
Water cooler show
We interrupt this
  broadcast
What's on

Symbols and Metaphors

Bowl of popcorn
Rabbit ears

Recliner
Remote

Roof antenna
Satellite dish

Sofa
TV dinner

Theater

Synonyms

Broadway

Community theater

Off-Broadway

Show

Related Words, Phrases, and Expressions

_____ nights only

Act

Act natural

All the world's a stage
  (William Shakespeare)

An evening at the theater

Auditions

Backstage

Balcony

Cast

Casting call

Comedy

Costumes

Culture/cultural

Curtain call

Curtains

Dinner theater

Directed

Drama

Electric

Ensemble

Exit stage left/right

Extravaganza

Front and center

Front row seats

Funny

Greasepaint

It's just a stage

Let's put on a show

Live

Loge

Make a date

Matinee

Mezzanine

Musical

Now playing

Now showing

On stage

On the aisle

On the scene

Orchestra

Orchestra pit

Performance

Play ball

Play fair

Players

Produced

Props

Rolling in the aisles

Save the date

Scenery

Script

Showbiz

Showtime

Stage fright

Standing ovation

Standing room only

Star

Starring

Summer stock

Take a bow

The play's the thing
  (William Shakespeare)

The show must go on

There's no business like
  show business*

Tickets are going **fast**

Upstage

Your ticket to _____

Symbols and Metaphors

Comedy and drama masks

Curtain

Lighted makeup mirror

Marquee

Spotlight

Toys/Games

Synonyms

Playthings

Related Words, Phrases, and Expressions

_____ batteries required

A world of their own

Ages _____ and up

Batteries included

Board game

Budding artist

Budding artist/
    musician/scientist/etc.

Build

Building blocks

Children

Children at play

Classic

Computer game

Create

Daydream

Develop

Dream

Easy to assemble

Educational

Enjoy

Fair play

Family **fun**

Favorite

Fun

Fun and games

Get in the game

Grow

Hours of fun

Imaginative/imagination

Inspire

Involve

Kids

Let's pretend

Make believe

Master

No assembly required

No batteries required

Play along

Play house

Played out

Player

Playground

Playtime

Rainy day fun

Realistic

Safety-tested

Save it for a rainy day

Share

Skill-building

The play's the thing
    (William Shakespeare)

Toy box

Unbreakable

Word games

Symbols and Metaphors

Blocks

Dice

Teddy bear

Toy box

Transportation

Synonyms

Air travel	Buses	Transport
Airlines	Mass transit	
Boats	Railroads	

Related Words, Phrases, and Expressions

A departure from the ordinary	Flying high	Save gas
Adventure	Full speed ahead	Save time
Along the way	Getting there is half the **fun**	Scenic route
Arrival	I've been working on the railroad	Shipping
Beat the traffic	Journey	Sleep
Catch some shut-eye	Legroom	Take your time
Chauffeur	Leisurely	That ship has sailed
Choo choo	Make your connection	The **easy** way
Come along for the ride	Off the beaten path	The road less traveled
Come with us	Passenger	The road not taken
Comfortable	Point A to Point B	Tour
Departure	Railroad crossing	Travel in comfort
Destination	Read a **book**	Travel light
Don't miss the boat	Ready, set, go	Traveling companions
Don't miss the bus	Redeye	Trek
Downtown train*	**Relaxing**	Watch a **movie**
Express	Road trip	We'll take you there
Fast		Window seat
		Wings

Symbols and Metaphors

Anchor	Little red wagon	Sleeping passenger
Backpack	Luggage	Tandem bicycle
Headphones	Open road	Tickets
Horn	Porthole	Tracks
Laptop	Sky	Wheel

Travel

Synonyms

Holidays   Tours   Vacations

Related Words, Phrases, and Expressions

A different world

A world apart

Abroad

Across the pond

Adventure

All over the map

Around the world
  in 80 days

Arrival

Bask

Beach bum

Beach bunny

Bed and breakfast

Bicycle tour

Blissful

Book

Border crossing

Borders

Break

Challenge

Change of scenery

Check out

Cities

Citizen of the world

Climate

Climb

Coast to coast

Conquer

Continents

Countries

Cruise

Cuisine

Culture

Culture shock

Day trip

Decompress

Departure

Destination

De-stress

Disappear

Discover

Drop anchor

Escape

Escape the
  everyday

Escape the routine

ETA

Exotic

Experience

Explore

Extended tour

Far-flung

Fellow travelers

Flight

Fly south for the
  winter

Foreign

Four corners of the
  earth

Gate

Get outta Dodge

Getaway

Globetrotter

Go

Gone fishing

Goof off

Guesthouse

Hang out

Having a wonder-
  ful time, wish you
  were here

Here, there, and
  everywhere

Hideaway

History

Home away from
  home

Hospitality

Hotel

I have a feeling
  we're not in
  Kansas anymore*

Indulge

Inn

International

International date
  line

Investigate

Itinerary

Jaunt

Journey

Landmark

Lazy days of
  summer

Leave it all behind

Local

Local color

Local customs

Memorable

Miles

Motel

Nap

Nations

Native

Near and far

Nestled

No plans

No schedules

Off

Off the beaten path

Off the map

On the road

On tour

Open road

Out-of-office reply

Out of this world

continues

Travel (continued)

Related Words, Phrases, and Expressions

Overseas
Pack
Pack animal
Pack your bags
Peace and quiet
Play
Poolside
Port of call
Postcard
Quest
Recover
Recuperate
Regions
Relax
Reservation
Resort

Retreat
Road less traveled
Road not taken
Road to nowhere
Roadside attraction
Run away
Sabbatical
Sandy
See
See the world
Setting
Seven wonders of
   the world
Shop
Ski bum
Souvenir

Split
Spur of the
   moment
Stay
Sunbathe
Take in the sights
Take off
Territory
The good life
The last resort
Time off
Tour guide
Tourist attraction
Tourist trap
Transportation
Travel is broadening

Trek
Tucked away
View
Visit
Walking tour
Wander
Weekend
Welcome
Well-traveled
What I did on my
   summer vacation
Where in the
   world
Where the action is
Where the wind
   takes you
World tour

Symbols and Metaphors

Backpack
Beach bag
Beach chair
Camera

Lift ticket
Loaded-up **car**
Luggage
Map

Pail and shovel
Postcard
Slides
Snapshots

Sunglasses
Tent
Tropical drink

Utilities

Synonyms

Electricity   Heat   Power

Related Words, Phrases, and Expressions

Advanced
Appliances
Bright idea
Burn the candle at both
  ends
Charge
Clean
Conservation
Cool
Dependable
Efficient
Fixture
Fuel

Full power
In **hot** water
Juice
Let there be light
Night light
Payment plan
Plug in
Power to the people
Power up
Reliable
Running hot and **cold**
Running smoothly

Safer
See the light
Service
Smarter
Solar power
The power of _____
Thermostat
Warm welcome
Warming up
Wind power
You have the power
You light up my life*

Symbols and Metaphors

Faucet
Light bulb

Plug
Sun

Vision Care

Synonyms

Eye care

Related Words, Phrases, and Expressions

20/20

A sight to behold

A vision of _____

Adjustable

Astigmatism

Black eye

Blurry

Brown-eyed girl*

Clear

Clear advantage

Clear difference

Contact high

Contact lens

Correction

Distance

Enjoy the view

Envision

Eye drops

Eyes on the prize

Farsighted

Focus

For your eyes only

Framed

Frames

I can see clearly now*

I see what you mean

Lens

Look

Look again

Look at the bright side

Look at things in a whole **new** way

Look for a solution

Look sharp

Looking for love

Looks

Make contact

Men don't make passes at girls who wear glasses

Must-see

Nearsighted/ myopic

Not a pretty sight

Opera glasses

Ophthalmologist

Optical

Optical illusion

Optician

Optometrist

Pink eye

Point of view/ viewpoint

Preview

Private eye

Read the chart

Reading glasses

Red eye

Restore

Review

Revision

Room with a view

Second sight

See for yourself

See the difference

See the light

See the world

See-saw

Sharp

Sight for sore eyes

Sightseeing

Smart

Sturdy

Stylish

Suitable for framing

Sunglasses

Take another look

Tinted

View

Visionary

Visualize

Visualize world peace

We've got our eyes on you

Symbols and Metaphors

Binoculars

Clark Kent*

Eye chart

Glasses on neck chain

Monocle

Mr. Magoo*

Weddings

Synonyms

Ceremony

Civil union

Commitment

Marriage

Matrimony

Union

Related Words, Phrases, and Expressions

All the days of your
life

Anniversary

Bachelor party

Bands/disc jockeys

Best man

Best wishes

Betrothal

Big day

Blushing bride

Breaking the glass

Bridal shower

Bride and groom

Bridesmaids

Caterers/**catering**

Catering halls

Chuppa/canopy

Cold feet

Congratulations

Dearly beloved, we
are gathered here
today

Engagement

Favors

First dance

First kiss

Flower girl

For better or for
worse

For richer or for
poorer

From this day for-
ward

Get me to the
church on time*

Going to the chapel*

Happiest day of your
life

Happy couple

Holy matrimony

Honeymoon

Hope chest

I now pronounce
you husband and
wife

I thee wed

I'm getting married
in the morning*

In sickness and in
health

Invitations/stationery

Joined in holy matri-
mony

Jumping the broom

Maid/matron of
honor

Mazel tov

Mr. and Mrs.

Music

Our song

Photographers/
videographers

Reception

Ring bearer

Sacrament

Something old,
something new,
something bor-
rowed, something
blue

Special day

The honeymoon is
over

Throwing rice

'Til death do us part

To love, honor, and
cherish

Trousseau

Unity candle

Ushers/groomsmen

Veil

Vows

Wedding attire

Wedding bells

Wedding **gift**

Wedding march

Wedding party

Wedding rings

Wedding song

Wedding toast

What God has
joined together, let
no one put asunder

White wedding

With this ring

You may now kiss
the bride

Symbols and Metaphors

Car with Just
Married sign

Engraved invitation

Orange blossoms

Rice

Rings

Two candle flames
joining to light a
third

Wedding cake/bride
and groom fig-
urines

White dress

Promotional Power

Act Now	Established	Open 24 Hours
Announcing	Exclusive	Recommended
Attention	Fall	Refund
Available	Father's Day	Reminder
Best	For More Information	Sale
Better	Fourth of July	Sample
Bonus	Free	Selection
Change	Gift	Service
Child-Friendly	Going Out of Business	Spring
Christmas	Grand Opening	Summer
Color	Halloween	Tell Your Friends
Compare	Improved	Thank You
Contest	Limited Offer	Thanksgiving
Convenient Location	Makes a Great Gift	Try
Coupon	Months	Value
Credit	Mother's Day	Winter
Deal	New	
Delivery	New Year's	
Enjoy	Numbers	

Act Now

Synonyms

Call today

Don't miss this opportunity

Don't wait

Related Words, Phrases, and Expressions

A journey of a thousand miles begins with one step

A stitch in time saves nine

Don't miss the boat

Don't put off until tomorrow what you can do today

Don't wait another day

Get started

Grab the brass ring

Here today, gone tomorrow

If not now, when?

Make it a priority

Make your move

No better time than the present

Opportunity knocks

Ready, set, go

Start now

Start today

Stop procrastinating

Strike while the iron is hot

Take the first step

The clock is ticking

The time is now

What are you waiting for?

While you still can

Why wait?

Symbols and Metaphors

Calendar

Checked-off item on list

Clock

Green light

String tied on finger

Announcing

Synonyms

Introducing   Presenting

Related Words, Phrases, and Expressions

Alert the media

Allow us to introduce ourselves

Announce your intentions

Announcement

Announcing the arrival of

Attention

Debut

Discovery

Drop date

Extra, extra, read all about it

For immediate release

For the first time

Guess what?

Hear ye, hear ye

In stores now

May we have your atten-
tion, please

Never before available

New

New arrival

Now

Now available

Now it can be told

Official announcement

Opening

Our newest

Premiering

Stop the presses

Street date

Unveiling

Visitors must be announced

We are pleased to
announce

We are pleased to present

We have an announcement
to make

We interrupt this broadcast

We want you to know

We'd like to share

We're shouting it from the
mountaintops

We're shouting it from the
rooftops

Symbols and Metaphors

Birth announcement

Bullhorn

Microphone

News anchor

Newspaper headline

News ticker

Stock ticker

Wedding announcement

Attention

Synonyms

Alert	Listen up	Notice
Check it out	Look	Yo
Hey		

Related Words, Phrases, and Expressions

Attention span	Here it is	Pay attention
Attention-getter	May we have your attention, please	We interrupt this broadcast
Center of attention		

Symbols and Metaphors

Alarm	Highway sign	Spotlight
Arrow	Podium	Traffic cone
Flare	Red flag	

Available

Synonyms

Accessible

For **sale**

In stock

In stores

Obtainable

On the market

Plentiful

Related Words, Phrases, and Expressions

Available around the clock

Available for immediate
  delivery

Available for purchase

Easy to find

Find it at _____

In stores everywhere

Instant

No waiting

On demand

On premises

On sale now

On the shelves

Readily available

Ready and waiting

Ready to move

Ready to ship

Supply

Take it home today

There for you

Waiting for you

Yours for the asking

Symbols and Metaphors

Delivery truck

Key

OPEN sign

Shopping bag

Shopping cart

Stockroom

Store display

Antonyms

Back-ordered

Discontinued

Hard-to-find

In short supply

Out of stock

Sold out

Unavailable

Best

Synonyms

#1	Peerless	Unmatched
First	Preeminent	Unparalleled
Finest	Ranking	Unsurpassed
Foremost	Top-ranked	
Leading	Ultimate	

Related Words, Phrases, and Expressions

Accept no imitations	In the lead	The best things in life are **free**
Best friend	King of the hill	The first name in _____
Best man	Leader of the pack	Top notch
Best option	Leading edge	Top of the heap
Best practices	Most	Top of the line
Best seats in the house	No competition	Top quality
Champion	No one can compete	Top shelf
Don't settle for cheap imitations	Nobody does it better	Tops
Don't settle for second best	None better	Triumph
First choice	Nothing but the best	Ultimate
First class	Only the best	Valedictorian
First place	Preferred	Victory
First prize	Setting the standard	We are the champions*
Head and shoulders above the rest	Superior	You've tried the rest, now try the best
	Take the lead	

Symbols and Metaphors

Blue ribbon	Trophy
Gold medal	

Antonyms

Also-ran	Inferior	Second-string
B-team	Second-best	
Imitation	Second-rate	

Better

Synonyms

Improved	Preferable	Superior

Related Words, Phrases, and Expressions

A better place	It gets better	Outclasses
A better tomorrow	It's getting better all the time*	Outdoes
Better deal		Outperforms
Better half	Leaves the competition behind	Outranks
Better than ever	Leaves the competition in the dust	Outshines
Better than nothing		Refined
Better your lot	May the better man win	There's got to be a better way
Better yourself	Nobody does it better	
Improves with age		You can do better

Symbols and Metaphors

+

Antonyms

Inferior	Lesser	Worse

Bonus

Synonyms

Extra	Gift	Plus
Fringe benefit	Perk	Premium

Related Words, Phrases, and Expressions

Added benefit	Extra feature	The icing on the cake
Additional	**Free** inside	With a cherry on top
Add-on	Free with purchase	You also get
Extra	More	

Symbols and Metaphors

+

Change

Synonyms

Alter	**Improve**	Transform
Convert	Redo	
Evolve	Remodel	

Related Words, Phrases, and Expressions

180	Change your mind	Switch-hitter
A change in the weather	Change-up	The more things change, the more they stay the same
About-face	Costume change	
Change clothes	Exchange	The only constant is change
Change gears	Make a change	The times, they are a-changin'*
Change lanes	Make change	
Change planes	Makeover	Times change
Change purse	Metamorphosis	Trade in
Change sides	Presto chango	Trade up
Change teams	Quick change	Turnaround
Change the system	Shift	
Change trains	Small change	

Symbols and Metaphors

Before and after pictures	**Hair** dye
Falling leaves	

Child-Friendly

Synonyms

After-school	Family-style	Kid-friendly
All-ages	G-rated	Wholesome

Related Words, Phrases, and Expressions

Bring the kids	Fun for the whole family	No baby-sitter needed
Children's menu available	Highchairs available	**Safe** environment
For all ages	Kids welcome	The kids will love it

Symbols and Metaphors

Balloons	Changing station	Playground
Car seat	Children at Play sign	Stroller

Antonyms

Adults-only	Quiet	Stuffy
After-bedtime	R-rated	
Elegant	Sophisticated	

Christmas

Synonyms

December 25

Holiday

Jesus' birthday

Noel

Season

Related Words, Phrases, and Expressions

Advent

Bearing gifts

Birth

Carol

Christmas card

Christmas comes but once a year

Christmas Eve

Feliz Navidad

Ghost of Christmas past

Gift

Gold, frankincense, and myrrh

Hark the herald angels sing

It came upon a midnight clear

Joyous

Lights

Manger

Mary and Joseph

Merry

Midnight Mass

Nativity

No room at the inn

Ornaments

Peace on Earth, goodwill toward men

Silent night

Star of Bethlehem

Stringing cranberries

Stringing popcorn

Three wise men

Tinsel

Tiny Tim

Tree

'Twas the night before Christmas and all through the house, not a creature was stirring, not even a mouse

Twelve days of Christmas

White Christmas

Winter

Symbols and Metaphors

Bells

Candy cane

Elves

Manger

Mistletoe

Poinsettia

Red and **green**

Reindeer

Santa

Sleigh

Star

Stocking

Tree

Wreath

Color

Synonyms

Hue   Tint
Shade   Tone

Related Words, Phrases, and Expressions

Assorted colors   Every color of the rainbow   Palette
Color scheme   Favorite color   Rainbow
Color-coded   In full color   Spectrum
Color-coordinated   Local color   True colors
Coloring book   One in every color

Symbols and Metaphors

Artist's palette   Crayons
Autumn leaves   Rainbow

Compare

Synonyms

Contrast   Shop around

Related Words, Phrases, and Expressions

Before and after   Comparison shop   Preference
Can't hold a candle to   Consider your options   See for yourself
Compare and contrast   Examine your options   See the difference
Compare for yourself   Experiment   Side-by-side
Compare to the higher-   Head-to-head   Test
  priced brand   No comparison   **Try**
Comparison chart   Nothing else compares   Weigh your options

Symbols and Metaphors

Old-fashioned scale

Contest

Synonyms

Battle
Challenge
Competition
Drawing

Game
Lottery
Playoff
Race

Raffle
Showdown
Sweepstakes

Related Words, Phrases, and Expressions

And the winner is
Around and around it goes, where it stops nobody knows
Baby needs a new pair of shoes
Battle it out
Chance
Contestant
Entry
Everyone wins
First prize
Gamble
Game show
Games of chance

Get in the game
Grand prize
It ain't over 'til it's over
Jackpot
Lucky
Lucky number
May the best man win
No contest
Odds
Payoff
Prize
Take your chances
Throwing down the gauntlet
Ticket

To the victor go the spoils
Triumph
Try your luck
Victor
Victory
Win, place, and show
Win big
Winner
Winner-take-all
Winning hand
Win-win situation
You bet
You win some; you lose some

Symbols and Metaphors

Boxing ring
Carnival midway

Dice
Poker chips

Roulette wheel

Convenient Location

Synonyms

A location near you   In the neighborhood   Nearby location
A short drive away   **Local**

Related Words, Phrases, and Expressions

Around the way   Just around the corner   Stop in
Close by   Just down the road a piece Within driving distance
Don't fight the traffic   Near public transportation Within walking distance
Don't go out of your way   On your way home
Drop by   Right off the highway

Symbols and Metaphors

Map   You Are Here sign

Antonyms

A long trek   Far away   Not worth the trip
An all-day affair   Long distance   Out of the way

Coupon

Synonyms

Cents-off coupon   Discount coupon

Related Words, Phrases, and Expressions

Buy one get one **free**
Cash in
Cents off
Clip and save
Cost-cutter
Coupon-clippers
Coupon-cutters

Cut it out
Dollars off
Double coupons
Good for _____
Handy
Paper **money**
Redeem

Save
Ticket to savings
We accept all coupons
We accept competitors' coupons
Worth

Symbols and Metaphors

$ ¢
%   Scissors

Credit

Synonyms

Installment plan   Mortgage
Loan   Payment plan

Related Words, Phrases, and Expressions

Account

Buy now, pay later

Charge

Charge account

Charge it to my room

Check your credit

Convenience

Credit card

Credit or blame

Credit or debit

Credit rating

Credit report

Credit-worthy

Down payment

Easy payments

Extend

Extra credit

Get the credit you deserve

Give credit where credit is
  due

In good standing

Installment plan

Layaway

Low monthly payments

Low-interest

No payments until _____

Open a line of credit

Open a tab

Payment method

Payment plan

Put it on my account

Put it on my card

Put it on my tab

Run a tab

Sign for it

Store credit

Taking credit

We accept _____

Zero down

Symbols and Metaphors

%   Credit card
Calendar   IOU

Deal

Synonyms

Bargain	Offer
Buy	Steal

Related Words, Phrases, and Expressions

A real find	Dealer's choice	Shop around
Agreement	Dealt a winning hand	**Special** offer
All offers considered	Haggle	Strike a deal
An offer you can't refuse	Hammer out a deal	The best deal
Best offer	Let's make a deal*	What a deal
Big deal	Name your price	Wheeling and dealing
Deal maker	Negotiate	You've got a deal
Deal me in	On good terms	
Deal of a lifetime	Opportunity of a lifetime	

Symbols and Metaphors

Flea market	Handshake	Price tag

Antonyms

Racket	Rip-off	Sucker deal

Delivery

Synonyms

Home delivery   Shipment

Related Words, Phrases, and Expressions

Arrival

At your doorstep

At your service

Avoid the crowds

Avoid the traffic

Carry

COD

Convenience

Courier

Deliver on our promises

Delivered to your door

Delivery man

Delivery room

Delivery service

Delivery truck

Driving it home

Fast

Flowers

Free delivery

I wouldn't send a dog out on a night like this

Immediate delivery

In the comfort of your own home

Long-distance

Mail-order

Operators are standing by

Order in

Overnight delivery

Phone it in

Pizza

Place your order

Quick

Save yourself a trip

Schlep

Send

Shop at home

Shop online

To your door

Unburden yourself

We deliver

We ship anywhere

We're waiting to take your order

When you can't be there in person

Symbols and Metaphors

Delivery truck

Doorbell

Doorstep

Mail carrier

Mailbox

Package

Paperboy/papergirl

Santa

Enjoy

Synonyms

Delight in	Groove on	Relish
Dig	Indulge in	Savor
Get into	Make the most of	Take pleasure in

Related Words, Phrases, and Expressions

A joyous occasion	Escape	Let yourself go
A time to rejoice	Follow your bliss	Live it up
Be in the moment	Get **happy**	Play
Enjoy life	Get your kicks	Pleasure
Enjoy the experience	Grab life by the horns	Sit back and enjoy the show
Enjoy the ride	Have a blast	Stop and smell the flowers
Enjoy the scenery	Have **fun**	Take a bite out of life
Enjoy yourself	Having a wonderful time; wish you were here	Take a break
Enjoyable		Thrill
Enjoyment	Jump in a puddle	Treat yourself

Symbols and Metaphors

Balloons	Party	Snapshot
Feet up on desk or railing	Postcard	Windsurfer
Ice-cream sundae	Smile	

Established

Synonyms

Born

Founded

Longstanding

Related Words, Phrases, and Expressions

A name you can trust

A part of history

An established authority

An established name

Anniversary

Bedrock of the community

Built on a **strong** foundation

Centennial

Firmly established

Generations

Golden anniversary

Inheritance

Our founder(s)

Part of the establishment

Respected

Serving the public for
_____ years

Silver anniversary

Since _____

Since your grandparents'
time

Still

Through the years

Tradition

Trust

We've established a
reputation

Symbols and Metaphors

Engraved cornerstone

Framed portraits

Antonyms

Fly-by-night

Johnny-come-lately

Newfangled

Trendy

Untested

Exclusive

Synonyms

Choosy	Private	Selective
Competitive	Rare	**Unique**
Elite	Restricted	VIP

Related Words, Phrases, and Expressions

Black-tie only	For select customers only	Not available anywhere else
By invitation only	High standards	Only at _____
Cream of the crop	Member of the club	Privilege
Exclusive interview	Membership requirements	Qualified applicants only
Exclusive offer	Need-to-know basis	Scoop
Exclusive opportunity	No one else has it	The exclusive story
Find it exclusively at _____	No shirt, no shoes, no service	

Symbols and Metaphors

Ivy League school	Velvet rope

Antonyms

Dime-a-dozen	Open-to-the-public

Fall

Synonyms

Autumn   Back-to-school

Related Words, Phrases, and Expressions

Autumn leaves	**Gold**	Spring forward; fall back
Autumnal equinox	November	Stock up for winter
Brown	October	The days are growing shorter
Chill in the air	**Orange**	The holidays are approaching
Cool off	**Red**	The leaves are turning colors
Fall foliage	School's open; drive carefully	
Fall wardrobe	September	
Falling leaves		

Symbols and Metaphors

Autumn leaf   School supplies   **Thanksgiving**

Father's Day

Related Words, Phrases, and Expressions

Adoptive father

Biological father

Breadwinner

Daddy long-legs

Dear old dad

Devoted father

Father figure

Father knows best

Father of the year

Father Time

Father-in-law

Godfather

Grandfather

Honor thy father and mother

Involved father

It is a wise father that knows his own child

Old man

Padre

Papa

Pop

Provider

Single father

Stay-at-home dad

Stepfather

Sugar daddy

Who's your daddy?

You've been like a father to me

Symbols and Metaphors

Driving lessons

Fishing trip

Pipe and slippers

Recliner

Remote control

Tie

Toolbox

For More Information

Synonyms

Find out more

Get the details

Learn more

Related Words, Phrases, and Expressions

Any questions?

Ask for our free brochure

Call for more **information**

Click on _____ for more
information

Discover how

Get filled in

Get the full story

Get the scoop

Get your questions
answered

Interested? Find out more
at _____

More details

Questions?

Tell me more

There's more to the story
at _____

Visit our website

Want to know more?

Symbols and Metaphors

Computer mouse

Phone

Fourth of July

Synonyms

Independence Day   July 4   The Fourth

Related Words, Phrases, and Expressions

13 colonies
50 states
1776
All-American
America
"America the **Beautiful**"
Barbecue
Baseball and apple pie
Beach party
Born on the fourth of July
Bottle rockets
Bunting

Cookout
Declaration of
  Independence
Firecrackers
Fireworks
Founding Fathers
Freedom
Happy Birthday, America
Let freedom ring
Liberty
Made in the USA
Nation
Patriot

Pledge of Allegiance
Red, white, and blue
Sparklers
Stars and Stripes
"The Star-Spangled
  Banner"
Three cheers for the red,
  white, and blue
USA
Uncle Sam wants you
We, the people
Yankee Doodle Dandy

Symbols and Metaphors

American flag   Fireworks

Free

Synonyms

At no charge

At no cost to you

Bonus

Complementary

Gift

Gratis

Related Words, Phrases, and Expressions

Absolutely free

At no additional cost

Born free

Butterflies are free

Buy one get one free

For the taking

Free and clear

Free and easy

Free as a bird

Free at last

Free for all

Free lunch

Free movement

Free of charge

Free prize inside

Free rein

Free ride

Free speech

Free spirit

Free throw

Free time

Free to go

Free will

Free your mind

Freedom of choice

Freestyle

Giveaway

Hands-free

It's a free country

It's on us

No obligation

No strings attached

On the house

Our gift to you

Pay nothing

There's no such thing as a free lunch

With our compliments

Antonyms

At an additional cost

At an extra charge

Gift

Synonyms

Bonus
Keepsake
Memento

Offering
Present
Souvenir

Token

Related Words, Phrases, and Expressions

All wrapped up
Bestow
Birthday
For you
Gag gift
Generous
Get
Gifted
Give
Good things come in **small** packages

Gracious
Gratitude
It's better to give than to receive
It's the thought that counts
Just what I wanted
Open
Registry
Remember
Ribbons and bows
Stocking stuffers

Surprise
Thank you
That's a wrap
The gift of _____
The gift that keeps on giving
Token of appreciation
Unwrap
Wish list
With a bow on top
With love
Wrap

Symbols and Metaphors

Birthday cake
Bows
Christmas list

Christmas tree
Santa Claus
Wedding bells

Wrapped package

Going Out of Business

Synonyms

Closing our doors   Final days   Liquidation

Related Words, Phrases, and Expressions

All items discounted   Everything must go   Retiring
All sales final   Everything's for **sale**   Selling out our inventory
Clearance   Final markdowns   Selling to the bare walls
Closeout   Final opportunity   Store must close
Closing this location   Last chance   Time is running out
Countdown to closing   Must sell

Symbols and Metaphors

Lock

Grand Opening

Synonyms

Debut	Opening	Unveiling

Related Words, Phrases, and Expressions

A star is born	**New**	We'd like to make your acquaintance
Be the first	New arrival	We'd like to meet you
Celebrate	New location	Welcome
First day	Now open	What you've been waiting for
Give us a try	Open for business	You have to see it to believe it
Greet	Open to the public	
Join us	Opening our doors	
Joining the community	Pay us a visit	
Meet and greet	Ready	

Symbols and Metaphors

Champagne bottle broken against ship	Open doors	Ribbon-cutting

Halloween

Synonyms

All Hallow's Eve

Related Words, Phrases, and Expressions

Black cat

Bobbing for apples

Boo!

Costume party

Doorbell

Dress up

Fright night

Ghost

Goblin

Graveyard

Halloween candy

Halloween costume

Halloween party

Mask

Masquerade

Monster

Pirate

Pranks

Pumpkin

Scary

Spooky

Trick or treat

Trick or treat, smell my feet; give me something good to eat

Vampire

Werewolf

Witch

Zombie

Symbols and Metaphors

Bag

Black cat

Ghost

Jack-o'-lantern

Witch

Improved

Synonyms

Better	Refined	Revised
Redesigned	Reformulated	Updated
Re-engineered	Remastered	

Related Words, Phrases, and Expressions

Better than ever	Makeover	Now _____ -free
Changing for the better	More **convenient**	Now with more _____
Changing with the times	Most improved	Now without _____
Develop	New and improved	Smarter
Easier	New feature	Stronger
Even better than before	New formula	Tinkered with
Evolve	New recipe	You can't improve on perfection

Symbols and Metaphors

+

Antonyms

Old	Out-dated

Limited Offer

Synonyms

Limited opportunity

Limited run

Limited supply

Restricted offer

Related Words, Phrases, and Expressions

Act now

Don't miss out

For a limited time only

Get 'em while they last

Get it while you still can

Get while the getting's good

Grab the brass ring

Limited to the first _____ to call

Offer good until _____

One night only

One to a customer

Only _____ in stock

Opportunity only knocks once

Postmarked by _____

Prices good through _____

Respond before _____

Respond by _____

Strike while the iron is hot

Time is running out

While supplies last

Symbols and Metaphors

Calendar

RSVP

Ticking clock

Makes a Great Gift

Synonyms

Ideal for **gift**-giving

Makes a great present

Makes a thoughtful gift

The **perfect** gift

Related Words, Phrases, and Expressions

A token of your love

Easy to carry

Easy to ship

Easy to wrap

For someone
  special

For the hard-to-shop-for

For the kids on your list

For the person who has
  everything

Gift cards **available**

Gift receipts available

Gift wrapping available

Give the gift of _____

Just what they wanted

Make their dreams come
  true

Make this birthday special

On everyone's wish list

Pre-wrapped for conven-
  ience

Put it under the tree

Remember that birthday

Remember them

Show them you care

Something they wouldn't
  buy for themselves

Stocking-stuffer

Stuck for a gift idea?

Surprise someone

Their eyes will light up

They'll appreciate it

They'll love it

They'll **thank you**

What they're hoping for

What they've been hinting
  for

Symbols and Metaphors

Bow

Christmas list

Months

Related Words, Phrases, and Expressions

January

Martin Luther King Jr. Day

New Year's Day

February

28 days

American Heart Month

Black History Month

Groundhog Day

Leap year

Lincoln's birthday

Presidents Day

Valentine's Day

Washington's birthday

March

Beware the ides of March

Easter/Passover (sometimes)

March comes in like a lion and goes out like a lamb

March hare

March on Washington

March to the beat of a different drum

Marching band

On the march

Purim

St. Patrick's Day

Vernal equinox

Women's History Month

April

April Fool's Day

April in Paris

April is the cruelest month

April showers bring May flowers

Easter/Passover (sometimes)

Opening Day

May

April showers bring May flowers

Cinco de Mayo

Darling buds of May

May Day

May-December romance

Memorial Day

Mother's Day

The merry month of May

Victoria Day (Canada)

June

Father's Day

Flag Day

Graduation

June is bustin' out all over*

Last day of school

O, my luve's like a red, red rose, that's newly sprung in June (Robert Burns)

Summer solstice

July

Canada Day

Fourth of July/Independence Day

August

Dog days of summer

September

Autumnal equinox

Back to school

Labor Day

Rosh Hashanah/Yom Kippur (sometimes)

September morn

October

Columbus Day

Halloween

October revolution

Thanksgiving (Canada)

World Series

November

Day of the Dead (Mexico)

Election Day

Remembrance Day (Canada)

Thanksgiving (United States)

Veteran's Day

December

Boxing Day (Canada)

Chanukah

Christmas

Kwanzaa

May-December romance

New Year's Eve

Winter solstice

Mother's Day

Related Words, Phrases, and Expressions

A face only a mother could love

A mother's love

Adoptive mother

Biological mother

Den mother

Full-time mom

Godmother

Grandmother

Honor thy father and mother

Mama

Mom

Mom's apple pie

Mommy

Mother Earth

Mother hen

Mother knows **best**

Mother of pearl

Mother of the year

Mother-in-law

Nurturing

Single mom

Soccer mom

Stay-at-home mom

Stepmother

Supermom

Working mom

You've been like a mother to me

Symbols and Metaphors

Breakfast in bed

Candy

Chicken soup

Flowers

Jewelry

New

Synonyms

All-new	Latest	Updated
Avant-garde	Mint	**Up-to-date**
Brand-new	Never-before-**available**	Up-to-the-minute
Cutting-edge	Next-generation	
Fresh	Unprecedented	

Related Words, Phrases, and Expressions

Ahead of the curve	New Age	The latest in _____
Factory-fresh	New and **improved**	The new trend
Farm-fresh	New angle	There's a new sheriff in town
Fresh take	New era	
Fresh twist	New kid in town	There's nothing new under the sun
Hitting the shelves	New wave	
Hot off the presses	News	Today
Latest and greatest	Now available	Tomorrow
Latest craze	Now on the market	Unheard-of
Leave the past behind	On top of the trends	What's new?
Makes everything else obsolete	The future has arrived	What's new, pussycat?*
	The future of _____	What's next?

Symbols and Metaphors

Newborn chick emerging from egg	Shrink-wrap	Small tree roped off for protection

Antonyms

Last year's model	Outdated	Out-of-favor
Obsolete	Out-of-date	Stale
Old-fashioned	Out-of-fashion	Tired

New Year's

Synonyms

January 1

Related Words, Phrases, and Expressions

"Auld Lang Syne"	Lose weight	Start fresh
Celebration	Midnight	Start over
Champagne	New Year's Day	Stay up late
Countdown	New Year's Eve	Stop smoking
Dick Clark*	Party	Stroke of midnight
Guy Lombardo*	Resolutions	Time zones
Kiss at midnight	Resolve	Times Square

Symbols and Metaphors

Baby New Year	Clock at midnight	Noisemaker
Champagne glass	Confetti	Times Square

Numbers

Related Words, Phrases, and Expressions

One

All for one and one for all

Once

Once in a lifetime

One and only

One for the money

One in a million

One is the loneli- est number

One night only

One shot

One true love

One way

One-off

Only

Single

Singular

Sole

Solo

Two heads are bet- ter than one

Two hearts beat as one

Unicycle

Unique

Uno

We're number one

You're the one

Two

Bicycle built for two

Couple

Double

Duet

Duo

Eating for two

It takes two to tango

Pair

Second chance

Table for two

Take two, they're small

Tea for two

There are two sides to every story

Two for the show

Two heads are bet- ter than one

Two hearts beat as one

Two of a kind

Two-way street

Two's company; three's a crowd

Two-by-four

Two-minute warning

Two-timer

Two-tone

Three

3-D

As easy as 1-2-3

Hat trick

Ménage à trois

Once, twice, three times a lady*

Power trio

There are three sides to every story: yours, mine, and the truth

Third time lucky

Third wheel

Three meals a day

Three of a kind

Three on a match

Three Stooges*

Three strikes

Three Tenors*

Three to get ready

Three-day week- end

Three-legged race

Three-part har- mony

Three-piece suit

Three-star restau- rant

Three-toed sloth

Triangle

Trifecta

Trio

Triple

Triple threat

Two's company; three's a crowd

You and me and baby makes three

Four

10-4

And a one, and a two, and a three, and a four

Barbershop quartet

Fab Four*

Four bases

Four corners of the earth

Four of a kind

Four on the floor

Four score and seven years ago

Four seasons

Four to go

Four Tops*

Four-wheel drive

Four-in-hand

Four-star movie

Fourth of July

Four-way stop

Four-year term

Four-year univer- sity

Quad

Quadruple

Quartet

Two-by-four

continues

Numbers *(continued)*

Related Words, Phrases, and Expressions

Five

Beethoven's "Fifth"

Cinco de Mayo

Fifth Avenue

Fifth of scotch

Five Easy Pieces*

Five-card draw

Five-dollar bill

Five-star **hotel**

Nine-to-five

Quintet

Quintuple

Take five

Six

Half dozen

Six continents

Six feet under

Six of one, half a dozen of the other

Seven

Lucky seven

Seven Brides for Seven Brothers

Seven seas

Seven-course meal

Seventh heaven*

Eight

Eight ball

Eight days a week*

Pieces of eight

Nine

A stitch in time saves nine

Baseball team

Dressed to the nines

Ninepins

Nine-to-five

On cloud nine

Possession is nine-tenths of the law

The whole nine yards

Ten

Count to ten

Perfect ten

Ten command-ments

Ten fingers

Ten toes

Ten-dollar bill

Tenpins

Top Ten

Eleven

Eleventh hour

This one goes to eleven*

Twelve

Dozen

Dozen donuts

Dozen eggs

Midnight

Noon

Twelve Angry Men*

Twelve astrological signs

Twelve months

Twelve-step program

Open 24 Hours

Synonyms

Around-the-clock **service**   We never close   24/7

Related Words, Phrases, and Expressions

All night long

All through the night

Always **available**

Always open

Any time of day or night

Call anytime

Convenience

In the middle of the night

Late-night emergencies

No matter what your
  schedule

Oasis

We'll be there

When the time comes

Symbols and Metaphors

Beacon   Clock

Recommended

Synonyms

Acclaimed	Endorsed	Prescribed
Approved	Praised	

Related Words, Phrases, and Expressions

Enthusiastically recommended	Recommended course of action	The experts agree
Fully approved	Recommended daily allowance	The verdict is in
Heartily endorsed		We come recommended
Highly recommended	Recommended dosage	What they're saying about us
Letter of recommendation	Satisfied customers	Word-of-mouth
Putting in a good word	Seal of approval	
Recommended by the experts	Singing our praises	
	The critics are raving	

Symbols and Metaphors

Stars	Thumbs-up

Refund

Synonyms

Credit   **Money** back   Reimbursement

Related Words, Phrases, and Expressions

Backed by our 100 percent
  guarantee

Bring it back, and we'll pay
  you back

Buy it and try it

Fully refundable

If you're not fully satisfied

If you're not **happy**

Money-back guarantee

No questions asked

No risk

No worries

Nothing to lose

Refund policy

Return for cash

Return for full credit

Return for store credit

Return it if you're not satisfied

Returnable at any of our
  locations

Risk-free

Satisfaction guaranteed or
  your money back

Save your receipt

Test run

Trial basis

Try it for _____ days

We put our money where
  our mouth is

We stand behind our
  products/service

We will credit your
  account

Reminder

Synonyms

Don't forget   Remember

Related Words, Phrases, and Expressions

A friendly reminder   It's that time again   Save the date
A **gentle** reminder   Just a reminder   Second notice
Bear it in mind   Keep it in mind   To refresh your memory
Forget-me-not   Make a note   We're waiting to
In case it's slipped your   Mark it on your calendar   hear from you
  mind

Symbols and Metaphors

Appointment book   Circled date on calendar   String tied around finger
Bell   Note on fridge
Checklist   PDA

Sale

Synonyms

Blowout

Clearance

Closeout

Event

Related Words, Phrases, and Expressions

% off

Anniversary sale

Bake sale

Bargains

Clearing out our inventory

Customer appreciation sale

Deductions

Deep discounts

Discount

Everything must go

For sale

Garage sale

Get it cheaper

Get it for less

Going-out-of-business sale

Grand opening sale

Half-price

Holiday sale

Huge savings

Hurry before it's over

Incentive

Liquidation sale

Look for our **special** tags

Love for sale

Low price

Make the sale

Markdowns

More **affordable** than ever

More for your **money**

On sale now

One-day sale

Pay less; get more

Pre-inventory sale

Price-cutting

Priced to move

Priced to sell

Reduced

Reductions

Sale rack

Sample sale

Save **big**

Save money

Seasonal sale

Selling out

Sidewalk sale

Special buy

Special event

Special offer

Special opportunity

Special purchase

Special sale

Stock up and save

Stock up during our sale

Storewide sale

Tag sale

This week only

This weekend only

Was $_____, now $_____

We're slashing prices

Yard sale

Symbols and Metaphors

Balloons and streamers

Price with X or slash mark

Sample

Synonyms

Example	Preview
Excerpt	Taste

Related Words, Phrases, and Expressions

A little taste of _____	Sample our wares	**Try**
Audition	Sample size	Try before you buy
Bite-size	Some of what you'll find in	Try something **new**
Free sample	_____	Tryout
Give it a try	Take a bite	
Have a taste	Trial size	

Symbols and Metaphors

Listening station	Test drive	Tray of hors d'oeuvres

Selection

Synonyms

Assortment	List	Range
Catalog	Medley	Smorgasbord
Choice	Mélange	Stock
Collection	Menu	Stuff
Fare	Merchandise	Variety
Goods	Mixed bag	Wares
Inventory	Potpourri	
Items	Quantity	

Related Words, Phrases, and Expressions

A to Z	It takes all kinds	Thousands of
Alternatives	Miles of	Variety is the spice of life
Browse	Options	We've got it
Choose wisely	Quantity and quality	What you want
Diverse	Rainbow of **colors**	What you're looking for
Dozens of	Sizes from ____ to ____	Wide range of
Everything but the kitchen sink	So much to choose from	Your choice
Hundreds of	Something for everyone	Your search ends here
	Take your pick	

Symbols and Metaphors

Buffet	Menu
Library	Warehouse

Service

Synonyms

Assistance   Help

Related Words, Phrases, and Expressions

Around-the-clock service
At your service
Car service
Church service
Customer service
Customer support
Delegate
Dinner is served
Don't do it yourself
Door-to-door service
Expert staff
Fast service
Friendly service
Full-service
Goods and services
Guest service
Happy to serve you
Helping hand
Here to help

Here to serve you
Hired help
How may I help you?
Knowledgeable staff
Leave the work to us
Lend a hand
Let us do it for you
Let us take care of it
May I be of service?
May I help you?
Military service
Now serving
On premises
On staff
On-site
Personal assistant
Professional services
Put the job in our hands
Self-service

Servant
Serve your country
Service charge
Service for 12
Service provider
Service station
Service with a smile
Serving a purpose
Serving the community
Serving your needs
Table service
The server is down
They also serve who only
   stand and wait
Unobtrusive service
You can't get good help
   these days
You've been served
Your serve

Symbols and Metaphors

Bell
Butler

Concierge
Waiter/waitress

Spring

Synonyms

Springtime

Related Words, Phrases, and Expressions

April

Bedsprings

Blossoming

Cinco de Mayo

Easter

Flowers are blooming

I love Paris in the spring-time*

If winter comes, can spring be far behind?

In bloom

In spring a young man's fancy lightly turns to thoughts of love (Alfred, Lord Tennyson)

Lent

March

May

Passover

Prom

Put a spring in your step

Spring forward; fall back

Spring has sprung

Spring into action

Spring training

Spring wardrobe

Spring water

Thaw

The merry month of May

Vernal equinox

Warm up

Symbols and Metaphors

Budding tree

Bumblebee

Crocus

Daffodil

Easter lily

Groundhog

Melting snow

Tulip

Summer

Synonyms

Summertime

Related Words, Phrases, and Expressions

Ain't no cure for the summertime blues*

Air conditioning

August

Barbecue

Baseball

Beach

Dog days of summer

Family vacation

Fourth of July

Fun in the sun

Graduation day

In the good ol' summer-
  time

July

June

June is bustin' out all over*

Long, hot summer

Memorial Day to Labor
  Day

No more pencils, no more
  books, no more teachers'
  dirty looks

School's out for summer

Shall I compare thee to a
  summer's day? (William
  Shakespeare)

Summer breeze

Summer fling

Summer hours

Summer house

Summer nights

Summer of '42*

Summer of '69*

Summer of love

Summer romance

Summer school

Summer solstice

Summer vacation

Summer wardrobe

Summertime and the livin'
  is **easy***

Summertime blues*

Sun

Surfers

The boys of summer

The last rose of summer

Where do you summer?

Symbols and Metaphors

Backyard barbecue

Beach umbrella

Beach ball

Fan

Flip-flops

Lemonade stand

Open window

Sandcastle

Sunglasses

Swimming pool

Tell Your Friends

Synonyms

Pass it on

Spread it around

Spread the news

Spread the word

Related Words, Phrases, and Expressions

Do you know someone who might benefit from _____?

Do you know someone who might like _____?

If you're unsatisfied, please tell us ... if you're satisfied, tell someone else

If you've enjoyed _____, please recommend us to a friend

No need to thank us—just tell a friend

Please take an extra menu/brochure/catalog for a friend

Put in a word for us

We rely on our satisfied customers

Word of mouth

You're the best advertisement we could have

Symbols and Metaphors

Megaphone

Telephone

Thank You

Synonyms

Gracias

Merci beaucoup

Much obliged

Thanks

We appreciate your business

Related Words, Phrases, and Expressions

Customer appreciation

Giving thanks

Gratitude

I have so many people to thank

I owe you one

I'd like to thank the Academy

Indebted

Our sincere thanks

Thank heavens

Thank you, come again

Thank you for a lovely evening

Thank you for not smoking

Thank you **gift**

Thank you note

Thank your lucky stars

Thankful

Thanks a lot

Thanks a million

Thanks for coming

Thanks for everything

Thanks for nothing

Thanks for the memories*

Thanksgiving

We couldn't do it without you

We're counting our blessings

You're welcome

Symbols and Metaphors

Acceptance speech

Thank you note

Thanksgiving

Synonyms

Turkey Day

Related Words, Phrases, and Expressions

A lot to be thankful for

All the trimmings

Appreciate

Count your blessings

Cranberry sauce

Drumstick

Feast

Football

For these **gifts** we are
  about to receive

Gathering

Gobble

Grateful

Gratitude

Home for the holidays

Leftovers

Native Americans

Pilgrims

Pumpkin pie

Say grace

Sharing

Stuffing

Thankful

Thanksgiving dinner

Thanksgiving table

Tofu turkey

Turkey

What are you thankful for?

Wishbone

Symbols and Metaphors

Cornucopia

Crowded airport

Football game

Pilgrim hat

Table laden with food

Turkey

Wishbone

Try

Synonyms

Check out	Experiment	Test
Evaluate	**Sample**	

Related Words, Phrases, and Expressions

A good try	Keep trying	Try it on for size
Audition	Run it up the flagpole, and see who salutes	Try something different
Challenge yourself		Try something new
Give it a chance	Take a chance	Try your best
Give it a go	Take it for a spin	Try your luck
Give it a try	Take it for a test drive	Tryouts
If at first you don't succeed, try, try again	Try again	You never know until you try
	Try another tack	

Value

Synonyms

Esteem   Price   Worth

Related Words, Phrases, and Expressions

A better value for your
   money
Appraised value
Assessed value
Bargain
Best value
Estimated value
Family values

Great value
High value, low price
Market value
More for your money
Retail value
Valuable
Value pack

Value size
Valued
Valued customer
We value your business
Worth every penny
Worth the investment
Worthwhile

Symbols and Metaphors

Price tag   Safe

Winter

Synonyms

Wintertime

Related Words, Phrases, and Expressions

A long winter's night

Baby, it's **cold** outside*

Blizzard

Bundle up

California dreamin' on a
  winter day*

Chanukah

Chilled to the bone

Christmas

December

Dress in layers

February

Frozen

Hibernation

Ice

Insulate

Jack Frost

January

Keep the cold at bay

Keep **warm**

Martin Luther King Jr.
  Day

New Year's

Old Man Winter

President's Day

Shovel

Snow

Temperatures are plunging

Valentine's Day

Winter solstice

Winter storm warning

Winter wardrobe

Winter **white**

Winter winds

Winter wonderland

Symbols and Metaphors

Boots

Fireplace

Hot cocoa

Icicle

Mittens

Scarf

Skier

Sled

Snowflake

Snowman

Quilt

Part 2

A Quick Course in Copywriting

Unless you have a marketing degree, copywriting is something you're most likely to learn through on-the-job experience or by looking at ads and catalogs to try to pick up the gist. Part 2 is a brief but thorough introduction to the art and craft of copywriting and will help ground you in the basics and get you ahead of the game. Included here are guiding principles, tricks, and shortcuts professional copywriters use all the time to get fast, effective results. I also give you illustrative examples, skill-developing exercises, interesting facts about consumer behavior, and tips for those pursuing copywriting as a career.

Chapter 4

Seven Qualities That Make a Great Copywriter

In This Chapter

- ◆ Ways to master the language—and your ego
- ◆ The importance of speedy turnaround
- ◆ Reasons for learning more about people and the world
- ◆ The need for imagination and integrity

I work in publishing, and I've had many chances to observe a surprising phenomenon: being brilliant at writing mysteries or self-help books or lyrical literary novels doesn't automatically mean being brilliant at copywriting. (And vice versa.)

What makes somebody a great copywriter—as opposed to a great writer? Of course, anything that makes an individual a great writer helps when it comes to writing copy. (And again, vice versa.) But some qualities are particularly important in the world of professional marketing writing.

Some of these qualities might not have an obvious connection to copywriting at first glance, but they are the traits shared by the majority of excellent copywriters I know. Having the right combination of these qualities is the key to succeeding in this field. Fortunately, these strengths aren't just inborn—they all can be developed. In this chapter, I present each of these skills to you and offer several simple ways for you to develop them.

Mastery of Language

Words are your tools. And as you increase your skill, you'll be more and more able to "hit the nail on the head" … and avoid those painful, swollen thumbs.

A musician has an ear for different notes and how they work together, and a painter has an eye for colors and their combinations. A writer is the same way, but his or her tools are words. When you have a mastery of language, you feel comfortable in the world of words—comfortable and in control. You can feel the relative weight of different words and make them fit neatly and beautifully together, like tiles in a mosaic.

> **The Experts Agree**
>
> Mastery of language makes you all-powerful.
>
> —Mike, former copy chief, current magazine editor

As with any task, from cooking to cutting hair, various tools can help you master the art of writing. Let's look at some essentials to keep in your writer's toolbox.

Vocabulary

What's the first thing that comes to mind when you hear the word *vocabulary?* Those awful SAT tests? Pretentious speeches filled with five-dollar words?

One of the most common (and best) pieces of advice handed out to writers is "Don't use a fancy word when a simple one will do." But it's also true that the more words you have at your disposal, the more likely you are to avoid dull, repetitive writing. That's especially true in ad copy where you're likely to find yourself searching for a hundred different ways to say a certain food product is "delicious" or a certain service is "helpful"—and competing against all the other ads trying to tell consumers the same thing about their products.

When you know lots of words, you also have better odds of knowing the just-right word choice for any given situation. A chef might use saffron or rosemary or coriander only once in a year's worth of menus … but isn't it exciting and delicious when that unusual spice turns up in the appropriate dish? Here are some ways to fill up your wordly spice rack:

- Subscribe to some challenging reading matter—a "serious" magazine about a topic that intrigues you or a high-quality general interest magazine like *The Atlantic* or *The New Yorker*. Then read it—with a dictionary at your side, if necessary.

Why Pay More?

See Appendix A for examples of good dictionaries and other reference materials handy for copywriters.

- Develop a crossword puzzle habit. And if you have to cheat and look at the answers, that's okay—it's educational!

- Look up the pronunciations—not just the definitions—of words in the dictionary. Sometimes we avoid stretching our vocabulary for fear of mispronouncing a word and sounding silly. Roll the words around on your tongue a little bit, and say them out loud so you own them. Then save them. You never know when they'll come in handy.

- Make up words, just for fun. Hey, if no one ever made up a word, we wouldn't have any. *Webster's* added 10,000 words to its dictionary in just a decade—someone had to come up with them all.

Brevity

Ad space is expensive. And buyers—whether individual consumers racing through the mall or business executives perusing catalogs—are busy. A copywriter must be keenly aware of the need to pack as much power as possible into a small number of words. "Brevity is the soul of wit," said Shakespeare—it's also the soul of copywriting.

The Experts Agree

I have made this letter longer than usual, because I lack the time to make it short.

—Pascal

An important thing to remember about brevity is that it doesn't always mean your copy should be *short*. It means your copy should be *efficient*—achieving its goals in the smallest number of words. If you're selling something that requires a significant investment—a major purchase the consumer is going to consider or research at length—they will be more willing to read a longer piece of copy about it. And if you really have five different terrific sales points to make, it makes sense to write a little more. Try these suggestions for keeping your writing short and snappy:

◆ **Think before you write.** When economy-minded musicians head into the recording studio, they come prepared—with songs written and rehearsed. If they don't, those bills for studio time can really add up. Professional chefs don't walk into the kitchen at the last minute to chop all the vegetables. Likewise, as a copywriter, you've got prep work to do before you start writing. Meditate on the tangible product you're selling. Meditate a little more on the intangibles you're selling. Speed? Safety? Style? Depending on how much direction you've gotten from your client, you may already have a strong sense of what your goals are. But you also bring your own insight and creativity to the job, and that means approaching the blank page without a blank mind.

◆ **Edit mercilessly.** Your copy shouldn't have an ounce of excess fat. You need to read it word by word, phrase by phrase, sentence by sentence, asking yourself all the while, "What purpose does this word/phrase/sentence serve? Does it inform, clarify, or add emotional impact? Is there a shorter way to say the same exact thing and have the same effect?" Weigh the relative value of your words, and remember that they are all serving one main purpose: to sell. So sometimes longer is better—because *a hot bowl of soup* sounds a lot more inviting than just *soup*. On the other hand, *a hot bowl of soup* is better than *a hot, steaming bowl of soup fresh off the stove*. Editing is like sanding down a piece of wood—it's close, slow work, but when you get into it, both the process and the results can be extremely satisfying. In careful reading, you might find you've made the same point three times in the course of your copy, and you can whittle it down to one. (Unless, of course, you're using repetition deliberately—see Chapter 6.)

CAUTION

Accept No Imitations!

Don't waste your reader's time—and risk his boredom—by saying in 50 words what you can say in 5.

◆ **Text message your copy.** Modern communication tools—cell phones billed by the minute, e-mail, and especially text messaging—have given brevity a new value. Even if you don't use these tools, you probably can think back on your last long-distance call and the effort you made to say what you needed to say without time-wasting small talk or digression. In the old days, people had to do the same thing on telegrams, and newspaper headlines continue to be great examples of packing information into the smallest number of words—or even the smallest number of letters. (Just think of all those words you usually see only in headlines—*tot* instead of *child*, for example.) As an exercise, write out your message as if you were paying a dollar per letter to send it. It will force you to think about what really needs to stay and what you can afford to throw out. Then you can try a "reverse edit," building on the copy-cake you've created and adding just enough frosting and filling to make it special—no more, no less.

- ◆ **Eliminate the obvious.** Sometimes copywriters seem to have term paper flash-backs, starting out their copy with grandiose, general introductions. Or they make statements such as, *Many people today want to save money, due to high unemployment and stagnant salaries.* It's a given that many people want to save money (even where there's low unemployment and salaries are soaring). Or in an attempt to establish a sense of sympathy with the reader, copywriters describe the reader's problem at length: *You've tried and tried to lose weight. No matter how many diets you follow, you just can't seem to lose those extra pounds. You want to look good, but you just don't have the time to exercise 4 hours a day.* The reader already knows this. He wants to know what you're going to do about it.

- ◆ **Remember the advice of the society ladies.** "Get completely dressed and then take off one piece of jewelry," is said to be the rule for achieving elegance in your attire. Keep this in mind when you're writing—especially in copywriting, where a common tendency is to overhype and take things one superlative too far. Mark Twain offered similar guidance on the subject of writing itself: "As to the adjective, when in doubt, strike it out."

Try editing this copy. See my edited version in the box on the next page and compare:

When you're sitting in front of your computer, talking to someone on the telephone, and trying to keep an eye on your little baby in the playpen, you don't have a lot of time to think about what you're going to feed your family for dinner tonight. That's why millions of busy, overburdened work-at-home moms have turned to RobotChef for help. RobotChef assists you by creating dinners for your family while you are at your desk working. Just aim the remote, program your RobotChef to make roast chicken, mixed vegetables, and mashed potatoes for four—and take care of your many other priorities while the RobotChef prepares your family's dinner. In these modern-day times, a woman's work is never done—but RobotChef can give you the help you need!

How did you do on the edit exercise on the previous page? Here's my edited version:

You're at your computer *and* on the phone, and the baby's next to you in the playpen. You don't have time to think about dinner. That's why millions of work-at-home moms have turned to RobotChef. RobotChef makes dinner for your family while you're busy—just aim the remote, program "ravioli for four," and take care of your other priorities while RobotChef does the work. Nowadays a woman's work is never done—but RobotChef can help!

Connotation

What's the difference between a cooking *aroma* and a cooking *odor?* A cooking aroma comes from your house—and a cooking odor comes from your neighbor's.

Most copy must appeal to the senses and the emotions as well as to the logical intelligence of consumers. A person who's already in the store can run her fingers down the satin sleeve of a dress or smell the cinnamon buns; your job is to get her into the store in the first place. Understanding word connotations is crucial to that task. Even if you haven't consciously thought about "connotation" since high school English class, you're probably much more sensitive to it than you realize. (For example: ladies, think about your reaction when the guy you've been seeing for 3 months introduces you as his "date" instead of his "girlfriend.")

The Experts Agree

The difference between the almost-right word and the right word is ... the difference between the lightning bug and the lightning.

—Mark Twain

To build that sensitivity, you have to go below the surface of words and actually *feel* them. This helps you choose the just-right word for your copy—a powerful tool that can make all the difference. Try deepening your sense of connotation with the following methods:

- **Free-associate.** Take two or three words that essentially mean the same thing—for example, *travel, journey,* and *trek.* While in some ways interchangeable, these words can call subtly different images and feelings to mind. *Travel* might make you think of fun, adventure, and exotic locales. *Journey* might imply movement toward a goal—a religious pilgrimage or a struggle through a long illness toward healing. *Trek* can suggest a hard hike through a dense jungle. No one is likely to have the exact same set of connotations because they're formed in part by our individual experiences. But they are also shaped by common usage—and often, without realizing, we grow to understand and accept a set of associations for different words that at first seem simply to be synonyms.

◆ **Read poetry.** Good poetry has a lot in common with good copy. A poem evokes vivid images and strong emotions through very careful word choice. Spend a rainy afternoon reading a website such as poets.org, run by the Academy of American Poets. Try printing out a poem and rewriting it by replacing key words with synonyms. How does it read differently before and after?

Free Sample!

Farm fresh. Dirt cheap.

This ad for freshdirect.com is an excellent example of using connotation well (not to mention brevity). By starting out with "farm fresh," the copywriter puts the image of just-grown vegetables in the reader's mind. In this context, the "dirt" in "dirt cheap" brings a vivid image of the outdoors and clean air and the lovely springtime smell of earth. You have to admire an ad that makes the word *dirt* appealing!

Rhythm

Rhythm is a quality of good writing that often goes unappreciated. Poetry is known for rhythm—even if it's not written in any strict meter—but rhythm is also an important part of even the most straightforward, purely informative prose. Say you stop along the road to ask someone directions to a gas station, and he replies, "Well … hmmm … you've got to make a left and then a right and then another right and then go two lights and then go down the road a piece …." That monotone could cause you to drift off in the middle, miss that crucial second right turn, and the next thing you know you're out of gas and calling AAA for a tow. You don't want to give your reader that opportunity to drift off, even for a second. Follow these guidelines for writing copy that's music to your readers' ears:

◆ **Recite it out loud.** If it's hard to read or sounds unnatural as you read it out loud, it's probably hard to read and unnatural on the page.

◆ **Vary your sentence structure.** Too many long sentences in a row leaves a reader feeling a little breathless and overwhelmed. Too many short sentences can have a staccato effect that drowns out the meaning. Experiment with short/short/long or with short/long/short/long/longer. This applies to individual words, too. You want a flowing, gentle beat with a little twist here and there, and rearranging your words and sentences can be the key to achieving it and keeping your reader's attention. Try breaking a sentence in half. Avoid using similar sentence structures one after another. For example, instead of:

> Exhausted by the holidays, you're dreaming about a January getaway. Looking at your holiday bills, you might think you can't afford it. Featuring cozy accommodations and great skiing, Winter World could be the solution.

Try:

> Exhausted by the holidays? You might think getting away is impossible right now—especially with all those holiday bills to pay. Think again. Winter World offers cozy accommodations and great skiing—at a budget-friendly price.

◆ **Punctuate with precision.** Words get all the attention, but for a bunch of little dots and symbols, punctuation can have a significant effect on how your work sounds and reads. Read it out loud, and include the punctuation. Do you want the reader to pause where that comma is? Does that line sound flat with a period at the end? You might want to join two sentences with an ellipsis (…) or an em dash (—), two valuable tools for the copywriter. Ultimately, you want your copy to read—to sound in the reader's head—the same way it would sound if someone were naturally and unrehearsedly speaking the words. Keep in mind that when taking in information, readers need time to digest, and punctuation gives little tiny breaks to do just that. It can also clarify meaning and add emotional cues—an ellipsis suggests suspense; an exclamation point indicates surprise and excitement.

> **CAUTION**
>
> **Accept No Imitations!**
>
> Don't treat punctuation as an afterthought but as a consequential part of your writing.

Mastery of Ego

Everyone's a copywriter! Do you see many people grabbing the wrench out of a plumber's hand and taking over a repair job? Or trying to perform their own orthodonture? Not many. But most people do know how to write, with one degree or skill or another. So it won't be unusual for you to have others—such as bosses and clients—editing you. Take a deep breath because it's part of the job. The better you are at dealing with being edited (and sometimes, badly edited), the more successful you'll be in the professional copywriting world. Just as important, your Buddhalike chill can prevent ulcers, high blood pressure, and other stress-induced symptoms, lengthening not just your copywriting career but your life as well! Following are some techniques to help you stay humble, handle frustration, and assert yourself, when necessary, in a gracious and professional manner.

Take Advantage of Your Critics

Hidden inside what you might consider your critic's woefully clueless comments, you might just find something valuable. Absorb his observations, and reread your copy from a different angle. Oops—does it turn out Mr. Doesn't-Know-His-Adjective-From-His-Elbow is onto something? Lucky you! Accept it; adjust the copy … and be sure to say "thank you."

Why Pay More?

I've learned that the bright side of "everyone's a copywriter" is that you never know where help and inspiration will come from. In my work, I've seen great copy ideas come out of the sales department, the editorial department—and even from a summer intern in the art department.

Write Your Own Stuff

If you've got novels, plays, or poems inside you crying to get out, it's very easy to let all that creative energy boil over when your copywriting efforts hit a brick wall.

Save a good chunk of precious time in your schedule for the writing that's deep and meaningful to you, even though it may never earn you a penny. During work hours, keep in mind that you're being paid to get somebody else's message across—not yours.

The Experts Agree

All it takes to edit ad copy is a pen.

—Sarah, creative manager

The Experts Agree

When I started I was near-obsessed with being the "original" source for all the writing I handed my supervisors. I actively did not want help from fellow writers, friends, etc. As I got more mature and more secure, I realized that my job was to take and use the best idea, whether it had sprung from my brain or not.

—Peter, former copywriter

Practice Humility

Even if you've been at it for years and have supreme confidence in your skills, it's a good habit to routinely ask others for their opinions—and not just fellow writers whom you "respect." As a copywriter, you're trying to communicate with large numbers of people, and they're not all going to have M.F.A.s in creative writing. Many writers try, consciously or subconsciously, to avoid feedback. Sometimes it takes years for them to realize what they're missing out on and how rapidly their talents can grow once exposed to the light of day.

> **The Experts Agree**
>
> One thing I had to force myself to get over was my perpetual desire to turn my copywriting into a masterpiece. I would imagine most people who envision themselves when they're young as becoming "writers" have the same problem. I had it, and I saw it in people I supervised a few years later.
>
> —Peter, former copywriter

Remember, the main purpose of any type of writing is *communication*. Ultimately, your readers are your judges—and if they "don't get it," you have to consider the possibility that it's your failure, not just theirs.

Read *The Artist's Way*

The Artist's Way by Julia Cameron (Tarcher, 2002) is oriented toward artistic, not commercial, writing. But its thoughtful examinations of subjects such as self-image, criticism, and ego can benefit just about anyone.

Be Assertive—but Don't Roll Your Eyes

There will be times when you're convinced the client's changes are a bad idea. And because you want the job done right, it's not unreasonable to make your case. Do it calmly, pleasantly, and diplomatically, though. Be specific, give a reason, and offer an alternative. "Hmm. That is another option we could consider. But I'm concerned that this phrase might confuse people. What if we said it this way instead?" If you're truly alarmed about the factual inaccuracy or legality of what he's insisting upon, make that clear—you just might save him from a lawsuit. If you sense you're not going to win the argument, let it go. Maybe you're wrong. Maybe he's wrong. But when it comes down to it, he's paying for the ad space, not you.

Finally, look at it this way: you've got a fun job, writing copy. No wonder everyone wants to join in!

Speed

Acclaimed novelists are sometimes known to fuss over their manuscripts for years while their publisher and their public wait with bated breath. But no matter how acclaimed a copywriter you become, your clients probably aren't going to show the same patience.

Perhaps more than any other quality discussed in this chapter, speed can be a determining factor in your copywriting success. For one thing, the more you write, the more you get paid! Plus, copywriting jobs usually can't wait. Even if you're not working on some timely or seasonal product, you're probably working for a business (your own or somebody else's) that depends on a very tight schedule. Inventory must be sold and shipped on a reliable basis, and there's no time for writer's block, procrastination, or tinkering with that sixteenth draft. Follow these tips to build speed and make yourself a more valuable copywriting professional.

Get Over It

If you're plagued by perfectionism or performance anxiety, you'll be sabotaging yourself constantly. If you find yourself with repeated "deadline crises," maybe you need to take a step back and address your problem. These tendencies can destroy careers, and even if you keep muddling through and pulling it off at the last minute, do you really want to keep pulling all-nighters and popping antacids? Self-help books on procrastination and perfectionism can get you on the right track.

CAUTION

Accept No Imitations!

If you suspect your self-defeating behavior is a little more intractable, look into cognitive-behavioral therapy. This type of therapy is especially quick and effective for changing bad habits, and if your career is suffering, the investment pays for itself.

Be a Worker, Not an Artist

Saying to yourself "I'm a pro" or "I've got a job to do" takes away a lot of the anxiety that gets stirred up when you think in more artistic terms. As artists, we seek to express ourselves or bring truth and beauty to our audience. We want our creations to be unique, and we hope for praise and recognition. That's a lot of pressure. When you approach your keyboard or pick up your pen to write some copy, switch into professional mode. This is business. Hey, Shakespeare wrote some great plays, but did he move product?

Count on Feedback

Naturally, you want your copy to be as close to perfect as possible when you hand it in. And you certainly should keep it professional-looking—free of spelling errors and the like. But the fact is, even superb copy sometimes needs revision for reasons that have nothing to do with its inherent quality. Sometimes the client's business goal has changed and you need to adjust accordingly. Sometimes the client isn't quite sure what she's looking for until she sees the copy in front of her—and suddenly, you've got a whole new set of directions. Sometimes a change in an art concept requires a corresponding change in the copy concept. So if you're fiddling with your copy and having trouble letting go, go ahead and let it go. It will likely come back to you anyway.

The Experts Agree

I was once told to write copy about library tape and to make it sound "sexy." This took a lot of creative thinking on my part ... and the end result didn't fly anyway. My idea of "sexy" and librarians' idea of "sexy" were wildly different. The finished (not by me) copy read something like "This roll holds 60 feet of 1-inch-wide tape."

—Beth, writer/editor

Psychological Insight

Copywriters aren't just writers—they're salespeople. Expanding your psychological understanding is a worthwhile activity for both writers and salespeople; so if you're both, you'll benefit twice as much. Try the following activities to improve your people sense.

Build Empathy

Naturally, most of us live in our own heads a majority of the time and form friendships with people similar to ourselves. The more different people seem to be from us, the harder it is for us to "get" them—at least, at first. The value of empathy goes far beyond copywriting, but it's very important to anyone who needs to reach a wide variety of people as a part of his job.

There are lots of ways to build this skill. Next time you find yourself sitting on a train or waiting in line, look at each person around you. Ask yourself what might be bothering this person right now. Use your imagination: maybe the cold weather is aggravating that elderly woman's arthritis; maybe that teenager carrying the gigantic backpack has way too much homework.

If you don't have kids, listen carefully when your friends who are parents tell you their woes. If you're single, consider the downside of being married, and if you're married, consider the downside of being single. Remember something that made you feel better when you were lonely or sad as a child. Seek out memoirs or articles by members of minority groups unfamiliar to you, or by the opposite gender, to get a taste of the cultural, physical, and emotional experiences that might never even occur to you. Aside from growing as a person, you'll probably find it a lot easier to think of ideas and strike the appropriate tone the next time you have to write an ad for diapers or a dating service, acne medication, or a retirement community—regardless of whether you've ever used the service or product yourself.

Know Thyself

Learning what we all have in common is just as important as learning what makes us different as individuals. If you never took Psychology 101, pick up a used textbook—you might even find one at a yard sale—and discover some fascinating facts. There's valuable information for the copywriter in there—not just about our emotional reactions but about the ways our brains work. You'll find out about what makes us retain (or not retain) information, what motivates us (or deters us) from trying something new, and how we make our decisions about what's important to us—which can translate into what we're willing to spend our money on.

Monitor Your Own Reactions to Copy

Can you remember the last time a TV commercial or a description in a catalog persuaded you to buy something? Spend a month being extra-mindful of the pitches aimed at you (there are a lot of them!) and what effect they have on you. You'll likely discover some negative effects, too: an ad might make you feel pressured or manipulated or skeptical. Analyze which specific words, phrases, ideas, and tones jump out at you and provoke either positive or negative feelings. You can perform this analysis not only on copy, but on visual images, music, or any part of advertising as well. This analyzing will improve your marketing sense … and make you a smarter shopper along the way.

> **The Experts Agree**
>
> Stop Tivo-ing over the commercials. Watch them. … These things are being sold to you. Are you buying? If so, why? If not, where did they fail?
>
> —Mike, former copy chief, current magazine editor

Wide-Ranging Interests

As with psychological insight, having a broad understanding of many topics helps the copywriter by making him or her capable of working on a larger variety of jobs. (Copywriting is a job that comes in handy when you've had one of those impractical liberal-arts educations.) You don't have to be a CEO to write an ad for business software, an M.D. to write an ad for decongestant, or an Olympic athlete to write an ad for sporting goods. But having a firm grasp of many fields of interest makes you a more adaptable and confident copywriter. The following activities can help.

Why Pay More?

Reading a variety of sources and types of media keeps you timely. After all, you don't want to use any dorky, outdated slang when writing for teenagers or refer to happenin' trends that actually stopped happenin' in 1994.

Read Every Section—at Least Once in a While

Business, sports, reviews of movies you wouldn't dream of seeing: whatever you usually thumb past in the paper, try reading those sections thoroughly, even if it's just once or twice a month. You'll pick up not only basic jargon used in various fields, but also a better understanding of what makes each of these things interesting to others (even if you're personally bored silly by them).

Don't Pick Up Your Usual Magazines in the Dentist's Waiting Room

Find out what all those foodies are going on about by glancing through *Gourmet*. Or familiarize yourself with computer lingo and cutting-edge gadgets by browsing through something the techies read. Try *Teen People* or *Modern Maturity*. Now you've turned that wasted time into a career-building activity and taken your mind off your upcoming root canal.

Don't Zone Out

Has the party conversation drifted into a debate over nicotine gum vs. the patch? If you're a nonsmoker (or a smoker who really doesn't want to think about quitting), you'll probably start composing your grocery list in your head or scoping out the other guests rather than hearing this conversation. Try listening instead. This is the kind of consumer research companies pay big money for, and you're getting it for free.

Imagination

We all have our weak points, and this is one of mine. I'm amazed by people who can spin stories and scenarios, seemingly out of nowhere. How do they do it? This has been a quality I've had to work on, so let me share some of what has worked for me.

Throw All the Pieces Up in the Air

Creativity isn't really about creating something entirely new—it's about taking the existing pieces and putting them together in a new way. In observing imaginative people, I've learned that they're good at scanning their environments, jumbling things up, and putting them back together, sometimes in extraordinary ways. It's a skill that makes for good jokes and poems—and creative advertising.

Free Sample!

One very famous ad from a couple of decades ago placed a baby inside a tire. It's an odd, startling image, and that's part of what made it so effective at getting attention. It also suggested a sense of safety and security and added an element of humanity and fun to what would otherwise be a rather mundane product. This technique can work with images, words, and even abstract ideas, and practicing it helps you break out of the habitual thinking that limits your imagination.

Play Games

Game-playing can be especially helpful when you're looking for a snappy headline or slogan. Think of every word you can that rhymes with the brand name. Make up a silly song about the product or a brief story in which the product has a starring role. As children we had great imaginations, but the daily grind can knock that out of us as we get older. So bring a sense of play into your work, and you might rediscover that inner 5-year-old. Just don't hand in your copy written in crayon.

Take a Walk

Ever notice how a lot of your creative breakthroughs seem to come at the moments when you're not trying? You could be washing your hair or painting a wall when

inspiration strikes. The ability to focus on a goal or multitask can serve you well in other situations, but "productive" mind-sets aren't necessarily the most productive when it comes to creativity. Do something that's not too mentally demanding, and give your brain a chance to stretch along with your muscles.

Integrity

Advertising has a (sometimes well-deserved) reputation for sleaziness. It's not hard to twist words and fiddle with facts and numbers to suit your persuasive purpose, and you will probably be tempted to do so on occasion. Don't give in—although it might make your copy seem more powerful and impressive in the short run, in the long run it undermines both your credibility and the client's, and that's not good business. (That's aside from it being just plain wrong.)

Sometimes we can compromise our integrity without even being fully aware of it. So be on guard and make the right choices by keeping the following things in mind.

Fact-Checking Is Essential

This includes checking your numbers if you're using numbers to sell your product. If a store gives a 50 percent discount and then an additional 20 percent discount, that doesn't mean consumers are getting a 70 percent discount. The second discount is taken off the *reduced* amount, not the *original* amount. So if the product started out at $100, the first discount would bring it to $50. Then, the second discount would take 20 percent off the $50 price for a final price of $40. That's an overall 60 percent discount, not 70 percent.

Accept No Imitations!

Don't play fast and loose with your math or your facts.

Suppose you've done some research and you want to mention that a million Americans have already lost weight on the Snack Cake Diet. You better read your source carefully and be sure it doesn't actually say a million Americans have *tried* the Snack Cake Diet—but 95 percent of them actually gained weight as a result; or that a million copies of *The Snack Cake Miracle Diet Handbook* have been sold—just because somebody bought the book doesn't mean they tried the diet, let alone lost weight on it.

You also want to be sure your sources are reliable. Statistics from MySnackCakeDietBlog.com may not pass that test. (And note: if you're writing copy for a Snack Cake Diet, you may be compromising your integrity simply by accepting the assignment.)

You Don't Have to Say Yes to Every Job

If you don't feel comfortable with a particular product or service, or feel pressured to write seriously misleading copy, you can bow out gracefully. Putting something into the most positive possible light is one thing; misrepresentation is another. There are a lot of gray areas between facts, lies, and opinions, and it's not always easy to identify the thin lines, but if you start feeling like you need a shower while you're working on a sales brochure, that might be a clue.

Sales Relationships Suffer from Dishonesty

This is important on two levels. First, if you create sleazy, sloppy copy, upstanding businesses will not want to put their own reputations at risk by using you. They want to know they can put the job in your hands and not be required to scrutinize your work every time for unacceptable content. Second, a short-sighted business that tries to foist inferior products on buyers or uses questionable sales methods will eventually find itself unwelcome in the marketplace … if not investigated by the Federal Trade Commission. We all want to deal with people we can trust, and part of that is accomplished by being trustworthy ourselves.

The Least You Need to Know

- Good copywriters share some of the same skills as novelists, reporters, or poets … but not all the same.

- Think of words as your tools: choose the right ones for the job, and use them the right way.

- Be considerate of your reader's valuable time.

- Don't forget your main goal is to sell.

- Be open to ideas from everywhere and everyone.

- Do an honorable job, and earn the trust of those you deal with.

5

The Mind of the Market

In This Chapter

- A step-by-step look at the art of persuasion
- Summaries of different generations—and hints about what gets their attention and motivates them to buy
- Tips for appealing to media-wise younger consumers
- Theories about gender differences—and what they might mean for marketers

As a marketing copywriter, you're trying to persuade. That is, you're trying to get people to do something—buy your brand of potato chips, contribute to your foundation, see your movie. But how exactly do you accomplish that?

The Four Phases of Persuasion

Decades ago, a psychologist named Carl Hovland and his team of researchers identified four distinct parts of the process of persuasion:

- Attention
- Acceptance
- Comprehension
- Retention

Let's consider what you as a copywriter can do to help each of these parts of the process along.

Attention

We live in an age of media overload. And we may be even more overloaded with advertising than we are with media. After all, we don't just get ads from TV, radio, magazines, newspapers, and the Internet—we also get them on the sides of buses, on coffee cups, in restroom stalls, on billboards, and even woven subtly into our movies in the form of product placement. Nowadays there's even a new trend in which marketing companies recruit people to work products into their casual, everyday conversations. It's no wonder consumers have learned to tune out.

In his book *Confessions of an Advertising Man* (1963), David Ogilvy—who started out as a copywriter and became one of the biggest names in the modern advertising world—listed words and phrases that would "work wonders." In addition to *free* and *new*, which he considered the most powerful words you could put in your headline, he offered the following must-use words as well:

advice to	important development	offer
amazing	improvement	quick
announcing	introducing	remarkable
bargain	it's here	revolutionary
challenge	just arrived	sensational
compare	last chance	startling
easy	magic	suddenly
how to	miracle	the truth about
hurry	now	wanted

More than 40 years later, his list still holds up pretty well. But let's face it, we've been battered by some of these words so much in the intervening years that they've lost a bit of their impact. Also, another trend in American life over the past 40 years is that people are working longer hours. In fact, just in the past 20 years, reports Juliet B. Schor in *The Overworked American*, our working hours have increased on average by 163 hours a year—that's an entire extra month of work! And of course, a lot more outlets are competing for the few leisure hours we have left: video games, more cable channels, 24-hour online shopping. So the competition is fiercer than ever when it comes to getting the time and attention of the American consumer, and that means big challenges for copywriters. To help you cut through the clutter, here are some tips to keep in mind:

- **Keep it short.** This applies especially when you're producing point-of-purchase materials, such as packaging and store signs. In many cases, you have literally just a few seconds to make an impact.

- **Use nonstandard wording.** I was recently convinced to buy gel insoles for my shoes by a simple phrase on the package: *outrageous comfort*. It may sound silly, but something about the word *outrageous* convinced me there was something special going on here and it was worth my spending a few dollars for the chance to experience it. (They are indeed quite comfortable.)

- **Go low-key.** When everyone's yelling, a whisper really stands out. The trick, of course, is to be low-key in an attention-getting way, not in a way that gets drowned out. You might try being gentle in your language and tone and using an unusual, old-fashioned adjective such as *lovely*. Or inject a little sincere emotion into your message instead of striving to make an impression.

Free Sample!

Please try my product.

The "Video Professor" looks directly at the camera and makes this request in his commercial for software that teaches beginners how to use computers. In a world of slick pitches, it comes across as so low-key, heartfelt, and humble that it makes me want to try his product—even though I already know how to use computers.

Comprehension

Succeeding in getting people to read your message won't do you any good if they don't understand it. And they don't necessarily have to be slow-witted to not get it. We're all busy and stressed today, and that means we're easily confused. Don't make your audience work too hard to figure out what you're saying. They have enough work to do already. Use these ideas to ensure your ad is not just seen but also understood:

- **Be conscious of your vocabulary.** The words in Chapters 1 through 3 are, for the most part, commonly used. It's been a long time since most of your audience studied for the SAT, and one obscure word can make them lose the thread and

The Experts Agree

Sometimes you have to ask yourself: *Am I just trying to show how clever I am? Does this headline really sell the product or am I just showing off?* Cleverness just for the sake of being clever can be really annoying to the reader.

—Beth, writer/editor

give up (or completely misunderstand your message). Remember that as a writer, you probably have a larger vocabulary than the average person. Some copywriters sneer at having to "dumb down" their copy, but with so much information to process on a daily basis, I appreciate having things "dumbed down" for me—that is, having them presented as simply and clearly as possible. That's the philosophy behind *The Complete Idiot's Guides*, and before I became a *Complete Idiot's Guide* author, I was a *Complete Idiot's Guide* reader—very grateful for the "dumbed-down" advice on a variety of topics.

◆ **Don't misdirect.** In the quest to get attention, you may be tempted to write a funny or intriguing headline, but that only works if the rest of the copy follows naturally. If your headline says *Get rid of blemishes and scars* and the ad turns out to be for a photo-retouching product, the people who continued to read, hoping to discover a useful skin-care product, are likely to be first confused and then disappointed. And the people with problem-free complexions who might be in the market for a photo-retouching product will not have continued to read.

◆ **Don't overwhelm the reader.** If you have a lot of facts to impart, present them in an easily digestible way. Keep your headline straightforward and simple. See Chapter 6 for hints on attention-getters such as bulleted lists and bursts. In addition, Chapter 7 offers hints on structuring your sentences and using punctuation in ways that make your message clear instead of confusing. People want a chance to breathe and absorb what they're taking in. Overselling or throwing too much at them all at once will just make them shut out your copy for the sake of their own sanity.

Acceptance

Why should consumers believe *you?* That's a good question! If you're tempted to answer, "Because this product or service is really good, and I'm telling the truth," that's a wonderful place to start. Unfortunately, it doesn't necessarily mean your consumer will be persuaded. Lots of studies have been done on what makes a message likely to be accepted, and this data can help guide you:

◆ **People consider the source.** That's a big disadvantage for copywriters. After all, when people read an ad, they go into it knowing you're trying to sell them something and, therefore, they keep their guard up. That's why testimonials can be so powerful (see Chapter 6). Take advantage of opportunities to let others do the talking—ideally, not paid endorsers but objective third parties. A good recommendation from a former employer can help a candidate much more than a resumé or interview filled with self-praise.

When writing marketing copy for books, I have often shortened or even eliminated my own copy to make room for good quotes from newspapers and magazines. No matter how good my writing might be, I know that my telling you the book is compelling doesn't hold a candle to *People* magazine or *The Minnesota Star-Tribune* telling you the same thing.

♦ **A source is most likely to be believed if it's regarded as knowledgeable, trustworthy, and attractive.** A caution comes attached to this, however. Coming off as too much of an "expert"—that is, an overconfident know-it-all—can turn off your audience, so don't write in a condescending tone. Don't use the term *of course* to imply something is obvious if there's a chance it might *not* be obvious to your reader. As for trustworthy, remember, saying "trust me" is an easy way to make someone *not* trust you. *Be* trustworthy instead of saying you are. And be aware that *attractive* doesn't always have to mean physically or sexually attractive—sometimes using spokes-hunks and spokes-babes can be counterproductive if you're selling the kind of item that isn't particularly sexy or shrouded in fantasy. People respond well to those who are pleasant and likable—and to those who remind them of themselves.

The Experts Agree

Put yourself in the mind and the speech of your subject. Honing this requires hours of reading because you need to call on these voices at will, on deadline. Absorb books and magazines across diametrically opposed genres. Patricia Cornwell and *Texas Monthly* this week. Joyce Carol Oates and *Maxim* next week. William Faulkner and *Glamour* the next.

—Mike, former copy chief, current magazine editor

Write in a conversational, down-to-earth tone. If your reader identifies with you, he or she is more likely to listen to what you say. That's why a lawnmower commercial is going to work better if it features an ordinary-looking suburban homeowner instead of a glamorous 20-year-old pop singer. (This example can also apply to the matter of expertise. Will anyone really believe said pop singer mows her own lawn?)

♦ **Consider presenting both sides.** If you're writing to a more sophisticated or educated audience, you are likely to be more effective if you acknowledge complexity and potential objections. A reader with a lot of formal education has been trained to look for holes in your argument. So address possible downsides and doubts while still placing your overall emphasis on the positive. *Is a health club membership worth the price? Consider that X% of health club members maintained their weight loss, compared to Y% of those who didn't belong to a gym.*

Likewise, allow a more educated audience to draw its own conclusions, rather than telling it what conclusion to make. Their educations have taught them to question authority and use their own logical skills, so they will feel more persuaded if they have made the deduction themselves, rather than just taking your word for it.

Retention

Your job isn't done when the reader has finished the ad. He has to take the next step and take action, and the more memorable the message, the more likely he is to do so. Based on scientific studies of how our memories work, these facts can help you create ads that stick in people's heads:

The Experts Agree

In the fascinating book *Freakonomics*, authors Steven Levitt and Stephen Dubner crunch some data to reveal that in real estate ads, terms like *granite* and *maple* correlated to higher eventual sale prices for the house in question. Words such as *fantastic* and *charming* correlated to lower prices. Vivid, concrete details help!

♦ **We remember it if it means something to us.** Our brains recall information in several ways. We remember things through sound—which is why, as will be discussed in Chapter 6, rhyming and rhythm can make a piece of writing much more memorable. We remember things visually—thus the advice often given to writers to include concrete examples and descriptive details so a picture is formed in the reader's head.

But when it comes to long-term memory, meaningful content is crucial. When you're creating copy, think about the meaning of your product or service to the reader. How will it make him feel better? How will it change her life? What will he experience as a result of using it?

The more they can imagine and relate to these meanings, the better. Saying your product will help them lose weight is virtually meaningless at this point because there are probably 50 other ads telling them the same thing. But if you can make them mull over the feeling of slipping into a slim pair of jeans, walking into a party with confidence, or having lots of endurance and energy when they play with their kids—now that's meaningful.

♦ **Organization is key.** We use a technique called "chunking" to help us remember information. The average person is capable of retaining only seven bits of information at a time in short-term memory, so our brilliant brains find ways to overcome that limitation by forming larger "chunks." One common way businesses take advantage of chunking is by creating 1-800 numbers that form words. How often would you call 1-800-FLOWERS if you had to remember the actual digits?

Likewise, we tend to sort things into categories to improve our recall. When you present information to the reader, don't do it randomly. Follow a logical sequence. For example, telling them they can spray on the oven cleaner, wait until morning, and then wipe it off allows them not only to remember the content of your ad because of its step-by-step information, but it also makes it more meaningful and memorable to them because it allows them to picture themselves cleaning their oven and to see how this product can make their lives easier. If your product comes in five colors, list the colors one after another in a separate box. Even the messiest people, deep down, like order and symmetry—it's a part of human nature. How many times have you heard someone with a chaotic desk explain that he has his own "system" for knowing where everything is?

♦ **Context creates cues.** Experiments have shown that we remember things much more easily when they're presented in their original context or when they're linked to cues that help prompt our memory. Marketers know this and coordinate their campaigns by carrying the same words, pictures, and logos in ads, on product packages, and on in-store signs.

You can provide cues that enhance memory in simple ways. Saying *Look for Brand X shampoo* is good, but saying *Look for Brand X shampoo next time you're at the drugstore* is better. A day or two after reading your ad, the consumer might walk into the drugstore thinking, *Wasn't there something I was supposed to pick up here?* Describing or showing the context in which your product or service can be used turns it into a part of the picture—you might mention how your frozen bagels are *perfect for a leisurely Saturday-morning breakfast* or how your inventory service can help store owners *be prepared for the after-Thanksgiving holiday rush*.

◆ **Things take time to sink in.** In one experiment, subjects who tried to remember lists of random words read out loud to them did a lot better when there were a few seconds of silence in between each word. Our brains are like computers, and data overload can make them freeze up. Allowing people to pause and breathe lets them process and store what you're saying in their long-term memory. Keep some visual and mental space between your important points: start a new paragraph, divide points with a line, or add a dingbat in between pieces of information.

The Experts Agree

More white space. Less clutter.

—Lisa, newspaper promotion director, on what makes a good ad

◆ **Anxiety makes us forgetful.** Don't use scare tactics in your ads. Explain how your tax service will ease the consumer's anxiety. Don't tell them they better use your tax service or the IRS will be at their door with a battering ram come April 16.

◆ **Emotion helps us remember—as long as there isn't too much of it.** Simply put, we think more about things with emotional content, and thinking about them ingrains them into our memory. (No wonder that romantic tearjerker you saw as a teenager still stays with you while your high school chemistry lessons have vanished into thin air.)

Intense emotion, however, tends to interfere with and distort our memory, while mild emotional arousal helps our mental performance, making us interested and alert. Avoid dry text, even if what you're selling is on the mundane side. FedEx has very successfully used humor over the years, and there's nothing inherently funny about shipping. And you can show nearly any product in an emotional context if you use your imagination—from a refrigerator covered with children's artwork to a cleaning product that helps make your house spotless before your friends and family arrive for a joyful get-together.

Copy for All Ages

Much effort has gone into figuring out how to sell to different age groups—you've probably heard expressions like "the crucial 18 to 34 demographic." Being aware of the different mind-sets and motivations among younger and older consumers is important for marketers, and it takes ongoing effort because history and society is always evolving, and what's true about 18- to 34-year-olds today might not be true tomorrow. With a disclaimer to that effect—and a reminder that these are generalizations with plenty of exceptions—in the following sections I give you a rundown of some of the traits and trends that have been observed about consumers of different ages.

Seniors

Seniors are identified as cost-conscious, practical, conservative, and religious. They're not expected to respond well to hedonistic messages such as *indulge yourself* or *splurge*. With the Great Depression and World War II shaping their generation, they tend to be savers, not spenders, and they tend to be idealists and sacrificers, putting family and community above selfish concerns and comforts. But get ready for a changing senior population because those infamous baby boomers are getting older every day …

Boomers

Born between 1946 and 1964, baby boomers are a huge force in the population, and marketers have been courting and coddling them since the earliest days of television. Having grown up in an unusually prosperous era, they spend pretty freely, not worrying too much about the future. Personal sacrifice isn't a big theme for them—it's not something they had to learn much about, being born into smaller, more affluent postwar families where shared bedrooms and hand-me-downs weren't as common.

Their milestone events were things such as Vietnam protests and Woodstock, and they identify with attitudes like those expressed in the sayings *Question authority* and *Do your own thing*. Boomers have fond memories of their rebellious younger years, and appealing to that self-image has helped a lot of companies make millions, even after the "hippie generation" had already morphed into the "yuppie generation." David Brooks's book, *Bobos in Paradise*, is an interesting exploration of the way this generation's contradictions have affected marketing and culture in general.

Generation X

It's a sign of just how much boomers dominate the culture that this smaller generation is often referred to as the post-boomers. Born between 1965 and 1975 (some extend the range to 1980 or 1981), Gen-Xers are a sharp contrast to the generation before them, a generation whose shadow they have always lived in. The media has associated them with fads like grunge music and tattoos, but more serious studies have revealed the events, both personal and historical, that set them apart.

For one thing, they came of age in a recession and face poorer economic prospects than their parents did. As a result they are very practical and cautious with their money. They are the offspring of the first generation to get divorced in such huge numbers, and as a result, sociologists have argued, they're also cautious about committing to relationships, marrying later than generations before them, if they marry at all. AIDS made them a bit skeptical about the previous generation's utopian visions of free love, and growing up in a media-soaked world made them cynical. Many of them have returned to traditional religious observance or some sort of spiritual endeavor, probably for complex reasons having to do with the highly materialistic era they emerged from and what they perceive as the damage that resulted. (But they don't approach religion as unquestioningly as seniors might because they saw the televangelist scandals of the 1980s unfold before their eyes on TV.)

When they look around, they see broken families, STDs, mounting personal and national debt, and looming environmental disaster, so their outlook can be a lot bleaker than that of the sunny Woodstock generation. Gen-Xers are quite comfortable with having friends of the opposite gender and are also more comfortable with different races, religions, and sexual preferences than their older counterparts. And they are not the sort to feel a sense of loyalty to a corporation or a brand name—observing the downsizings and mergers and hostile takeovers of the past couple of decades have put an end to any illusions about that.

As with boomers, though, this generation has its contradictions. Despite their spiritual interests, they may be more materialistic than any generation before it, thanks to the inescapable consumer culture we live in. And though they may look beyond outward appearances when it comes to issues of prejudice and multiculturalism, one suspects that this generation can't help but be highly appearance-conscious in a different way, having grown up in the age of MTV, supermodels, plastic surgery, and celebrity obsession.

Generation Y

Sociologists—and marketers, of course—are already zooming in on the next batch of young consumers coming down the pike, those born in the late 1970s and onward (I'm sure Generation Z will be announced any day now). They've commented that Gen Y is marked by multiculturalism (growing up on the Internet has allowed them to be in touch with the world in a way no generation before them ever could), comfort with rapid change as technology evolves around them with lightning speed, attention deficit (thanks to their love of video games), and low literacy (they don't read a lot of books—probably because they're too busy with the Internet and the video games). Only time will tell how much merit these generalizations and predictions have.

And today's kids will most certainly be shaped to some extent by September 11—but how? Will they be more fearful or decide to live for today? Will they be hostile to foreigners or will their multicultural outlook allow them to accommodate and accept the complexities and gray areas of world politics?

These Kids Today ...

Generations X and Y present special challenges to advertisers, for several reasons. They're the generations most inoculated against sales pitches—many boomers can still recall the advent of TV and are actually still a little in thrall to its magical glow, but kids today have been channel-surfing since they were old enough to hold a remote. That's another reason they're a tough market: they know how to work that remote very well. They'll change the channel or press the mute button when an ad comes on unless it grabs their interest right away. They know how to fend off spam and close pop-up ads, and they have iPods and satellite and Internet radio, so there's no need to sit through a string of noisy commercials on WBUY.

So what can you do to get through to these tough customers? Try these tips:

- **Play it straight.** Telling them they've been *specially selected* for this credit card offer will just make them laugh. Implying that *all the cool kids are doing it* will probably make them *not* want to do it. Get to the point, and be honest.

- **Don't pretend your corporation has a soul.** These markets *know* they're markets, and they know marketing is about making money. Don't play sappy music and try to convince them that your company "cares." Just tell them what you're offering. If you really want to convince them you care, change your policies and practices and try to get yourself onto one of those lists of the most socially responsible companies.

- **Entertain them.** Remember Kurt Cobain's line: "Here we are now, entertain us"? Younger consumers have had no shortage of entertainment options, and they're more likely to pay attention to ads that are funny or at least fun. Avoid the same old same-old. (Just don't make the mistake of letting the fun drown out the main message.)

The Experts Agree

Most advertising is so bland that you can smell the fear coming off of it.
—Mike, former copy chief, current magazine editor

I respond poorly to overused ideas, like "Think *(insert just about any phrase here)*? Think again." That has got to be the most overused idea in advertising. I'm sure I've used it at least 10 times.
—Beth, writer/editor

♦ **Don't condescend.** Perhaps it's a result of following on the heels of the monolithic—and sometimes self-righteous—boomers, but for whatever reason, Generations X and Y are prickly about being talked down to or trivialized. One of the mistakes marketers made when they discovered Generation X was falling all over themselves to market to Generation X—too often in shallow, stereotyped ways that made Gen-Xers feel mocked instead of understood. Suddenly everyone had a skateboard, and everything was *extreme*.

The Experts Agree

When an ad doesn't talk down, when an ad is obviously taking a risk, I respect that.
—Sarah, creative manager

Never forget that successful sales come from making a one-on-one connection, and relying too much on caricatured perceptions about younger consumers (or older ones, for that matter) can damage your chances of making that connection, just like any other stereotype.

♦ **Don't fall into the irony trap.** Young folks today have a reputation for sneering and jeering at anything corny or kitschy, and many presume that copping a snotty attitude is a good way to sell them something. In reality, I believe, there's a certain anger at the contrast between the glossy, idealized images of 1950s and 1960s pop culture and the ugly realities that have replaced them, leading to some eye-rolling and sarcastic comments. But that doesn't mean young people don't wish for what's represented by those corny images. They might know that *The Brady Bunch* is imaginary and unrealistic, but at the same time, they might find the idea of a large, intact family very emotionally appealing, especially considering the odds are low they had anything like that themselves.

One of the authors most popular today among young people is Dave Eggers, whose writing is highly personal and emotional. Be aware that corniness might turn off twentysomethings, but genuine feelings might not.

That's a good overview of the age demographics out there—but remember that while history keeps changing, some distinctions between old and young are a lot more constant. No matter what the political trends of the day, younger people always tend to be less conservative—in the sense that they are more willing to try new things, are more open-minded, and are less set in their ways, simply by virtue of the fact that they've been knocked around less by life. They tend to be less concerned about their health and about money because even those who grew up worrying about carcinogenic foods and the future of Social Security are still *young*—unlined, unsettled, unburdened by stiff joints, unable to imagine that one day they actually will want to retire. And they tend to dream about sex, romance, and adventure—while older folks dream about getting a good night's sleep.

Selling to the Sexes

It's not just marketers who are constantly trying to figure out what makes men and women different—psychologists, educators, standup comedians, and just about everyone has been doing it since time immemorial. Plenty of mysteries remain to be solved, but here are some common theories that might help guide you as a copywriter.

Women Like Shopping More

Women make most of the purchases. Women spend more time in a store than men do and are more likely to browse and try things on. So when all else is equal, you're safer aiming your product at women, if you have to choose—but modern marketers must keep some trends in mind. Paco Underhill's book *Why We Buy* (see Appendix B) points out that because people get married later and divorce more often—and because women more commonly work outside the home—those selling traditionally "feminine" products have to be careful not to get too frilly because it just might be a man who's actually buying it.

Underhill observes that kitchen appliances have become more masculine and high-tech-looking, that ads for smaller appliances tend to emphasize their "power," and that even paper towels are sold under the name "Brawny." On the flip side, he notes that sisters are doin' it for themselves—a trend, he argues, that's partly responsible for the huge success of The Home Depot, a friendlier, more style-conscious sort of hardware store.

Before you take anything for granted about who's buying your product, look for solid information and write your copy accordingly—or play it safe and make your pitch gender-neutral.

Women Are More Verbal; Men Are More Visual

There's still plenty of debate on the differences between men's and women's brains, but as someone who works in the publishing world, I can tell you that women are much bigger readers than men are. And it's often been noticed that men find sexy pictures and images way more compelling than women do. (You hardly ever hear jokes about women driving into trees because they were distracted by the cute guy walking down the street.)

I myself don't fit into every gender stereotype, but I do fit into the one about women being less visually spatially oriented—maps, for example, befuddle me, and I'd much rather have a set of directions written out on a piece of paper. So if you're addressing women, you may have more leeway verbally—you can use more words, bigger words, and a greater degree of verbal complexity. But if your campaign is aimed at men, it might be more effective to use a chart or a graph (along with a picture of the product—maybe with a pretty lady next to it).

Another interesting observation in Underhill's *Why We Buy* is that women look at price tags when they shop more than men do. It could be that women are just more skilled, practical shoppers, but Underhill theorizes that looking at price tags makes men feel unmanly. ("Who cares about the price? I can afford it!") If this is true, a print ad or catalog aimed at men might be a good place to include price information—so men can comparison-shop without letting anyone see them doing it.

Men Are More Competitive; Women Are More Cooperative

True? Well, one could argue that women just compete in more subtle ways (talking about other women behind their backs rather than dissing them to their faces) or that plenty of women are up for a good fight—just watch an episode of *Jerry Springer*. You could even point out that the military and team sports—traditional male activities—show that men have a superior sense of cooperation. But reports from scientists give some credence to the theory, with some even speculating that it's as much a result of our biological natures as our social conditioning.

So what might this mean for advertising and marketing? It could mean that men are more tuned into hierarchy and, thus, more responsive to products that are (or claim to be) the best, the most, or the first. It could mean that men will respond better to stories about winning, whereas women will respond more to stories about settling differences in ways that preserve relationships.

But as with any generalization, take it with a grain of salt. And keep in mind that we all yearn for balance, so what shows on the surface isn't necessarily what we truly long for—sometimes it's the opposite. Men who are constantly pressured to "win" or "be the best" (whether by society or by their genes) might be more open than you'd expect to a message that emphasizes friendship and family. Women who are expected to be "nice" might welcome an opportunity once in a while to take charge or grab the spotlight. As always, understanding what makes us different—young or old, male or female—can be valuable, but understanding what makes us the same—what makes us human—is even more so.

The Least You Need to Know

- Get to know the four steps to persuasion—attention, comprehension, acceptance, and retention. Neglecting any of them can decrease the effectiveness of your copy.

- In tailoring your message to different age groups, be aware of large-scale trends, but don't put too much stock in stereotypes.

- Old assumptions about male and female shoppers don't always hold true, so think carefully when trying to appeal to one gender or the other.

- Remember that what shows on the surface doesn't always reflect what's really going on in the consumer's mind and heart.

Chapter 6

Tricks of the Trade

In This Chapter

- ◆ Features of your ad, from the headline to the call to action
- ◆ Bullets, bursts, and other attention-getters
- ◆ Techniques to try: rhyme, repetition, wordplay, and more
- ◆ Cautions: tricks can backfire

Everyone loves a shortcut. And many shortcuts are available to copywriters—fast, simple ways to make ads read better and work better. Some are techniques poets or novelists also use, such as rhyme and alliteration. Others, such as lists and taglines, are more visually oriented and have to do less with the words than with the way you present them.

In this chapter, I give you 18 shortcuts, with advice on when, where, how, and why to use—or not use—them.

Headlines

The headline is, in almost all cases, the most crucial part of your presentation. For just a few words, it's doing a lot of work—grabbing attention, subtly identifying and attracting your target customers, and conveying information that encourages them to read on. Not every headline is going to accomplish all these goals every time, but these are the goals you need to keep in mind when you're cooking one up.

Let's start with grabbing attention. Certain words grab attention all by themselves, like *free, celebrity, money, sex, power, beauty.* (Thus the classic joke headline: *SEX … now that I've got your attention.*) Unfortunately, these powerful words have lost some of their power—mainly thanks to all the copywriters out there using them in headlines. There's so much advertising and media around nowadays that it seems people see and hear these words every 12 seconds or so, and they're a little jaded. That's not to say these words can't still be very effective, but you might have to do a little more work than just plunking them into your headline.

You'll need to find ways, both straightforward and subtle, to make busy, harried people slow down and take another look. Here are some ways to do that:

- ◆ **Attract them** with language, images, and possibilities that are so marvelously appealing they want to stop and dwell on your ad for a while. For example: *Sit back and relax. A ray of lemon-fresh sunshine. Fall in love all over again. Finally, relief from nagging headaches. Ripe, sweet strawberries … in any season. Work less— earn more. Never go hungry again.*

- ◆ **Provoke them** with words and phrases that kick-start the mind and the emotions, making them feel a need to act or respond. Use strong statements or questions. *How many times have your health-care premiums gone up in the past 5 years? Facts the fat cats don't want you to know. Are you really satisfied with your broker's performance? What would you do if you were the president? You don't have to go broke heating your house this winter.*

- ◆ **Intrigue them** with a touch of mystery and a promise of interesting information to come. *I never thought it would happen to me. Do you have any of these symptoms? Three ways your bank may be failing you. Who loves you more? What's hiding in your backyard? All you need is …*

Attracting attention isn't always difficult to do. But when you're marketing a product or service, your task goes far beyond attracting attention. After all, plenty of things succeed in attracting our attention every day—a motorcycle roaring by, a playful puppy taking his morning walk, a gigantic pile of trash. It doesn't mean we want to buy the motorcycle, the puppy, or the pile of trash, though.

You want to get not just anyone, but *potential customers,* to invest the time in reading what you have to say, and tailoring your headline to those particular people is important.

A sign in the window of the hardware store that says *Great prices on tools* is good. A sign that says *Great prices on screwdrivers* might be better. Attract the attention of people who are already in the market for screwdrivers, and you're halfway there. It's like placing a personal ad that says *Great-looking guy, many interests, looking for relationship with free-spirited young woman* vs. one that says *5'10" bearded-hippie-type who likes jazz and Asian cooking looking for no-commitment fun with artsy woman under 30*. The second ad is going to result in a lot less wasted time for everyone.

Likewise, if no one under 50 is likely to be interested in your product or if you're on a mission to increase a company's market share among the over-50 crowd, don't waste your time trying to get *everyone* to read it. Suppose a phone company wants to appeal to older people who are resistant to using cell phones. Target the ad to these buyers by saying *Now you can talk to your grandchildren everywhere you go* rather than just *Enjoy the convenience of portable phone service*. Or emphasize the ease of use, because impatience or difficulty with new technology is a common obstacle standing between many older people and newfangled gadgets. You might say *Press the green button and talk away*. Or *If your 5-year-old granddaughter can use a cell phone—so can you!*

Why Pay More?

When you're seeking to zero in on the people most likely to respond to your offer, targeted placement sometimes does the work for you. If you own a small business, advertise your wares with demographics in mind. Who are your best bets: teenage girls? Churchgoers? Parents of elementary-school children? Overweight adults? Determine what your target customers read, watch, and listen to. Figure out where they spend most of their time and what they like and dislike. Then build your efforts around their lifestyles to make them far more likely to come across your message. If you're working with a large client, get information about their overall strategy and where they plan to buy ad space, and tailor your ad accordingly. If your ad for a set of Civil War figurines is going to appear in *Civil War Buffs Monthly*, you can skip some of the preliminaries and get right to the nitty-gritty.

When you've gotten the attention of the right people, you want those people to stay with you. A headline that asks *Are you over 50?* will indeed strike a chord with someone over 50—especially someone who turned 50 fairly recently and still hasn't quite gotten over it. But by giving them a further incentive to listen to your pitch and holding their attention, you're less likely to lose them to a private reverie: *Why yes, I am over 50. Unbelievable but true. Where did the time go? Hey, 50's not so old. So I'm feeling a little stiff and flabby lately, so what? I really have to get back to the gym …*

So suppose your ad or brochure just happens to be for a new gym specially designed for mature customers? Start out with something such as *Keep fit after 50* or *Get the body of a high school cheerleader ... just in time for your fortieth reunion.* That way, the flabby, 50-something potential customer continues focusing on your ad, rather than being distracted and drifting away.

No matter what your headline, you'll want to keep it short, simple, and snappy. With all the text flying at them in the course of a day, people make very quick decisions about what to skim and forget about and what to keep reading. Confuse them, bore them, or annoy them, and you'll risk losing them—fast.

Taglines

Taglines are the little "kickers" at the end of your copy, and their main purpose is to leave a lasting impression. They might just be a catchy slogan designed to stick in the reader's head, they might summarize the overall message of the ad, or they might echo your ad's headline or repeat a piece of the copy to reinforce it. If you succeed in getting someone to read your whole ad—and that's a great accomplishment—you don't want them to finish with a mental shrug or a "So what?" A good tagline is your way of saying "That's what!"

Continuing with one of the examples from the "Headlines" section, here's an ad in which the headline, body, and tagline work together:

Are you over 50?

More important, do you feel over 50?

Stiff? Sore? Slower than you used to be? It doesn't have to be that way—and at Body Wisdom, you'll find everything from saunas to sculpting classes to renew your strength, energy, and endurance. All in a relaxed, luxurious atmosphere where you can set your own pace ... and see rejuvenating results in just weeks.

BODY WISDOM

Feel fabulous

Lists

People love lists. The *Billboard* charts, *The New York Times* best-seller list, the *Fortune 500*—the evidence is everywhere. The people who published the smash bestseller *The*

Book of Lists in the 1970s knew it; David Letterman knows it; and every copywriter should know it, too.

Some ads have even used Letterman's Top Ten List format for inspiration, creating entertaining (or not-so-entertaining) versions pertaining to what they were selling. You needn't be that ambitious if you're not up to comedy writing just yet. Simply by using lists when they make sense in your copy, you greatly increase the likelihood of attracting readers. Perhaps it's the sense of order implied by a numbered list, or perhaps it's the simple fact that short bits of text with space in between are easier to digest. If your assignment lends itself to a list, make use of the opportunity. You might list …

- **Benefits of the product:** All the things it will do for the customer.

- **Features of the product:** Stain-resistant surface, removable leaf, skid-free security for a kitchen table.

- **Contents of a package:** The songs on a CD, the types of treats in a gift basket, the stops on a local walking tour. It says "look at all you get!"

- **Choices:** A nice way to get the reader involved. A recent campaign to increase tourism to the Bahamas tells us to find ourselves on one of its 700 islands. No, it doesn't list all the islands, but it offers a variety of photos and descriptions, which can really get you engaged in figuring out which is your perfect island. Once you've discovered it, you might as well book the trip, right?

Bullets

Bullets—short items preceded by some kind of icon or dingbat (sometimes a simple bullet shape, hence the name)—follow many of the same principles and are effective for the same reasons as lists. However, a single bullet can stand on its own if you just want to highlight something (much like the star you draw in the margin next to something important). Bullets can also be a way to put plain old body copy into a more accessible, quick-hit form.

Instead of:

Discover new places and make new friends on About Town Tours—our fleet of five boats sails every weekend, offering food and drink, dancing, and day trips to fantastic destinations!

You might try:

- Drink

- Dance

- Dine

- Discover new places and people

ABOUT TOWN TOURS

You can also make bullets informational and mix and match them with more "selling" bullets:

◆ Drink, dance, dine

◆ Discover new places and people

◆ A great day trip for under $50

◆ Five boats to choose from—five fantastic destinations

Bullets are also handy as a way to break up longer text within a brochure or sales letter. If you were making a pitch for the aforementioned Body Wisdom, the gym for the over-50 crowd, you might use bullets to highlight some sales points:

◆ Special knee- and back-strengthening equipment

◆ Low-impact classes available

◆ On-site moisturizing treatments and massage

◆ Certified physical therapist on-site

Bursts

You've seen bursts, even if you didn't know that's what they were called. They're the circles on the box that say *SPECIAL DEAL 2.99*, the screen-shaped icon that reads *AS SEEN ON TV,* or the sun-shaped sticker that cries *NOW WITH 50% MORE CALCIUM!* Bursts give prominence of place to important selling points—the better to catch the customer's eye. The very fact that they appear in this form makes them seem automatically important—much like the way a news story seems more important when it's on the front page.

Keep any information you use in a burst very short and very straightforward. A burst negates its purpose if it's filled with tiny, unreadable type or a muddled message. *NEW AND IMPROVED* is classic burst content. *MADE WITH WHOLE GRAIN* or *VALUE SIZE* are burst-worthy. In most cases, bursts contain facts rather than fluff, but you can use bursts in playful ways as well. There's no law against putting a burst that says *SCRUMPTIOUS!* on a bag of cookies, so if something creative "bursts" into your head, give it a try.

> **Why Pay More?**
>
> Bursts often work well when they have a "newsy" feel, both in their clipped, breathless wording and their "late-breaking" feeling, as if the burst was slapped on at the last minute to announce new developments. Sometimes it was—as on CD packages that feature a *CONTAINS THEIR HIT "SO AND SO"* burst.

Rhyme

Rhyme helps people remember. Have you ever wondered what was up with all those ancient cultures constantly writing epic poems? Think of it this way: if you don't have printing presses yet and you have to pass on the tales and legends orally from generation to generation, wouldn't it be a lot easier to memorize something that rhymes? Nowadays rhyme is often recommended as a mnemonic, or memory-enhancing, device—if you meet a big muscular guy named Hank, remember his name by thinking of him as Hank the Tank.

> **Free Sample!**
>
> One ad campaign, now looked on with fond nostalgia, featured highway signs pushing Burma Shave. It lasted for decades, until 1963, and a set of the signs is even on display at the Smithsonian. These signs, meant to be read in sequence by drivers passing by, featured funny rhymes that became a part of the culture. Today, a TV commercial for a cholesterol medication tells a little story completely in verse.

Rhyme can be a fun technique for advertising, but approach it with caution. Too much rhyme can have a hypnotic, singsong effect that overwhelms the message, and that's not something you want. And in most writing—but especially copywriting—it's important not to use style at the expense of content. If you're busy trying to stick to a rhyme scheme, you're less likely to communicate clearly. You'll be choosing words for their phonetic qualities rather than their persuasive qualities. Rhyme can be done, but it's a serious challenge.

However, rhyme doesn't have to be a series of couplets and verses. You can use something called internal rhyme, in which the rhyming words appear close to each other rather than following that strict "A-B," end-of-each-line pattern you studied in high school.

> Skin feeling slack, dry, cracked? Try Filomena's Firming Lotion and get your supple skin back.

Okay, maybe I took it a step too far there, but I can't help it, rhyming is fun.

Another type of rhyme to keep in mind is slant rhyme, which essentially means an imperfect rhyme. Rather than *moon* and *June*, a slant rhyme involves words with similar sounds—*room* and *soon*. You can also use quick tricks (there I go again) to make your copy more memorable and enjoyable to read by inserting rhyming phrases, like *a whale of a sale*, *clean and green*, and the proven-effective-in-stadiums-across-America *Beer here!*

Numbers

There's something reassuring about numbers. Words can be vague, slippery, and tricky, but numbers are verifiable facts. When you have an impressive sales point that you can convey with an actual number, use it. It's much more persuasive than saying *lots of* or *many*.

> Over a million copies sold!
>
> 15 convenient locations
>
> Available in eight eye-catching colors
>
> 27" screen
>
> 95% customer satisfaction rate

In most cases, you'll want to put numbers in numeral form—*15* rather than *fifteen*—because numerals will be more noticeable in the text. And of course, the most important thing about using numbers in your marketing copy is that they must be accurate, so triple-check them before handing in your copy!

Testimonials

Testimonials are a time-honored technique for advertisers. After all, no matter how sincere and convincing you are, everyone knows an ad is trying to sell something.

Bringing in an objective third party to sing your product's praises can make a big difference.

The most convincing testimonial is independently verifiable. That is, it comes from a media outlet, an organization, or a prominent figure. I deal with testimonials all the time in the form of book reviews, and as a customer, I also know that I'm much more likely to consider buying a book when it's plastered with raves from *The New York Times, Chicago Tribune, Entertainment Weekly*, and the like. Or if I'm looking in the history section, quotes on the back cover from prominent, respected historians will convince me that this is a book I should take seriously.

Sometimes these testimonials come in the form of quotes, but they can also come in the form of an award or honor that implies an endorsement. For example, Combos tell us on the package that it's the cheese-filled snack of NASCAR. (I don't eat Combos because they're the cheese-filled snack of NASCAR—I just eat them because they're yummy.) Many products are the official so-and-so of the Olympics or Major League Baseball. Honors such as *New York Times* Notable Book, *Motor Trend* Car of the Year, and the *Good Housekeeping* Seal are all testimonials that help sell. That's why when the Academy announces its annual nominees, the ads for the movies immediately trumpet the nominations in gigantic type.

These types of testimonials, of course, aren't always readily available. They come at the mercy of such authorities as *The New York Times* or involve high-level corporate negotiations. But your product or service may have testimonials available to take advantage of. Look at community awards and honors or reviews in local papers. If the heroes at the local firehouse order in from your pizzeria all the time, you might be able to parlay that into fodder for an ad (just be sure it's legally permissible for them to publicly endorse your pizza). Celebrity endorsements work because of something known in psychological circles as the "halo effect"—the tendency of people to think that if someone has one positive quality (like good looks or a lovely singing voice), all their qualities are positive, including their judgment of the best peanut butter. Plus, celebrities— even relatively minor ones—are immediate attention-getters.

> **Why Pay More?**
>
> You needn't have a multi-million-dollar contract with a superstar to put the power of testimonials to work for you if you make the most of what's available and use your creativity.

There are two cautionary notes to keep in mind when using testimonials. One: whenever you are quoting or referring to an outside party, you must confirm that it is legal, acceptable, and wise to do so. For example, if you happen to overhear a major celebrity reflecting in a candid moment on how much he likes your potato chips, it doesn't mean you can rush back to the office and plaster his face on your company's ad. The Federal Trade Commission (FTC) website, listed in Appendix A, offers some guidelines about the use of testimonials. Two: you can't edit someone's quote. Anything between two quotation marks must be an exact reproduction of the original text. Ellipses and brackets can usually be used to adapt quotes into more manageable form if necessary, but you may not change the meaning of the quote in any way by editing.

> **CAUTION**
>
> **Accept No Imitations!**
>
> Use caution in all repro-duction of other people's words. For guidance on how quotes may be properly edited, refer to *The Chicago Manual of Style.*

Alliteration

Alliteration is the writer's technique of repeating the sound of a single letter—strictly speaking, the first letter of a word. It's frequently employed by copywriters and is a simple way to make your writing punchier. Enjoy our *superb steaks,* rather than our *delicious steaks. Make every moment count,* rather than *Make every second count.*

You can also go beyond the first-letter technique to achieve an alliterative effect. Try *blissfully soft* rather than *wonderfully soft* or *crisp, ripe apples* rather than *fresh apples.*

> **CAUTION**
>
> **Accept No Imitations!**
>
> Don't overuse allitera-tion. Used sparingly, it's very effective. Used too much, it turns your copy into a tongue-twister and detracts from the substance of your message.

The sounds of letters can carry subtle messages in themselves. In the previous examples, the *s* sound suggests softness and the *p* sound is crisp. They both reinforce the content of their respective phrases. When choosing words, you may want to factor in the way they sound, the "hard" or "soft" qualities of their actual letters, in relation to the sensual effect you're going for.

Onomatopoeia

Remember this one from high school English? Onomatopoeic words *sound* like what they *are.* The classic example is *buzz.* Onomatopoeia can be useful in advertising writ-ing, especially when you want something sensually evocative—like *splash* for a cold drink or *crunch* for popcorn.

Free Sample!

Plop, plop, fizz, fizz

Oh what a relief it is

Alka-Seltzer used onomatopoeia to great effect in this classic slogan. The actual sound of the tablets dropping into the water glass and dissolving is closely associated in our collective mind with the comfort of our bellyache going away, thanks to this ad.

Repetition

You memorize a poem by reading it repeatedly. You reinforce (or change) a habit with repeated effort. Repetition is often necessary for something to really stick, so even in a short piece of copy, you may need to emphasize and reinforce your message with repetition.

The downside of repetition? It's boring. Or at least it can be if not employed carefully. If you want to emphasize a point by repeating it, try altering the wording while keeping the meaning. If one of your main selling points is low price, you might use the word *bargain* in the headline and then work in the terms *low-cost* and *the inexpensive alternative* in the body of the ad. Or illustrate the message with a comparison chart showing your price vs. the competition's.

However, sometimes you can use repetition of exact wording deliberately, to good effect, as in slogans such as *Beautiful clothes—beautiful prices*. Deliberate repetition is deliberately noticeable and is sometimes meant to be dramatic in tone:

> You have auto insurance.
>
> You have homeowner's insurance.
>
> You have health insurance.
>
> But do you have the most important insurance of all?

Parody

A parody imitates the style of something else for humorous effect. Usually it's meant to satirize the original, but some parodies just use an existing work as a jumping-off point for their own purposes.

A crucial thing for advertising writers to remember about parody is that although it's protected by law for artistic works, commercial works are a whole different matter. You can't simply change the words of a hit song and use it in your ad.

Free Sample!

Don't stay home without it.

This delightful, just-plain-brilliant takeoff on one of the all-time classic advertising slogans, American Express's *Don't leave home without it,* appeared in an ad for the *TV Guide Film and Video Companion.*

However, some things, such as old proverbs or commonly used recognizable styles that are not specifically trademarked by anyone, can be safely parodied or used as jumping-off points for creativity. The insurance company Geico makes excellent use of parody in its series of commercials that make fun of commercials. A doctorly looking man pontificates about the problem of hair loss and then announces that there's good news. The good news is that he just saved a ton of money on his car insurance. Energizer Batteries did the same a while back, starting out with what appeared to be a cliché-laden commercial for another product, which was then interrupted by the marching Energizer Bunny.

You might be able to use a recognizable form like a commencement speech or a comic book to present your message in a lively, memorable manner, as long as it's not derived from someone's real speech or an actual existing comic. Parody is fun, and it offers an instantly familiar form that helps give the reader or viewer something to grasp onto, pulling him into the ad. Just tread carefully, and don't wind up in court.

Wordplay

People might groan at puns, but even those who roll their eyes often secretly enjoy them. What's good about puns is that they can wake up the brain a little. The experience of being thrown a little off-course by a pun is mildly startling and then getting it a half-second later is quite satisfying.

The key phrase in that sentence is *a half-second later*. Complicated or obscure puns turn people off more often than turn them on. People like to be a little challenged, but they don't want to get a headache or feel inadequate for not being able to figure out your clever little play on words. Use puns that are easy for the average person to get. Unless you're writing to a particularly sophisticated, educated, or specialized audience, avoid puns that play on foreign languages or little-known expressions.

Puns can add a touch of liveliness and playfulness to your copy and can help people remember your message and your brand name. Geico, the car-insurance company mentioned previously, uses a gecko as a mascot. This is especially smart advertising because Geico in itself is not a particularly memorable or meaningful company name, but the connection with *gecko* makes it much easier to recall.

The Experts Agree

There is a very fine line between a really bad pun and a really brilliant one.

—Beth, writer/editor

Humor

I just love a funny commercial. Some of them have me practically falling off the couch laughing. The problem is, when I tell other people about them, I often have to precede it with, "Have you seen that hilarious commercial—I don't know what it's for, but ..."

Humorous ads may become popularly beloved and even get awards, but your client won't be laughing if the ad doesn't serve its main purpose and increase sales. I would never discourage you from using humor (though you might want to avoid it if you're writing, say, a brochure for a chain of funeral homes), but if you do, follow these important guidelines:

◆ **Make the humor a vehicle for selling—don't make the selling a vehicle for humor.** Geico ads are quite funny, but their running punch line is directly related to the sales message, and that's what makes them good ads. Integrate the brand into the core of the message so that when the funny part is remembered, the brand is, too.

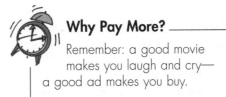

Why Pay More?

Remember: a good movie makes you laugh and cry— a good ad makes you buy.

◆ **Don't offend.** No matter how benignly it's meant, humor involving ethnic groups, controversial subjects, or other sensitive topics can backfire very easily. If you're a black copywriter working for a black-owned company and your ad's going to appear in a magazine for black audiences, you may be able to get away with some lighthearted ethnic humor, but in most selling situations do not use references to skin color, religion, national origin, gender, sexual orientation, or age in attempts at humor. You risk alienating your customers or making them wonder how your joke is really meant. Likewise, personal insults don't usually work well. Even if you're not directly insulting your target audience, humor that has a hostile tinge can be a huge turnoff. This may seem obvious, but sometimes advertisers don't realize the implications of their attempts at humor. They might try to appeal to a customer's ego by flattering his intelligence and in the process convey a snide attitude toward people who aren't so smart. These kinds of attitudes, rather than having a flattering effect, usually make people feel defensive and insecure.

◆ **Remember humor has an expiration date.** Some kinds of humor can be enjoyed again and again; other kinds go stale very quickly. In addition, humor that depends on current events or pop culture will fade as quickly as the news and trends it's based on. This won't matter so much in a one-time ad or quick-hit campaign, but if the sales material you're working on is meant to have some shelf life, be cautious about the kind of humor you use.

When going for laughs in an ad, you'll have the best chance of success with gentle, observational, universal humor. A good technique is to present the problem (a messy spill, being sleepy at work, trying to do your own taxes) in a humorous way and then lead immediately into the solution, which is, of course, your product or service. Essentially, a humorous ad should be more Ellen DeGeneres or Bob Newhart than Richard Pryor or Lenny Bruce.

Added Value

You're writing to sell something. But why not give something away in the process? Ads that include something valuable have a few strong advantages. First, they create a feeling of goodwill—the customer appreciates the little bonus. Second, they encourage interactivity and get the customer to spend more time on the ad. Third, they sometimes get clipped out and saved or posted on refrigerators or bulletin boards so that even more people see them.

Here are some things you can include as an "added value":

◆ A recipe

◆ A joke

- An inspirational or funny saying set in large, attractive type

- A how-to tip

- A checklist that people can use again and again, like "What to pack for an out-of-town weekend"

- A handy reference, like a tip-calculation chart or a list of ingredient substitutions for baking

If the added-value item is actually a sample of your overall service or product, all the better. If not, try to make your service or product a part of the added-value item by working the brand name into it somewhere or just including it near the text.

Gimmicks

The word *gimmick* has a bit of a bad connotation, often being associated with deception and trickery. But as long as your trick isn't *too* tricky, it can be a fine way to make your ad stand out.

Harmless gimmicks include, for example, "teaser" campaigns that offer mysterious messages leading up to the main advertisement. Another gimmick is to set up the copy in some kind of flashy form, making it read upside down or backward or modeling it after a resumé or a menu.

You can try gimmicks once in a while as long as they don't deceive (or disappoint, frustrate, or annoy) your audience. Be wary also of gimmicks that let the reader down or pull in the wrong audience—for example, a headline that says *Get Rich Now!* followed by an ad for rich, creamy salad dressing.

Questions

As a general rule, sales materials should answer questions, not ask them. But some types of questions can draw customers in and get them involved. These include provocative questions such as *Is your child's future secure?* or hypothetical questions such as *Why pay more?*

Another way you can effectively use questions is by posing them and then answering them:

> Why are dentists enthusiastically recommending Blinding Grin more than any other whitening system?
>
> *(Because it gets your teeth three shades whiter than other brands—in half the time!)*

What gives a great player the confidence it takes to win?

(Sturdy, comfortable sneakers ... like ours!)

You can also use *Wouldn't you rather ...* questions to compare your product or service favorably to others. Say you're trying to sell sensible cars to young, fashion-conscious female buyers:

Wouldn't you rather invest your money in designer pumps than gas pumps?

(Then buy our fuel-saving hybrid, not a huge gas guzzler, and drive straight to the mall!)

Calls to Action

An effective ad doesn't just inform—or even convince—the reader. It also spurs him to action. You might write a good ad that gets someone to believe that a weekend at your inn would be quite pleasant, but you will usually need a little extra push to get him on the path to making an actual reservation.

A call to action can be as subtle as a tagline that says *Look for it in your grocer's freezer* or *Try Shiny-Locks Conditioner today*. It can be a limited-offer alert such as *Sale ends January 15* or *Free gifts for the first 100 customers to respond*. It also can be a device that makes an immediate response easier: a toll-free number, website address, or coupon.

Some products and services pose a challenge to advertisers because of the natural human tendency to procrastinate. Making out a will, doing one's taxes, quitting smoking, joining a gym ... we'll get around to it one of these days. These might require putting extra thought into, and emphasis on, the call to action. Chiding the customer for tempting fate can sometimes work: *Don't pay late penalties ... there's still time to call Render Unto Caesar Tax Preparers.*

Don't get too carried away with scare tactics, though: *What are you waiting for, a heart attack? Join our gym now!* Motivating and encouraging is good; making people even more anxious about the situation usually backfires and sends them running back to the happy world of denial. Take it from one who's comforted herself with many an Oreo after receiving unpleasant news from the scale.

The Least You Need to Know

- Don't sacrifice substance for style—remember your job is selling, not entertaining.

- Put extra effort into your headline; so much depends on it.

- Techniques such as rhyme and humor are effective only if they don't overwhelm the message or the product.

- Use most tricks of the trade sparingly for maximum impact.

- Certain techniques, like testimonials and parodies, require legal research and extreme caution.

- Never get so clever that you make your reader feel clueless.

Chapter 7

Grammar and the Copywriter

In This Chapter

- Parts of speech and basic sentence structure
- The real purpose of grammar
- Which grammar rules you can break—and which you shouldn't
- Examples of grammar mistakes to avoid

You can be a brilliant musician without knowing how to read music, and you can be a naturally gifted writer without knowing the first thing about parts of speech or what the passive voice is. But in either case, learning the ropes and the rules will only enrich your skills. You might have absorbed a sense of what to do and not to do on your own, even if you spent your high school English classes doodling in your notebook and dreaming about the weekend. But knowing the grammatical terms and rules makes it far easier to collaborate with other writers or with editors because you can articulate what you're doing—instead of just saying, "I don't know, that word just doesn't seem right there."

Having a grasp of grammar will allow you to explain much more easily why you wrote something the way you did. And understanding the *why* behind the rules can also help you determine when you can break the rules without damaging the effectiveness of your writing. The real purpose of grammar is to make your writing clear to prevent miscommunication and confusion. That's why grammar rules exist. They're not there to limit your writing but to enhance it.

Unfortunately, even the rules meant to prevent confusion can at times seem confusing themselves. When it comes down to the nuts and bolts of grammar and style, plenty of ongoing disagreement and debate exist. Language is a living, changing thing, and different types of writing tend to follow different rules. Many professional writers use specific guides that tell them what standard style to follow. An academic writer might use the *MLA Handbook*, put out by the Modern Language Association. Journalists usually follow the *AP Stylebook*, from the Associated Press. In book publishing, *The Chicago Manual of Style* is the widely accepted reference.

The good news is that in copywriting, many of the rules don't apply and you don't need to pore over those kinds of texts and memorize everything. In fact, by-the-book grammar can often work against you in copywriting. But don't think you're getting off easy. You're still communicating with an audience, and that means you need to know and follow the basic rules so you don't wind up confusing or misleading your readers. Ground yourself in grammar, and you will be a more effective, adept, confident copywriter—it's worth the investment.

In this chapter, I do a quick review of the most essential points to know about grammar and talk about how grammatical and style rules relate to copywriting. Don't worry—I'm only covering the simple stuff here. But I do recommend you pick up one of the grammar books listed in Appendix A and spend a rainy Saturday with it sometime, learning about fun stuff like gerunds and intransitive verbs.

Grammar and Style Rules to Follow

You don't have to be Conan the Grammarian—just stick to the following guidelines, and most of the time you'll land on your feet.

Keep a Tight Rein on Your Sentences

At heart, grammar is really about logic. Words mean something, and their meanings can change depending on how they're combined with other words. As a copywriter, you want to keep your sentences short and simple because it makes them easier to read and digest. People reading ads want quick, useful, clear information. They don't want ads to make a lot of mental demands on them. If they enjoy language for the sake of language, they'll look for it in literature, not in a catalog. Artfully constructed paragraph-long sentences can be delightful in a literary novel, but rarely will they work in marketing materials.

Fortunately, keeping sentences short has an additional advantage—it helps you avoid the opportunities for error that can occur with complex sentences. The more complex your sentence, the better the odds that you'll make a grammatical error somewhere. It happens to the best of us. It may not be as challenging and fun to write short, simple sentences, but it's a necessity for a copywriter.

That said, a little complexity does make for livelier, more efficient writing, so you want to know the basic building blocks of a sentence. That way, when you write one, even a longer one, what you mean will still be completely clear. Here are the basic blocks:

- The foundation of a sentence is a *verb*—or "an action word" as your teachers might have called it. If there's no verb, there's no sentence. For example, in *The boy threw the ball*, the verb is *threw*.

- Building from the foundation up, the verb in a sentence always has a *subject*. And the subject is always a noun. The subject is what does the action. So in *The boy threw the ball*, *boy* is the subject.

- Next comes the *object* of the verb. That's what the action is done to. So the object in our sample sentence is *ball*.

- Sentences start getting fancier and more complex when you add things like *prepositional phrases*. Prepositions are those little words that place one thing in the sentence in relation to another thing. They usually deal with time (*after, before, until*) or space (*near, at, between, under*). Thus, The boy *on the pitcher's mound* threw the ball *to the first baseman*. In that sentence, *the pitcher's mound* is the object of the preposition *on*. *The first baseman* is the object of the preposition *to*. So verbs can have objects, and so can prepositions.

- Then you have adjectives and adverbs. *Adjectives* describe nouns, and *adverbs* describe verbs. So let's take that sentence to the next level: The *blond* boy on the pitcher's mound threw the ball *casually* to the first baseman. You can see why some complexity in a sentence is helpful—it enables you to convey a lot of information quickly. The reader learns a lot more from that sentence than he would from the original version, *The boy threw the ball*. And it would be pretty tedious if you wrote *The boy is blond. He is standing on the pitcher's mound. He throws the ball casually. He aims it at the first baseman.* Don't make your writing style too bare-bones and colorless just to avoid potential errors.

Why Pay More?

Use the imperative sentence frequently in copy. Not only does it sound authoritative and spur the reader to action, it saves on unnecessary words. If you find yourself writing, *You can save time by using our cleaning service,* try *Save time—use our cleaning service* instead.

The most important thing to remember is that while objects, adjectives, adverbs, and prepositional phrases are optional, a sentence *must* have a subject and a verb.

However, one type of sentence—used very, very frequently by copywriters—doesn't at first appear to have a subject. That's the imperative sentence, the kind that tells the reader what to do. *Buy now. Visit our new store. Taste the honey goodness.* Well, there actually *is* a subject here, and it's called "you understood." It's *understood* that *you* is the subject—*(You) buy now.*

Sentences can get *very* complicated. Back in the day, we used to have to diagram sentences in English class. We took a complicated sentence and broke it down into its parts, using lines and arrows and whatnot. We zeroed in on the main subject-verb construction, and then we had to figure out the clauses and conjunctions and all the other stuff that adds more information to a simple sentence. It was a terrific way to master the logical loop-de-loops of what could otherwise be a head-spinning piece of writing and to get comfortable with reading and processing information accurately (as well as for spotting errors in other people's writing). When you're breaking a complex sentence down into shorter sentences to punch up your copy, identify the main subject and verb of the sentence and work from there so you separate words and phrases and still make sense. Recognize what's the subject of what, what's the object of what, what's describing what, and how the words work together logically.

I've seen copywriters who tried to edit down grammatically-correct-but-too-long sentences quickly without paying enough attention to what they were doing, and they wound up with two or three shorter sentences—which unfortunately *didn't* make grammatical sense. A sentence that goes out of control is bad news. One tangled-up sentence can lose your reader for good. Keep them short and simple, and be sure the pieces are in the right place.

Keep Subjects and Verbs on Agreeable Terms

You're probably aware that *The dog drink out of the bowl* is grammatically wrong. But in more complicated sentences, subject-verb agreement can trip you up in sneaky ways.

One very common error is illustrated by the sentence *A group of women are waiting for the bus.* If you were diagramming that sentence, you'd realize that the subject is singular, not plural: *group*—not *women*. Therefore, the sentence should read *A group of women is waiting for the bus*. Another mistake I see frequently is *None are*. *None* is singular, and it should read *None is*.

The farther apart your subject gets from your verb, the more likely you are to lose track and have them disagreeing with each other. That's another argument for keeping sentences short and simple and keeping your subject and verb close together. But when you do have words in between, don't lose track of what's what. And remember that a sentence has to stand up grammatically when you remove any phrases within dashes or parentheses. Look at the following, and read it without the parenthetical phrase:

> My mother (along with her constant companions, Aunt Dorothea and our next-door neighbor) are attending the opera tonight.

Oops! That's not good. That *are* should be *is*.

Take Extra Care with Multiple Nouns and Verbs

As mentioned earlier, sentences get more complicated when you go much beyond the basic subject-verb-object construction. Errors in what's called *parallel construction* can creep in. This is such a widespread error that I've seen it in copy from major companies and organizations. Don't make the same mistake in your copy. Let's look at an example:

> Find out more by calling, writing, or visit our website.

All the stuff after *by* goes with *by*—or at least should. You can see something's gone wrong by inserting the *by*s:

> Find out more by calling, by writing, or by visit our website.

Clearly, *visit* needs to be changed to *visiting*. Filling in those "missing" words (words that are understood but don't need to be in the sentence) can help you figure out your mistakes and stay consistent in your construction. Here's another example:

> Try the bread that's soft, chewy, has lots of nutrients, and comes in a convenient resealable bag.

Now fill in the missing words, and you'll discover where the problem lies:

> Try the bread that's soft, that's chewy, that's has lots of nutrients, and that's comes in a convenient resealable bag.

As a copywriter, you have more options for fixing this sentence than someone writing in a more formal setting would have. For example, you can use bullets to present the information as a series of selling points:

- Soft and chewy
- Loaded with nutrients
- Convenient resealable bag

Or if you can't use the bullet option, you can rearrange the sentence:

> Try the soft, chewy bread that has lots of nutrients and comes in a convenient resealable bag.

You can also break it up into shorter, simpler sentences:

> It's soft and chewy. It's got lots of nutrients. And it comes in a convenient, resealable bag.

Don't Misplace Your Modifiers

The most entertaining grammatical errors I come across usually involve things called dangling participles or misplaced modifiers. Simply put, a *modifier* is something that describes something else—a word, a phrase, whatever. Look at the following:

> Swinging from branch to branch, I saw the monkey coming my way.

Swinging from branch to branch is supposed to describe the monkey, but because of the way the sentence is written, it seems to suggest that you, the writer, were swinging from branch to branch. I'm presuming this is not the case, unless you're Tarzan. I appreciate the laughs, but I still have to rewrite the sentence. You want your writing to be funny on purpose, not by accident. So place those modifiers with care.

Don't Get Tripped Up by Possessives and Apostrophes

Get your possessives straight, use apostrophes correctly, and don't mix up *who's* and *whose* and *it's* and *its*. Otherwise, you will irritate and confuse your reader and your writing will look sloppy. Yes, these things can be tricky—that's why you need to pay extra attention.

Hint: keep in mind that *it's* with an apostrophe always means *it is*. *Who's* with an apostrophe always means *who is*. Replace these words in the sentence, and if it doesn't make sense, you've got the wrong one.

Grammar and Style Rules You Can Ignore

Some rules of grammar just don't apply to copywriting. A sign in a window that says "Sale" isn't a complete sentence—but it is copy. Copy is kind of like the signs on streets and highways. It's there to get the message across clearly and quickly. It says "bump," not "There is a bump in the road ahead." When writing copy, you can put aside the following rules.

Don't Use Sentence Fragments

Wait a minute—didn't I just lecture you about proper sentence structure? Yes, if you are writing a sentence, it must be properly constructed. But as a copywriter, you don't always have to write a sentence.

Marketing copy—especially the direct-to-consumer kind—is supposed to be informal and conversational, and people rarely speak in full sentences, especially complex ones. (Bear that in mind if you're writing dialogue for a commercial.) As someone who has transcribed dictation, I can assure you of that—as a matter of fact, not only do people speak in incomplete sentences, but they also hem and haw, trail off in the middle of a thought, go on tangents, repeat themselves, stutter, and interject "you know" and "like" every five words or so. Of course, I don't recommend doing all of that in your copy. You're aiming for a conversational style—just not too conversational. It still has to be coherent.

Sentence fragments can be a useful tool for copywriters not only because they sound more natural but because they can add a sense of drama as well. *Mortgage payments. Credit card bills. Your kid's tuition. If you're feeling financially overwhelmed, we can help.*

Headlines, taglines, bullets, and bursts aren't usually in full-sentence form, and using sentence fragments as a quick, high-impact way to convey information can be advantageous. If you're getting feedback saying your copy is a little on the tedious side (or if you sense it yourself), try chopping up a couple sentences into pieces, and see if it helps.

Don't End a Sentence with a Preposition

Slowly but surely, this rule is falling out of favor in all but the most formal settings. But it's been so oft-repeated as conventional wisdom that some of us still feel a twinge of guilt when we do it. However, it's the way people talk—they say *Where are you calling from?* not *From where are you calling?*—and copy should sound like talking.

Who Is a Subject; *Whom* Is an Object

True, but hardly anyone ever says *whom*. (And when they do, they often wind up misusing it anyway in a misguided attempt to sound proper.) Use what sounds natural, which will almost always be *who*. Using an overly formal style can put people off, and that's not your goal in advertising and marketing.

Use "Correct" Punctuation

Your punctuation should be correct, but that doesn't mean it needs to be formal, especially in copy. Add drama by using an em dash (—) or finish with an ellipsis (…) for suspense or suggestiveness. Put a comma where you would naturally pause if you were saying the words out loud. Even if your headline is a full sentence, consider leaving off the period if you're looking for a "newsy" effect. (Newspaper headlines don't usually end in periods.) Don't overuse colons and semicolons—they're useful in more formal, complex writing but can give copy a stuffy feeling.

Don't Start a Sentence with "And"

So someone told you you're not supposed to do that. But it just sounds better that way. And you want your copy to flow naturally and smoothly. So I say feel free to start a sentence with *and, but, so,* or *or.* Or else you could wind up with less effective copy, because people start sentences that way in real life.

Never Use Clichés

In literature, originality is prized; in advertising, not so much. (Remember that in this job, selling trumps creativity every time.) Coming up with a new variation on an old idea can be effective, and when dealing with new products, new markets, or new circumstances, thinking outside the box is in order. But sometimes the best approach to take is "If it ain't broke, don't fix it."

Clichés can be helpful in copy in two instances. For one, clichés become clichés because they are so universally recognizable and true. It may be tired to say that something is as cold as ice, but the fact is ice is cold, and when you think ice, you think cold. (Of course, there are also the inexplicable clichés like "happy as a clam," and those might be less useful—although "happy as a clam" is included in Chapter 1 under "happy," just in case it comes in handy.)

Clichés also serve as a sort of shorthand, and because brevity is so important in advertising, they can be a quick way to get something across to your audience. Sure, it's silly to think that only smart people wear glasses, but if you want to suggest or signal a character's intelligence in a 30-second commercial, it's a lot easier to throw a pair of glasses on him than to have him deliver a lecture on Plato's *Republic*.

The Experts Agree

Déjà vu is part and parcel with this career: "Wait, haven't I *written* this already?!" Yes, you have and you will write it again … Don't rack your brains looking for a more unique and sensational word than "spectacular."

—Neal, English teacher and former senior copywriter

Accept No Imitations!

There's a fine line between an affectionate cliché and a negative or hostile stereotype—for example, *the ditzy blonde, the dumb jock,* or anything based on ethnic, religious, or other forms of identity. Avoid those types of clichés.

It's also important to remember that there are regular literary clichés and then there are advertising clichés. The sad fact is that most people nowadays have heard the advertising clichés a lot more often than they've heard, say, "happy as a clam," so make efforts to recognize and avoid them. Using the reference section in this book should help.

Avoid Contractions

Nonsense! People use contractions almost exclusively in speech, unless they're aiming for special emphasis: *You will not, under any circumstances, go to that party or I will ground you until you are 30.*

Unfortunately, some of us are still haunted by the glare of long-dead English teachers and tend to stiffen up when we have a pen in our hand. The result, especially in copy and dialogue, is a very unnatural sound. Unless you're writing the constitution of a country or something equally formal, go ahead and use contractions. Really, it's okay.

The Least You Need to Know

◆ Grammar's purpose is to make your writing clear and logical.

◆ At the heart of every sentence, no matter how fancy, is a subject and a verb.

◆ The way you use words affects their meaning, so use them carefully.

◆ Dashes and ellipses are okay, and so is starting a sentence with *And*.

◆ Good copy is concise, informal, and conversational, so don't shy away from sentence fragments, clichés, and contractions.

8

Show You're a Pro

In This Chapter

- ◆ Neatness counts
- ◆ Tailor your copy to different buyers
- ◆ Get ready to write some copy!
- ◆ What to do with deadline disasters

Whether you're a freelancer, full-timer, or aspiring copywriter, the career-building tips in this chapter can help you get more assignments and better positions. But even if you're just creating selling materials for your own business or as part of another job, those you work with, from office managers to typesetters, are sure to appreciate your effort.

Don't Make Me Clean Up After You

In my career, I've not only written copy but also edited it. I've had work handed in to me by more than 20 full-time copywriters and countless freelancers (and because I'm in the book business, by more than a few authors, book editors … and even agents). So I can tell you from the point of view of your client or boss what I *really* appreciate—not having to clean up after you.

On occasion, I give references to other employers, and if the job candidate in question writes clean copy, it's something I'm sure to mention because I know what a pleasure it is to work on clean copy. When I have to make decisions about hiring people or assigning jobs, I keep two words in mind: *fast* and *clean*.

The Experts Agree

It sounds obvious, but many freelancers don't adhere to word counts and fail to pay close attention to style/format guidelines ... Then they either end up having to rewrite, or not getting another assignment.

—Lana, senior copywriter

The Experts Agree

One of my pet peeves as copy director is when I get a piece of copy from a freelancer that looks slapped together or phoned in ... names misspelled, awkward turns of phrase, endings that fizzle—these are all signs that the copy was written in a rush.

—Susan, copy director

Clean copy, I would imagine, is even *more* important when you're working in industries that aren't focused on the printed word. In my business, there's no shortage of writing and editing professionals to find and fix mistakes. But if you're doing a professional writing job for a car dealer or a home-furnishings company, they're not going to be anxious to fix your grammatical errors. They expect professional work—something that's polished and ready for the typesetter. Before you hand in a job, proofread it twice—with at least a 5-minute break in between. When you reread immediately, it's easy to miss the same mistake you missed the first time. Taking a break gives you a fresher take. Look for all the following—and fix them.

Spelling Errors

When in doubt, look it up. Familiarize yourself with frequently misspelled words (see Appendix A for some books that list them), and commit the correct spelling to memory once and for all.

And although the spell-checks in word-processing programs haven't been perfected yet, they can help, so pay attention to those squiggly red underlines.

Grammatical Errors

You want your writing to be smooth. Grammatical errors are like rocks in the road. Read Chapter 7 and the grammar guides recommended in Appendix A. Also, like the spell-checker, the grammar-checker on your word-processing program could be a help, so check out those green squigglies.

Factual Errors

Fact-check your work—it's easier than ever with the Internet. The client will provide much of the information you base your copy on, but if you're using facts and statistics of your own, you have to be able to back them up.

It's not such a bad idea to fact-check some of the information you receive from the client, too. If they've made mistakes in preparing fact sheets and other materials, you might be saving them a headache later on. Remember, a simple typo by a harried office worker can turn a hundred into a thousand … and next thing you know, the Better Business Bureau is nosing around.

Are You Talking to Me?

Different kinds of copy serve different purposes and address different audiences. Think about who you're speaking to, and choose your words accordingly.

Direct-to-Consumer

If your copy is going to appear on a package or a sign in a store, in direct-mail solicitations, or in the pages of a consumer publication, the emphasis is on what the product can do for the end user. This is where you'll be using your appeals to the senses and relating the product to everyday life:

Thirsty? Enjoy a splash of Front Porch Lemonade!

Start your day the easy way—the 60-second Breakfast Burrito from Microfoods.

Tired of long lines? Order groceries online today.

Surprise your kids with a Presto Pizza tonight!

Free Sample!

We do it all for you. —McDonald's

Have it your way. —Burger King

Addressing the reader directly—as *you*—is crucial in direct-to-consumer copy. Clearly, the two big burger chains know this, and these classic slogans are simple, brilliant examples.

Direct-to-consumer copy is personal, conversational, and specific. It explains what the product or service in question will do for the reader, ideally in concrete, measurable terms. Sometimes those concrete, measurable terms are hard facts—miles per gallon, cost savings over a 1-year period, grams of protein—and sometimes they're other kinds of results: the smile on Mom's face when you send her flowers on Mother's Day or the feeling of confidence you'll have when you use a particular type of deodorant. Depending on the assigned job, you may be attempting to establish the brand name in consumers' memory, convince them to pick up the phone and order the product, or attract them to a special display of holiday items. But no matter what the goal, direct-to-consumer copy is about talking one-on-one.

Wholesalers and Retailers

Lots of marketing copy is never even seen by the public. It's used by salespeople or mailed out by manufacturers hoping to sell new items or establish new accounts in stores and consumer outlets. The people reading these materials do want to know what the product is and what makes it special—but their main interest is in its salability to their customers. Whether it's a mom-and-pop store or a regional buyer for a large chain, they ask themselves certain questions when they make decisions about buying:

Will this bring more traffic into my store?

Will it fly off the shelves?

Are my competitors having success with it?

They might also have other practical concerns in mind:

Is this company going to deliver the goods on time?

Is this product easy to store and display?

Is the product packaged the right way?

Is now the right time to order, or should I hold off?

How is the company going to advertise or promote the product?

The Experts Agree

I would say I get 15 to 20 catalogs a week ... more times than not, I don't really have time to look at them, so they wind up in "the pile."
—Anthony, buyer/purchasing agent

Copy written for these purposes is a bit more businesslike. Sometimes, if you've got a terrific product, that's all the reader needs to know—but the fact is, a great product doesn't always equal great sales, and this reader is a professional consumer who's attuned to hype and somewhat immune to emotional appeals. She might even find the product personally appealing but not consider it a moneymaker for her business. So in copy aimed at wholesalers and retailers, you might take approaches along the following lines:

> Lightfoot sneakers have taken the UK market by storm—and now they're available in the U.S.

> A handsome Pinpoint pen: the perfect graduation gift.

> Kids love Borscht Bites—the after-school snack that can't be beet!

> Don't miss the boat! Two million Yacht Club sweatshirts have sold already through mail-order.

> The author has been booked to appear on four major TV shows—including the #1-rated *Daytime Chat*, with 8 million female viewers.

Why Pay More?

Potential marketing tie-ins fill the calendar year, far beyond the usual holidays. Retailers might build promotions around Women's History Month, National Poetry Month, The Great American Smokeout, and countless other such events—and your product might fit right in. Special events might be scheduled for National Hispanic Heritage Month, National Aviation Day, or American Heart Month. Do an Internet search for "National Observances" to find a variety of sites with information.

Business-to-Business

A person buying supplies for a business has two important goals: he wants to please his bosses by getting the best deal, and he wants to be sure employees don't complain to his bosses about the stuff he's bought.

If you were selling a computer directly to a consumer, you might make mention of its sleek design. After all, she's going to look at it every day, and she wants it to fit in with her décor. If you were selling it to a retailer, you might refer to the promotional campaign planned for it so he knows his customers will be looking for this particular model. Neither of these things is of much interest to your reader in the purchasing department at XYZ

The Experts Agree

Avoid the outrageous, sensationalistic approach. Just have high-quality promo, but keep it simple. Tell me specifically why I should consider you, and offer testimonials, or a list of current satisfied clients.

—Anthony, buyer/purchasing agent

company, though. What he wants to know is what price can be negotiated to buy 700 of these computers, whether they're easy for the employees to use, and whether they'll give the company's tech support people migraines. Writing to this sort of buyer, you might say things like this:

Four out of five Fortune 500 companies choose us to take care of their networking needs.

We guarantee on-site service for our copiers—within 24 hours.

A smooth-running assembly line means a smooth-running company.

Imagine every employee producing 5% more—without any extra effort.

Is your lousy office coffee competing with the café down the block? Our premium blends will keep employees in the office—at a nonpremium price.

America's top firms have used Legal-Ease filing systems for more than 50 years.

Why Pay More?

One aspect of the product or service applies no matter who you're addressing: price. Tailor your message to the reader's situation—but keep in mind that *everyone's* looking to get the most for the least amount of money (except for certain "snob appeal" ads, in which a high price is actually a selling point). Even if no dollar figures are included, the message should always be *this is a good value for you*.

Think About the Next Step

Your copy will probably move through a lot of people on its way to becoming part of a finished product: artists, designers, perhaps actors or musicians ... and even the simplest text-only ad will have to be typeset by someone. If you don't have enough context to figure out the best way to construct and present your copy, ask your client to provide some, so you can prepare it with the appropriate people in mind.

Here are some tips to make your copy more presentable and helpful to those who touch it after you:

♦ Use the proper format, and include any necessary direction in a script. Tips are available in the "Writing Commercials" chapter of Robert W. Bly's *The Copywriter's Handbook*.

♦ For print materials, use bold, underline, and italic type and different font sizes to suggest what you think are particularly important points in the copy. Highlight more important and attention-getting elements because typesetters and designers will want to make these words larger, put them in a color that stands out, or place them where they are most likely to be seen first. The designers may not follow your every suggestion, but these cues will make their work easier.

♦ If you haven't received clear guidelines about the amount of copy you should produce, getting information or samples from your client can give you a better idea of what they have in mind. Depending on the medium you're working in, you have to take into account what kind of, and how much, visual and musical elements may be included. On more complex projects, you'll be part of a team that will—you hope—easily integrate the various parts of the puzzle. But if you're working at a distance from your "team," the more you know about the overall project and process, the more professional your results will be. Working for an agency gives you plenty of support, guidance, and help in asking the right questions of the client. An independent contractor—i.e., freelancer—has to take on that responsibility for him- or herself.

Don't Give Me Ten Choices

In some circumstances—perhaps in a meeting with clients early on in the process—there's nothing wrong with presenting a few different approaches. Having two distinctly different ideas or variations on a theme can be useful when a campaign is just beginning to take shape and things are still in the brainstorming stage. But when you have a clear assignment and you're supposed to hand in a brochure or a solicitation letter on March 1, don't hand in a list of slogans or a pile of drafts on March 1 and let me "see what I like best." If I had time to look through all the options and think about them, I wouldn't have asked you to take care of it in the first place.

As a copywriter, your job is not just to write, but to edit yourself and use your judgment. A good copywriter knows which idea on the drawing board is the strongest candidate and presents that idea—and only that idea. If you have a few others up your sleeve you think are pretty good, too, just hold on to them … in case your initial idea doesn't work out.

The Experts Agree

If, at a meeting to pitch taglines, you show up with 10 lines, chances are they will stare at you blankly and won't like any of them. Narrow it down to 3.

—Sarah, creative manager

Do Your Homework

The more you know about the product or service, the company providing it, the intended market, and the specifics of the campaign, the easier it will be to write effective copy. Take the following steps whenever possible.

Read the Materials

If the client provides you with relevant materials, read them. These can include in-house communications about the product or service, previous ads, market research data, press clippings, letters from customers, and more. Take notes, too—it's a great way to come up with ideas or review ideas discussed in the meeting later when you're trying to remember.

Don't Have Materials? Ask for Them

If the client doesn't provide you with relevant materials, ask for them. If there isn't as much material available as you'd like, ask questions. Don't worry about looking dumb. On the contrary, you'll look like a professional who cares about doing the best possible job. If you have trouble getting feedback, explain that you want to be sure you've got all the important information so you can represent the product or service in the right way.

> **CAUTION** **Accept No Imitations!**
>
> The web is a great source of fast, free information. But when you research online, exercise your skepticism. Take information only from respected and established sources whose identity and trustworthiness you can verify through other sites. Accredited universities, government websites, and recognized organizations (such as the American Red Cross or the American Psychological Association) are usually good bets. Sites that sell things aren't necessarily a good source of objective information. And be wary of opinion masquerading as fact, which is rampant in the unregulated online world (and the offline world, too, come to think of it).

Look at the Competition

Most companies educate themselves about the competition and, ideally, give you some information about it before you start writing. But smaller clients won't always have the time to do this thoroughly. And sometimes, the higher-ups in a company have a lot of knowledge about the competition, but that information doesn't always make its way to the people you're dealing with.

Look up the competition on the web so you can see what they're doing, and figure out how to distinguish your product from theirs. Look beyond the obvious competition, too. Everyone knows McDonald's competes directly with Burger King and Wendy's. But McDonald's also competes with other types of fast food such as Kentucky Fried Chicken and Pizza Hut. And on another level, McDonald's competes with inexpensive convenience foods that can be made at home or in the office microwave. Coke is not just competing with Pepsi; it's competing with water. Novels are competing with movies, magazines, and iPods for a consumer's leisure time. Foreign travel is competing with domestic travel—and both are competing with the pleasures and cost savings of skipping the vacation this year and just staying home.

The purpose of your research is to put the product or service in a context, and the broader and more nuanced that context, the more you will be able to zero in on a marketing approach that will work. If the trend is that families with young children aren't taking as many trips, emphasizing the educational value of bringing kids to historic sites might convince them to reconsider.

Know How the Copy Will Be Used

Who's on the mailing list for the catalog—older women? Teens? People who live in big cities? Where will the ad appear—in a newspaper? In home-decorating magazines? Are you trying to appeal to people who have never used a product like this before—or trying to get them to switch brands?

It's been said that a good copywriter knows that the goal is to sell, not to entertain. But a *great* copywriter knows the goal is to sell to single apartment-dwellers between 18 and 29 who eat out 8 times a week and have never owned a microwave.

If You Really, Really, *Really* Can't Make the Due Date

Stuff happens. Nobody's perfect. When circumstances are beyond your control, try to do the following to minimize the damage.

Give as Much Notice as Possible

As soon as you suspect you're not going to meet your deadline, give your client a call. It's the professional thing to do. Say you'll do your best but wanted to find out how much breathing room you have because you don't want to cause problems for others. Sometimes, you'll get an extension and a reassuring word—and your client will appreciate having a heads-up.

> **CAUTION** **Accept No Imitations!**
>
> If worse comes to worst and the work needs to be reassigned, you can recommend another copywriter you know—but do this only if you have confidence that the person you're referring has the right skills for the job and only after you are sure his schedule is open. Your client may turn down the offer, but it will at least show you're still thinking of his needs and taking responsibility. That might make you a lot more likely to keep him as a client.

Keep the Excuses Short and Simple

Your client really doesn't care *why* you can't do it. She just wants it done. You can explain the problem briefly—a family emergency, a computer crash, whatever it may be—but calling your client at the office and going on at length about your woes will make her less sympathetic, not more. Right now, she's focused on figuring out how to work around this delay. You can always drop her a note a week later, apologizing and hinting that you're still available for future jobs.

Consider the Possibility That You Really, Really, Really *Can* Make the Due Date

If the due date is approaching and what you've produced is not perfect, but of reasonable quality, you can submit it anyway—perhaps with a casual mention that you welcome feedback. Just because it isn't perfect doesn't mean it isn't finished. (See the "Speed" section in Chapter 4.)

> **The Experts Agree**
>
> If you need an extension, request one, but don't assume you'll get it. It's really important that a client be able to count on you.
>
> —Susan, copy director

There you go. Now you're ready to be a professional copywriter … or just write like one. Whether you're promoting the PTA bake sale or creating a Super Bowl spot, you've got the basics down. Go forth and write good copy—and don't forget to have some fun!

The Least You Need to Know

♦ Fix your own mistakes *before* you hand in your work.

♦ Think about your intended audience's priorities and motivations.

♦ Learn all you can about the product or service, the competition, and the target market.

♦ Don't hand in doodles and brainstorms—make a decision.

♦ Even if you have to give up an assignment, don't give up trying to help out your client.

Appendix A

Writing Resources

This appendix includes a range of resources that may help you in your work, whether you're a professional copywriter or just in search of that perfect word or phrase.

Books

Books on Copywriting

The Copywriter's Handbook: A Step-by-Step Guide to Writing Copy That Sells **by Robert W. Bly**
Although it was first published more than 20 years ago, the advice in this book is timeless—and priceless. It's sensible, thorough, and extremely easy to read, and includes full chapters on writing direct mail, public relations material, commercials, and more. His one-page "Checklist for Effective Headlines" is alone worth the cover price. Recommended for all copywriters, even experienced ones.

The Online Copywriter's Handbook **by Robert W. Bly**
Bly's earlier book, *The Copywriter's Handbook,* came out before the Internet boom. In *The Online Copywriter's Handbook,* he covers writing for the web, which was not covered in his earlier work.

Hot Text: Web Writing That Works **by Jonathan Price and Lisa Price**
Covering both creative and technical issues for the web copywriter, this book, according to *Library Journal*, "shines in its comprehensive coverage of online writing."

The Art of Writing Advertising: Conversations with Masters of the Craft **by Denis Higgins**
This is a compilation of interviews, first published in *Advertising Age*, with some of the giants in the field, including David Ogilvy, William Bernbach, and Leo Burnett.

Basic References

Merriam-Webster's Collegiate Dictionary, Eleventh Edition
This authoritative hardcover dictionary is available with a CD-ROM and a 1-year online subscription to Merriam-WebsterCollegiate.com, where you can find its thesaurus, encyclopedia, and Spanish-English dictionary. For slightly less, you can buy the book without the extras.

The New Oxford American Dictionary
New indeed, this work has a thousand new entries, including *low-carb* and *warblog*.

The Oxford Essential Dictionary of New Words
Want to stay up to date, but can't afford to buy those revised hardcover dictionaries every time they come out? This mass-market volume is packed with newly minted terms such as *McMansion* and *mullet*, as well as trademarks, identified as such, from *Allen wrench* to *Zyban*.

The Oxford Essential Thesaurus, American Edition
This excellent low-priced thesaurus also includes some handy references for writers, such as guides to punctuation and proofreader's marks.

The Oxford American Desk Dictionary and Thesaurus
Dictionary definitions and thesaurus synonyms appear together in the same entry in this two-in-one paperback. It's a great deal if cash is tight or for when you're working on the road.

Quotation Books

Bartlett's Familiar Quotations **by John Bartlett**

First published in 1855, this is the mother of all quotation books, and it deserves a place on any writer's shelf. Two caveats, though: for the modern-day copywriter, many of the quotes within will be rather obscure and written in the language of another era as the collection reaches back a few thousand years through history. In addition, it is organized by source rather than topic, though an index in the back does guide you to quotes with specific keywords.

And I Quote **by Ashton Applewhite, Tripp Evans, and Andrew Frothingham**

Although it's billed as a resource for public speakers, this hefty book is equally useful to copywriters. It has the advantage of being organized by topic, so you can look up quotes, sayings, and even jokes under headings including "Creativity," "Taxes," "Doctors and Dentists," "Babies"—and many, many more. Because it's oriented toward practical everyday use, its contents tend to be more contemporary and accessible than those in *Bartlett's.*

Specialized Quotation Books

The New Beacon Book of Quotations by Women **by Rosalie Maggio**

This may require some effort to find, but it contains approximately 16,000 quotations, organized by topic.

Words for the Wedding: Creative Ideas for Choosing and Using Hundreds of Quotations to Personalize Your Vows, Toasts, Invitations, and More **by Wendy Paris and Andrew Chesler**

… the "more" being writing copy for wedding-related businesses.

Books for Writers

Woe Is I: The Grammarphobe's Guide to Better English in Plain English **by Patricia T. O'Conner**

Grammar may seem a dry topic, but this book offers a thorough basic course disguised as a fun, lively read. Chapters on topics such as frequently misused words ("Verbal Abuse") and punctuation ("Comma Sutra") will help you avoid embarrassing mistakes and write better copy.

Grammar Smart

From The Princeton Review, this handbook is like an accessible, easy-to-follow introductory text with plenty of quizzes and examples.

***The Artist's Way: A Spiritual Path to Higher Creativity* by Julia Cameron**

This book, which includes a program of exercises, has become a classic. Some people are put off by its (nondenominational) references to God or its "12-step" approach, but many others feel the book has changed their lives for the better. I'm in the latter group; of all the books I've read in this category, it's probably had the most profound effect on me. I highly recommend it, especially for anyone struggling with his identity as an artist or with feelings of being stuck or blocked.

***The Business Writer's Book of Lists* by Mary A. DeVries**

This may be harder to find than some of the other books on the list, but if you can get your hands on a copy, it's a good reference with 80 lists of things such as "Crucial Factors to Consider in International Messages" and the most frequently misspelled English words. Some of the information in the "Resources" section is outdated, but the sections on word choices and business English can be very helpful.

Specialized Writers' References

***The Food Lover's Encyclopedia* by Sharon Tyler Herbst**

This book is meant for cooks, but if you write about food, it's a gem, packed with A-to-Z information on ingredients, cooking tools and techniques, and more.

***Dictionary of Legal Terms: A Simplified Guide to the Language of Law* by Steven H. Gifis**

Oriented toward nonlawyers, this reference contains definitions, and in some cases illustrative examples, of legal words and terms.

Merriam-Webster's Medical Dictionary

This inexpensive mass-market paperback includes 35,000 entries, and covers lots of specialized fields, including veterinary medicine.

***American Medical Association Manual of Style: A Guide for Authors and Editors* by Iverson, Flanagin, et. al.**

The AMA's standard for medical journals and books can also be useful for advertising writers working in the medical field.

Webster's New World Computer Dictionary, Tenth Edition by Bryan Pfaffenberger
The tenth edition includes 250 new terms relating to computers and the Internet, for
a total of nearly 5,000.

Online

Academy of American Poets

www.poets.org
Remember, good poems have a lot in common with good ads: they're evocative,
rhythmic, and say a lot in very few words. This site lets you browse for poems by keyword, among other things, and may get you back in creative mode when the words
just aren't flowing.

Other Resources for the Copywriter

These resources offer a bigger picture for copywriters, from psychological to sociological to business to legal perspectives.

Marketing, Sales, and Consumer Behavior

Why We Buy by **Paco Underhill**

Underhill is a consultant to retailers, and in this book he shares his research on the "science of shopping"—that is, the effect on consumer behavior of everything from store signage to aisle width. It's a fascinating read.

Think Like Your Customer by **Bill Stinnett**

A sales professional and consultant discusses how you can better understand—and serve—your customer.

A New Brand World by **Scott Bedbury with Stephen Fenichell**

This look at efforts by some major corporations (including Nike and Starbucks, where Bedbury has worked) to establish strong brand names is an enlightening look at what has and hasn't worked, useful for anyone in marketing.

The Tipping Point by Malcolm Gladwell
This is a thought-provoking discussion of trends and marketing. Gladwell, also the author of *Blink*, is popular among advertising copywriters and art directors.

The Overspent American by Juliet B. Schor
Here, Schor looks at the negative side of advertising and other aspects of modern American culture. Audiences today are more skeptical than in the past, and this will help you understand why slick, fast-talking marketing techniques can backfire.

Consumer Reports
Consumers have relied on this publication (and its website, consumerreports.org) for many years to find data on the relative merits of different products, with specific ratings and comparison charts. It can keep you informed about the marketplace and the competition—but what's especially relevant for copywriters is the regular feature that highlights ineffective or misleading packaging and advertising. Check it out for cautionary examples.

Adbusters
Become a more responsive—and responsible—copywriter by perusing this magazine (or its related website, adbusters.org), which dissects and critiques consumer culture and advertising.

NoLogo® by Naomi Klein
In a similar vein as *Adbusters*, this book takes a deep look at corporate branding, advertising, and consumer culture and makes some serious critiques.

Confessions of an Advertising Man by David Ogilvy
Get a glimpse at the heyday of Madison Avenue from one of its biggest names. This book has lots of how-to advice, and although some of it may be out of date, it's a worthwhile read for anyone considering an advertising career.

Information on Legal Issues

Federal Trade Commission
www.ftc.gov
This government agency looks out for the consumer, and reading its website will make you aware of the kinds of wording and practices that are unacceptable. You'll find much important information, including specific guidelines for weight-loss products, food, and jewelry; use of endorsements and testimonials; use of the word *free*; and more. Click on "For business" and then "Advertising guidelines."

U.S. Patent and Trademark Office

www.uspto.gov

Although not as consumer-oriented as the FTC's site, this site can guide you to information on what you may or may not use in your ad and what kind of uses are and aren't considered infringement.

Professional and Job-Hunting Resources

The Write Jobs

www.writejobs.com

Features lists of job openings for writers, some marketing-related, some not, located across the country.

Adweek

Published weekly in a well-designed, easy-to-read format, *Adweek* offers profiles of "creatives" in the advertising field, commentary on currently running campaigns, and news about the business, as well as job listings.

Advertising Age

A bit more business-oriented than *Adweek*, *Advertising Age* has been around for decades and provides extensive coverage of the advertising field and job listings.

A Deconstruction of *The Complete Idiot's Guide to Copywriter's Words and Phrases* Cover Copy

If you're reading this appendix, chances are you shelled out some dough to buy this book. Perhaps the copy on the cover helped persuade you? Let's take it apart and show why it says what it does …

The Front Cover Copy

- **Thousands of words and phrases** to make your copy more powerful

- **Lists of expressions and symbols** arranged by topic to spark creative new ideas

- **Expert tips** on writing effective ads, brochures, sales letters, catalog copy, and more

I wanted you to know right away that this book has a lot to offer. Note the use of bullets to convey this information quickly. In addition, the beginning of each bullet listing is in bold type to grab your attention.

I start out with "Thousands of …" because that's one of the best features of the book—it contains lots of entries in its reference section. Then I mention "expressions and symbols" to indicate that it's much more than just a thesaurus.

"Expert tips" hints that it's not just anyone writing this but someone with solid experience in the field. And because many potential readers might not automatically think of themselves as "copywriters," I also list a few kinds of writing activities they might relate to. Perhaps they're not copywriters per se, but they have to write sales letters as a part of their job. Or perhaps they run a small business and have to write their own marketing materials.

The front cover—where I'm hoping to get your attention, intrigue you, and make a good first impression that will lead you to read on—is not the place for complex explanations or long sentences. So although I use a couple subjective, nonessential words such as *expert* and *powerful*, I focus primarily on clarity, simplicity, and solid selling points.

The Back Cover Headline

Get their attention—and get their business.

I needed a headline that would tell you what you could achieve with this book in a clear, snappy way. Lots of topics are covered inside, and people in many different situations might find the book useful. This line unites all those topics and people and situations by stating what they have in common: they're all about selling.

And I used the repetition of "get" for extra impact.

The Back Body Copy

You're no idiot, of course. You're a pretty good writer. But writing sales and marketing materials—whether for your own business or someone else's—can be a real challenge. How do you find new ways to say the same old thing? What do you do when you're stuck for an idea?

The Complete Idiot's Guide® to Copywriter's Words and Phrases is here to help. This unique, all-in-one reference offers thousands of words and phrases, organized under more than 200 keywords to get your creativity flowing—plus gives you clear, jargon-free advice on how to create persuasive copy. In this *Complete Idiot's Guide®*, you get:

We always start out by acknowledging that you're no idiot. But if you feel like one when it comes to a particular topic, *The Complete Idiot's Guide*s can help, with down-to-earth, clear information presented in a lively manner. Here I explain something that many might not realize: copywriting has its own set of skills and rules that can puzzle even a skillful writer. Then I use questions to pique your interest, in the hope that you'll buy the book to find the answers.

The second paragraph restates and expands on some of the front-cover bullets. I made sure to use a couple phrases here—"all-in-one" to remind you just how comprehensive the book is and "jargon-free" to reassure you that this isn't a textbook for an advanced marketing course—it's easy to read and accessible. And "In this *Complete Idiot's Guide®*, you get" leads you into …

The Back Cover Bullets

- ◆ Synonyms, related words, phrases, expressions, symbols, metaphors, and antonyms.

- ◆ 18 tricks of the trade and tips on putting them to good use.

- ◆ Valuable chapters on how to write terrific copy, as well as advice for targeting specific markets such as men, women, and young people.

These bullets show you how much you're getting in a quick-hit format. I tried to avoid wordiness and hype here and focused instead on hard facts—and numbers. You don't just get "some" tricks of the trade; you get 18. And while the front cover refers to "targeting your market," here I have the opportunity to give specific examples of what those markets might be.

Note also the use of alliteration to make the main reference sections sound catchy: dead-on descriptions, buzzwords by business, and promotional power.

Why did I choose the examples I did, rather than others? Well, although the book includes keywords such as *pink* and *local* and *shiny* and *grand opening*, I felt that more commonly used words would draw in more people. Likewise, the examples of the buzzwords by business are the bigger industries where more copywriters are likely to find work. Most copywriters at some point are going to have to describe something as "affordable" or write about a sale, so they're more likely to see the immediate usefulness of the book by seeing things they're more likely to come across in their work. Plus, these words have large numbers of synonyms listed under them, so it's an extra chance to use impressive numbers.

Note that I use some numerals here because they stand out (and save space!).

The Blue Box

The book that does the brainstorming for you!

- Promotional power: new ways to say *Act now*, *Sale*, and *Bonus*.

- Words for seasons, holidays, months, colors, and numbers.

- Grammar and style: seven rules copywriters can ignore—and five to follow.

- The seven qualities of a great copywriter.

- Dead-on descriptions: 26 synonyms for *affordable*, 46 for *big*, 27 for *clean*.

- Buzzwords by business: special listings for different industries—cars, computers, cosmetics, financial, medical, and more.

The headline is another take on "what this book can do for you," this time with an emphasis on creativity. I think anyone who writes—copy or anything else—can relate to the painful, frustrating search for the right word or the right idea (and on bad days, *any* word or *any* idea). This line tells you that the book can save you time and stress— especially important when you're writing for business rather than pleasure.

Alpha Books designs its covers in a smart way, using different boxes and colors to prevent turning off customers with one overwhelming-looking block of type. This blue box gives me an opportunity to get into some nitty-gritty, with specific samples of what's inside. To re-emphasize that this is not just a thesaurus, I highlight an especially helpful feature for copywriters, in which you can find lists of words and phrases for the different types of businesses you might work for. I tell you that there are also entries for general phrases commonly used in advertising and marketing, like *Sale*, and for things that might tie into those sales, like seasons and holidays.

Because everyone looking at a how-to book is also concerned about how-not-to, I mention grammar and style rules to follow, as well as those to avoid. We all worry about making mistakes, so "what not to do" advice can be even more attractive than the "what to do" kind. And because you're interested in being a great copywriter, the "seven qualities of a great copywriter" should pique your interest!

The Author Bio

KATHY KLEIDERMACHER is the director of copy at a major publishing house and has been writing sales and marketing copy professionally for 16 years. Her writing has appeared in several publications, and her poetry has received an International Merit Award from the *Atlanta Review*. She has also been a book editor and guest-lectured at the New School on humor writing.

Writing your own author bio is a nice opportunity to brag on yourself, but this part of the copy also serves a selling purpose. It details the experience that makes me qualified to write the book and give you advice. And I also include extra details that suggest relevant experience and skills in editing, teaching, and leading because not everyone who can do something is also adept at showing others how to do it. I left out less relevant details, like the fact that I'm a compulsive Scrabble player or the writing award I won in fifth grade. The bio here is meant to serve as a sort of resumé, to help you decide whether you want to "hire" me as your copywriting coach, and those things probably won't impress you all that much.

The Whole Package

Overall, this copy …

- Shows why the product is different from or better than others on the market (with emphasis on the numbers of entries; mention of features such as buzzwords by business, expressions, and symbols, and clear indication on the front cover that it's *both* a reference book and a how-to guide).

- Avoids empty hype and fluff, focusing on specifics to demonstrate its practicality.

- Packs lots of information into a small number of words.

- Draws in its target market by referring to situations in which it is useful (writing copy for your own business or someone else's; writing ads, brochures, catalog copy, etc.).

◆ Encourages readers to browse through the book—and hopefully buy it—with the promise of lots more inside ("and more," "etc.," "18 tricks of the trade").

Not every copywriting situation will call for the exact same words and techniques. But these principles will serve you well when you set out to write effective copy—no matter what you're trying to sell.

And here's something important to note: my editor at Alpha Books looked over the first draft and made some smart suggestions for changes. So like I tell you in Chapter 4 … pay attention to your critics!

Index

Note: The bold entries are the keywords from Part 1.

Check Out These
Best-Selling
COMPLETE IDIOT'S GUIDES®

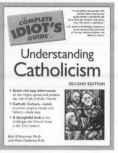

Understanding Catholicism
SECOND EDITION

1-59257-085-2
$18.95

Learning Spanish
THIRD EDITION

0-02-864451-4
$18.95

The Bible
SECOND EDITION

0-02-864382-8
$18.95

Being a Groom
SECOND EDITION

0-02-864456-5
$9.95

Grammar and Style
SECOND EDITION

1-59257-115-8
$16.95

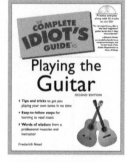

Playing the Guitar
SECOND EDITION

0-02-864244-9
$21.95 w/CD

Personal Finance in Your 20s & 30s
SECOND EDITION

0-02-864374-7
$19.95

Knitting and Crocheting
SECOND EDITION
Illustrated

1-59257-089-5
$16.95

The Perfect Resume
THIRD EDITION

0-02-864440-9
$14.95

Buying and Selling a Home
FOURTH EDITION

1-59257-120-4
$18.95

Low-Carb Meals

1-59257-180-8
$18.95

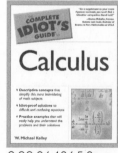

Calculus

0-02-864365-8
$18.95

More than *450 titles* in *30 different categories*
Available at booksellers everywhere

ALPHA